The New French Cooking

Minceur Cuisine Extraordinaire

The New French Cooking

Minceur Cuisine Extraordinaire

Armand Aulicino

GROSSET & DUNLAP
A FILMWAYS COMPANY
Publishers • New York

Illustrations by Peter Kalberkamp

Copyright © 1976 by Armand Aulicino
Published simultaneously in Canada
Library of Congress catalog card number: 76-1447
ISBN 0-448-12478-5 (hardcover edition)
ISBN 0-448-14418-2 (paperback edition)
Third printing 1977
Printed in the United States of America

Dedication

To my parents before me, to my wife and friends with me, and to my children after me, all of whom share Confucius' tenet that good food is "the first happiness."

Contents

Acknowledgment

It is only proper that I wholeheartedly acknowledge my indebtedness to the friends, fine cooks, chefs, and restaurateurs I have met, often in their own kitchens, in many cities and countries—many of whom, over the years, willingly shared with me their TOURS DE MAIN, their cooking secrets, and, of course, their precious recipes.

A special acknowledgment is due to Craig Claiborne, whose article in THE NEW YORK TIMES was substantially responsible for my writing this book. I also must thank Herbert Silverman, Paul Bonner, Tom Margittai and Paul Kovi (of The Four Seasons), Dr. David Schneider, Sidmore Parnes, Stanleigh Morris, and James Seligmann, my literary agent, who encouraged me in the pursuit of this project. I am particularly indebted to John Arvonio, whose expertise in human chemistry was invaluable to me, and to Dr. Arthur Seligmann, my personal physician for many years, who not only encouraged me to write this book but generously assisted with my presentation of medical information. And for special assistance, my thanks to Professor Carole Bisogni of the Division of Nutritional Scientists at Cornell University.

As in all projects of this kind, there are many people behind the scenes who were unstinting in their enthusiasm. First of all, I want to thank Peter Tonks, Kenneth Tam, Monique Gamet, Ayako Endo Langley, Ken Tsutsumi, Larry Dorion, Bonnell Irvine and many others for permitting me to adapt some of their favorite recipes to MINCEUR CUISINE. Since I wanted to be sure that all of the recipes were carefully tested, and in many cases retested to assure accuracy, I must thank the many avid cooks who participated in this endeavor, including: Gerald Aldi, Stefania Aulicino, George Drapeau, the Reverend Alan Freed, Terrin Levitt, Carly and Chris List, Jane McAuliffe, Carol Hauser, Adam Tihany— and for her extra-special devotion, Betty Silverman, who took time off from writing her own cookbooks to be of assistance.

And a most special acknowledgment to Jane Toonkel, my editor, and to the whole team of specialists at Grosset & Dunlap: their enthusiasm and dedication made a difficult and demanding project one of the greatest pleasures of my life.

Preface

There is no great mystery to MINCEUR CUISINE. Many of us, especially in the United States, have been approaching low-calorie and low-cholesterol concepts in our cooking for a number of years. Now with a little refocusing of our traditional cooking techniques and habits, we can easily prepare delicious and varied meals ideally suited to our personal tastes and preferences as well as to our contemporary way of living.

My intent in writing this book is to show how a busy homemaker can prepare simple and logical MINCEUR (slimming) CUISINE without necessarily resorting to unusual and expensive additional equipment. The techniques and cooking processes presented here are applicable not only to French dishes but also to other popular ethnic cuisines, such as Italian, German, Spanish—even South African. In fact, I have included a chapter that shows how to adapt famous international dishes, as well as favorite recipes, to the new MINCEUR style of cookery.

Many of you no doubt read and heard, as did I, about the fabulous new approach to HAUTE CUISINE practiced by great French chefs like Paul Bocuse and his Michelin-starred chef friends, who were no longer masking the basic ingredients of their dishes with opulent and overpowering sauces. But few of us had ever tasted these much-touted dishes.

Bill Collins, of THE PHILADELPHIA INQUIRER, wrote, "I have dined with Bocuse and several of his colleagues, but I never tasted the New French Cooking, either, until . . . I was part of a small group of journalists entertained by Armand Aulicino." This was also true of Craig Claiborne when he visited my home a year earlier, to first sample my MINCEUR dishes.

Of course, I am pleased with the wonderful reactions of the critics and media to this cookbook. However, probably the most gratifying reactions are those from readers who have written to me, as well as from the many listeners to radio interview shows throughout the country, who called in to ask questions and tell me of their excitement in discovering MIN-CEUR CUISINE. Generally, I have been impressed with how vital and stimulating the new slimming cookery is to the busy and dedicated homemaker who is concerned with nutritional value, as well as the overall goals of preparing and attractively presenting delicious and satisfying meals.

Also, a surprising number of letters mentioned that my MINCEUR dishes were their first attempts at cooking. Many of these letters were from busy people with exacting careers, including many men (my personal physician among them) who found preparing the recipes in this book stimulating, relaxing, and, above all, rewarding in terms of the reactions from their families and friends.

I hope this book will stimulate you as well to develop a repertoire of nutritional and delicious recipes suited to your particular tastes and needs. Remember, there are no absolutes in preparing MINCEUR CUISINE. You will find that the concepts and processes contained in this book can be easily and comfortably varied to create your own personalized and satisfying cuisine.

Armand Aulicino
Pelham, New York
April 1977

Introduction

The French generally use the term CUISINE to mean both the art of cooking or preparing dishes and the place in which the dishes are prepared—the kitchen. Traditionally, French cookery at its best has been distinguished as HAUTE CUISINE (fine cuisine) or LA GRANDE CUISINE (the great cuisine), both terms referring to the internationally famous cooking brought to its culmination by the great chef, Auguste Escoffier. Now there is a new type of French cooking: LA NOUVELLE CUISINE (the new cuisine).

It began auspiciously some years ago when Paul Bocuse, the Michelin-starred chef, initiated a new technique in his restaurant at Collonges, near Lyons. The new method emphasized the natural ingredients of each dish by not masking the basic taste of food with rich and superfluous sauces, as often found in LA GRANDE CUISINE. His influence proved so strong that soon he was joined in the new cuisine by other famous Michelin-starred chefs, including Michel Guérard, whose experiments and presentation of the new dishes have been acclaimed throughout the world.

LA NOUVELLE CUISINE is often referred to as CUISINE MINCEUR, or, as I prefer, MINCEUR CUISINE, which can be defined as "slimming" cookery. The two terms inevitably vary in nuance, but in the interest of consistency we will use MINCEUR CUISINE in this book to mean the technique that calls for eliminating or minimizing the use of such high-calorie and high-fat ingredients as oil, butter, cream, wheat flour, and sugar (other than the natural sugars found in fruits and vegetables).

In addition, we will use very little salt in the following recipes; we will, however, utilize herbs and spices judiciously to achieve a harmonious and satisfying blend of flavors, complementing the natural ingredients of each dish. Occasionally we will employ "bonus" recipes, which include acceptable but somewhat larger quantities of some of the higher-calorie and higher-cholesterol ingredients than would normally be used in MINCEUR CUISINE but would be consistent with the premises of the overall concept of LA NOUVELLE CUISINE. You will, for example, find two low-calorie, low-cholesterol recipes for mayonnaise in this book. One is EGG-LESS MAYONNAISE (page 124), which I find most satisfactory and pleasant, but requires neither oil nor egg yolks. The second is BONUS MAYONNAISE (page 124), in which one whole egg and two egg yolks are used to produce approximately one cup of dressing. You may wish to serve this richer, delightful mayonnaise on special occasions. Most doctors generally recommend no more than three eggs per week for adults interested in controlling or reducing their cholesterol intake. The BONUS MAYONNAISE recipe does not exceed this limit; and, of course, smaller amounts, which you would normally use, have even less cholesterol.

The recipes in this book are designed to assist you to create a personalized MINCEUR CUISINE—to assure you, your family, and guests of eating well and healthfully, in accordance with your own taste, judgment, and menu-planning needs. We are therefore including hundreds of recipes representative of MINCEUR cooking and the new style of French cookery. You will also find comprehensive instructions for converting traditional or favorite original recipes into MINCEUR dishes.

Before we begin learning MINCEUR CUISINE and the new style of French cooking, however, I would like to put them in historical perspective, showing how the new cuisine fits into the overall growth of cookery as an art based on and responding to the needs of a specific populace, be it national or regional.

I have found, and many experts agree, that the two most outstanding cuisines are the Chinese and the French. This is not meant to minimize other examples of fine, ethnic cooking, many of which have influenced—and have been influenced by—these two titans of the culinary world. These cuisines are outstanding because, in both cases, they have been developed into an art. Chinese cuisine, for instance, is almost ritualistic in nature and calls for precise rules, methods, and disciplines in the preparation of traditional dishes. I have often felt a sense of awe, of history, and an added and special sense of participation, as I have prepared some of the classic Chinese dishes.

But we must not lose sight of the fact that originally, and throughout their long periods of refinement, these fine cuisines were both developed primarily to meet the particular needs of the people who lived in each distinct, geographic locale. Each country had its own limitations of climate and resources, and there were other pertinent considerations—the absence of convenient refrigeration for the French and the insufficient supply and high cost of fuel for the Chinese.

Putting it very simply, the French developed rich and highly seasoned sauces to mask, as well as to enrich, their basic foods, and the Chinese developed extremely short cooking periods to economize on fuel. In the absence of forks and knives, Chinese cuisine further called for cutting all food into small pieces that could be managed with chopsticks. Even today, Chinese dishes call for a long period of preparation, including chopping and cutting, but only for a very few minutes of actual cooking.

One of the most stunning examples of the unusual Chinese cooking methods I have ever experienced is in a recipe I used for Velvet Chicken—one of our family favorites. Recipe instructions for this dish vary, from cooking the chicken for long periods of time to marinating it in a mixture of soy sauce, egg white, and cornstarch, then boiling for only one minute and letting it stand in the hot water for another minute or so, to cook further. The method that fascinated me most, however, called for placing a whole chicken in a pot filled with cold water, with a piece of ginger and some scallions. The secret is to place one or two metal spoons in the cavity of the chicken, after the latter has been rubbed with the juice of a lemon. (The metal spoons act as a conductor to hasten the cooking process.) The pot is then covered tightly, the water is brought to a boil, and the heat is immediately turned off. The pot is not opened until it has cooled—about four hours later. The result is one of the most delicately cooked chickens I have ever tasted, and, typically, the cooking method requires little fuel.

I would like to digress a moment here, because this recipe—as well as another favorite, Winter Melon Soup—taught me an important lesson the hard way concerning the cooking of large or bulky items in extremely hot water. None of the recipes I had encountered ever suggested how one was to remove the cooked, large items from the pot without getting scalded. As a result, I now carefully make a simple harness of strong twine, in which I cradle the item to be cooked—leaving a long, triangular length, knotted and looped at the end, which stays in the pot during the cooking process. When I am ready to remove the cooked item, I simply scoop up the triangular end or loop with a spoon, let it cool a bit as necessary, and then rather gingerly lift out my cooked masterpiece. It's fun and extremely practical.

Returning to our original discussion, I would like to point out other factors that influenced the development of the French and Chinese cuisines along particular lines. Like all good cuisines, each emphasizes the freshness of all foods utilized. Each has developed a method of cooking the various foods available in the principal regions of its own country. The Chinese, however, appear to be more aware of the necessity for selecting the most ideal method of cooking for each ingredient, rather than using a predetermined cooking process, and they are far more creative in varying their methods to suit the specific ingredients. (The Chinese WOK is probably the finest and most versatile cooking utensil ever devised by man.)

Chinese cuisine is, of course, far older than the French, and is intimately connected with the philosophers and scholars who are at the root of Chinese civilization. In China, the legendary Emperor Fu Hsi is said to have advanced basic concepts for hunting, fishing, and the cooking of food twenty-one centuries before Charlemagne did so in the first century A.D. in France. And before the birth of Christ, Confucius and his contemporary, Lao-Tze, the founder of Taoism, educated the populace in the fundamentals that have been refined into the finest cuisine in the world.

Confucius referred to good food as "the first happiness," and in his ANALECTS set down rules for the preparation of, as well as the protocol for serving and savoring, finely prepared foods. Indeed, food preparation was considered an art, both in harmony of taste and in decoration. A true Chinese gentleman was defined as an enthusiastic gourmet who prepared menus and served as an intelligent critic to the prized male chefs of the household. In the selection of a wife, the woman's culinary skill was considered a greater asset than her personal beauty. It is even reported that Confucius believed in his own precepts to the extent that he left his own wife, whom he considered an inferior cook.

Simultaneously, Lao-Tze and his fellow Taoists were advocating simplicity as an ideal and as the key to a more spiritual life. They sought harmony with nature and discovered and experimented with natural foods, plants, and herbs. Concerned with the nutritional value of foods, Lao-Tze was the first to advocate eating raw or only partially-cooked vegetables. Between them, Confucius and Lao-Tze were able to appeal to the instincts of the Chinese people— to their sense of tradition and reverence for wisdom—in order to establish what has been refined into and maintained as probably the finest and most cultivated cuisine in the world.

On the other hand, for centuries there was little development in French cuisine. Although in France, during the time of Charlemagne, the table was richly decorated with flowers and petals in lieu of a tablecloth, cooking was basic and far from refined. For example, a thick slice of bread—LE TRANCHOIR—was used to facilitate serving; before the pyramids of meat were heaped on the plate, the well-mannered diner would position the TRANCHOIR to absorb their fats and juices.

The first significant name to appear in French cooking was that of Taillevent (Guillaume Tisel), in the fourteenth century. He was head cook to Charles VI and was the author of one of the oldest cookbooks, VIANDIER. Many consider him the ancestor of all the celebrated French chefs who followed. However, there are many who believe—and others who disagree—that the turning point in the development of LA GRANDE CUISINE was the arrival of the fourteen-year-old Catherine de Medici, who went to France in 1533 to marry the future King Henry II. She brought with her Venetian chefs who had an exciting, experimental approach to new foods and cooking processes, a welcome by-product of exploratory voyages by the Venetian seafaring community. To grace her table, she brought with her as well many of the riches of the flowering Renaissance, including the work of such masters as Benvenuto Cellini. She sought not only to impress the aristocracy of France but also to captivate the ordinary people. And this she did triumphantly. Although Charlemagne had decreed it centuries before, it was Catherine who truly established women's right to eat at the same dining table with men.

Thereafter followed Brillat-Savarin and Antonin Carême, in the latter half of the eighteenth century. Brillat-Savarin, an influential politician and gastronome, published one of the finest works on the culinary art: LA PHYSIOLOGIE DU GOÛT. Carême, who insisted that cooking must be both healthful and decorative, is considered by many to be the real founder of LA GRANDE CUISINE, since his diligent writings methodically detailed everything one needed to know about the proper direction of the kitchen.

Finally, and most dramatically, "the Chef of Kings"—Auguste Escoffier—arrived on the scene in 1847. His TOUR DE FORCE of remaining active in his professional cooking career for over sixty years (most of them at the prestigious Savoy Hotel in London), and the publication of his writings, including MA CUISINE, have established him as the dominant influence in the refinement of LA GRANDE CUISINE. Emperor William II of Germany called him "the Emperor of Chefs."

The development of both the French and Chinese cuisines was determined by practical considerations. In France, from the Normandy coast, there was a good supply of fish, dairy products, Calvados, and Benedictine. There was also lamb and CHARCUTERIE from Brittany, cognac from Charente, and the famous Bayonne hams from the Basque provinces. In China, Canton, to the south, supplied most of the dishes we know in the West utilizing seafood, steamed rice dumplings, and the ubiquitous egg roll. Peking, to the north, utilized lamb and barbecues, scallions and garlic, wheat dumplings and wheat products rather than rice. Fukien, which includes Shanghai, reflects its coastal heritage, and fish and seafood are bountiful. Most recently, Szechuan-style cuisine—with its highly spiced peppers used for taste, medicinal reasons, and as a buffer against the damp climate of that area—has become popular in the West.

In China, whether it was the influence of Emperor Fu Hsi—who advocated the use of all available fish and animals—or the influence of Taoism, which explored the nutritious products of the natural world, the cuisine that evolved included items that some of us may consider rather extreme: sea slugs, birds' nests, shark fins, seaweed, and so on. Many of us in the past probably thought the French use of CHARCUTERIE somewhat bizarre, not to mention the use of brains and sweetbreads, and even cock's tongues. However, these exotic items of the past are becoming increasingly palatable and acceptable to our own tastes and, with variations, are employed in our own individual cuisines. Giblets, snails, pancreas—better known as sweetbreads—and steer's testicles are no longer considered exotic in many sections of the United States. Our sense of taste has become rather more cultivated.

At the same time, with the improvement of transportation and technical developments, our modern way of life has changed appreciably—not only in America, but more and more throughout the major cities of the world. We now have convenient refrigeration and freezing capabilities, more efficient cooking devices and utensils, greater availability of meats and vegetables not formerly common to our particular geography. Also, we live differently. There are fewer full-time homemakers and there is less domestic help in the home; we eat out more often—particularly our lunches while working away from home. We exercise less, and eat richer foods, more snacks and delicacies. Fine French restaurants have grown in popularity, especially for festive occasions that forgive extravagance. Chinese restaurants are in greater demand and consistently offer different, less expensive, and relatively large quantities of food. Yet, neither type of restaurant fulfills our basic needs in the twentieth century. Instead of considering our actual requisites, we have let tradition, habit, status, and national pride dictate our eating habits.

Much of this kind of thinking is simple misconception.

For years I, along with most people I knew who had visited Paris, raved about the great French HAUTE CUISINE, the marvelous and numerous restaurants, the great chefs—and always, the favorite, little-known discovery one had found on the Left Bank, Montmartre, or wherever. It was simply mandatory, for those who could, to spend at least a few days in Paris, to admire a most beautiful city, but especially to savor the great French food. We charted our day and entertainment in terms of our proximity to the great or favored restaurants.

Last year, however, I spent a major part of my time working and living in Paris, with regular visits to Milan, where my firm also had an office. During the first few days, I went out of my way to enjoy the fine restaurants whenever my work schedule and budget would permit. In a short time, however, the pressures of my work schedule placed the entire situation in a new perspective. I couldn't take several hours for a luncheon, or brave the formidable Parisian traffic to another section of Paris, so I learned, as we do in our own cities, to discover convenient little places. The quantity and selection of a meal was also necessarily influenced by the fact that I had to work afterwards, so I slowly learned, like the Parisians, that there is a world of cuisine far different from the one that visitors and tourists cram into a three-day or a week's stay in the famous City of Lights.

An amusing illustration of this point comes to mind. After I had been working abroad for several months, many friends would contact me as their expert "man in Paris." Could I suggest a fine restaurant, or would I please escort Miss So-and-So to dinner one evening? One friend called me from the United States to advise me that a young lady from his firm would be in Paris for three weeks. Would I contact her and possibly take her to dinner one evening? I agreed and did so.

It turned out that the young lady spoke only enough French to read restaurant menus but was adept at ordering a steak SAIGNANT (rare) or À POINT (medium-rare). She soon advised me that she had a long list of the famous and outstanding French restaurants, how many Michelin stars each had earned, and what the specialties of the house were in each case. Each year, and this was her third at it, she vacationed in Paris with the sole desire to eat every day in one or two of the fine restaurants. She knew virtually no one in Paris and planned her days to include a special luncheon and a more sumptuous repast at night. That particular evening we went to the Pharamond Restaurant in the old Les Halles section of Paris.

Although it is not a Michelin-starred restaurant, the

Pharamond is rather an "in" place among Parisians and the intelligentsia, primarily because it was reportedly one of Ernest Hemingway's favorites when he lived in Paris. Frankly, it was a pleasant evening and resulted in the discovery of a restaurant I frequented on other occasions. However, I became more and more amazed by the young lady's story and plans for her stay in Paris. She related what she had eaten, and where, during the first three days of her stay, as well as detailed plans for what specialties she would eat in restaurants scheduled for the next three weeks. Just the thought of her itinerary made me feel bloated.

The next day, I had lunch with a French client who had lived in Paris for years. Since it was a working lunch, we dashed around the corner from his office at the Rue de Berri to a little BISTRO with a few sidewalk tables overlooking a back alley. We were only two blocks from the Champs-Élysées and ten minutes' walking distance from dozens of well-known restaurants in the George Cinq area; we chose this small restaurant, however, and had a light, pleasant, and inexpensive meal.

When I related the story of the young lady I had met, Jean-Pierre looked at me in amazement. "How long did you say she was doing this kind of thing?" he asked. "Four days," I replied, "and plans to continue for about three weeks more." He looked at me unbelievingly, then added: "Amazing. When you see her again, in about another week, please tell me if she isn't so sick they had to transfer her to the American hospital."

I never did have an opportunity to check on what happened to the young lady, but I have often wondered. The main point, however, is that the French themselves do not subscribe to the idiotic and exaggerated concepts of eating that the many international visitors to Paris seem to take for granted. Actually, how many of us would do the same thing in our own country?

My main office and home is in New York, where there are many fine restaurants comparable to those in Paris. I have enjoyed Lutèce, La Caravelle, La Côte Basque, La Grenouille, The Four Seasons, and many others. However, regardless of the expense involved, it is inconceivable to contemplate going to these restaurants regularly for lunch and dinner. The food is simply too rich to satisfy my needs on a daily basis. I know a number of business executives who are expected to entertain regularly in these restaurants. Although many have PRIX FIXE luncheons and dinners, I have noticed that many of these executives select only small portions of food, skip courses, and merely nibble lightly on others.

It becomes obvious that—while on one level the luxurious and rich HAUTE CUISINE is discussed, promoted, and enjoyed by some—there has been a simultaneous and consistent evolution in eating habits by a majority of people. This has probably been most evident in the United States, where women's magazines and advertisements have been featuring more and more low-calorie and low-cholesterol recipes and healthful hints for eating more sensibly in order to meet our contemporary needs. However, I have found similar approaches in France and Italy, and in the larger cities of other countries.

In recent years, as we mentioned earlier, Paul Bocuse—whom NEWSWEEK magazine has called the "most influential and possibly the best chef in the world"—began cooking in the new French style, which features partially cooked, crisp vegetables and eliminates flour, cream, and other ingredients that mask the natural essences of the fresh meats and vegetables employed in his cuisine. Gradually, a group of talented chefs emerged as the "Young Bulls" of the new wave of cooking. Referred to as the BANDE À BOCUSE, the group includes Roger Vergé, the Troisgros brothers, Alain Chapel, Michel Guérard, and other chefs, all starred by Michelin. Unlike chefs in the past, the group members have become very friendly with one another; they exchange concepts, experiments, and ideas for recipes. As a result, new ingredients and new processes for cooking old favorites have been developed, and MINCEUR CUISINE or cooking in the new French style has gained international acceptance, and is now reflected in some of the hallowed menus of the famous Michelin-starred restaurants.

Many of us will wonder why the change took so long. The Chinese have been doing much of this NOUVELLE CUISINE for centuries. All of us have been adjusting traditional, favorite recipes and developing new ones to satisfy our individual and family needs, taste preferences, and other requirements. MINCEUR CUISINE is not all new; it has borrowed and developed from concepts and dishes of virtually every ethnic cuisine. Yet it requires discipline. It requires the perfecting of methods for preparing foods, enhancing them with spices and herbs, and garnishing them to present the final dish as attractively and satisfyingly as possible. It places an emphasis on natural ingredients and minimizes harmful and unnecessary calories and saturated fats that are damaging to our health.

Moreover, it is not a fad diet but a way of living, of savoring one's food and enjoying the excitement of developing personalized and individualized recipes. And, if in the process, as it has been with me, one loses excess weight and lowers cholesterol towards recommended levels, that's an extra bonus. I have even found my triglycerides were descending, though I never knew I had them at all until my doctor told me.

For me, this is the most satisfying and fun approach to eating well—to making foods, as Confucius says, "a first happiness"—and I want to share it with you.

Shall we proceed?

1.
Principles of Minceur Cuisine

Learning to cook in the new French style is a matter of preparing each dish simply and honestly, emphasizing the essence of the basic ingredients and presenting them in an appetizing and attractive manner, rather than masking them with rich sauces and unnecessary ingredients. This is a principle fundamental to both MINCEUR CUISINE and LA NOUVELLE CUISINE. Thus food in this new cuisine is not merely something to eat; our technique strives for maximum nutrition and maximum delight: food should be a harmonious blend of ingredients, which when cooked, should be presented as temptingly as possible, feasting the eye as well as the palate.

To achieve these aims—to create a personalized cuisine suitable to modern lifestyles, here are some basic principles and cooking instructions:

Use the freshest ingredients possible—meats, seafood, vegetables, fruits, and so on at peak flavor. Rather than foods that are not absolutely fresh and at their peak, it is preferable to use frozen ingredients.

Eliminate, or use only in minimal quantities, such high-calorie and high-cholesterol ingredients as oil, fats, butter, cream, egg yolks, wheat flour, or sugar (other than the natural sugars found in fruits and vegetables). If a small amount of oil or margarine is used, it should be the polyunsaturated variety made from corn, safflower, cottonseed, soybean, or sesame seed. Minimal amounts of peanut and olive oil are permissible.

Use little salt and more pepper, including green peppercorns, and other spices and herbs. These should be carefully measured and used judiciously to enhance, rather than to mask, the inherent essences of the fresh basic ingredients of each dish.

Sauces are generally made with a low-calorie FROMAGE BLANC, or white cheese. Iceland cheese, imported ricotta, yoghurt, and farmer cheese may be used, each mixed with lemon juice. Sauces can also be finished with purées of vegetables, seasoned and blended to the consistency of a mousse.

Egg white, cornstarch, and arrowroot can be used to bind ingredients and sauces, as required.

Wine and brandy are used for DÉGLAÇAGE (deglazing) and for reducing sauces by heating briskly until the alcohol content has evaporated.

When oil, butter, margarine, or fats are eliminated from a recipe, Teflon cookware and/or cookware spray are always used to avoid sticking.

Cooking AU SEC is a basic process involving the cooking of many items without added water in tightly covered cookware, utilizing the natural moisture contained in the ingredients themselves.

Sautéing is achieved by adding minimal amounts of water, stock or broth, and/or white wine or dry vermouth.

Meats can be browned or grilled without fat or oil, by dipping them beforehand for only a moment in cold water.

PK

This prevents them from sticking to the pan. Meats that have been marinated first can be cooked in the same manner, utilizing the marinade liquid instead of water.

Remember, satisfying the eye is important in the new style of French cooking. Be particularly conscious of the presentation of each completed dish, garnishing with carefully selected edibles in the colors, shapes, and textures that enhance and complement the basic ingredients.

To prepare MINCEUR CUISINE or LA NOUVELLE CUISINE dishes, it is not necessary to buy special equipment, other than those items generally found in kitchens equipped for preparing HAUTE CUISINE recipes. You are encouraged to use your ingenuity in adapting pots, pans, and kitchen utensils to the new style of French cooking, just as you are urged to create your own personalized MINCEUR recipes.

Most of the recipes in this book can be prepared on top of the range, in an oven, in microwave ovens, or in electric skillets, or by using steamers, clay pots, or crockery pots, or even, in some cases, by barbecuing outdoors over an open fire. However, like the Chinese, we will select the cooking process most suited to the individual ingredients, rather than arbitrarily impose any specific cooking process.

Many dishes can be prepared ahead, refrigerated, or frozen at specified steps in each recipe, and reserved until the desired time to complete the cooking, garnishing, and serving. Many completely cooked dishes freeze well; the recipes for these dishes will be marked with an asterisk (✱).

Vegetables should be cooked only until they are AL DENTE (pleasantly crisp)—as if they had been harvested recently.

The vast majority of classic recipes, and most favorite dishes, can be prepared in keeping with these principles.

MINCEUR CUISINE and LA NOUVELLE CUISINE are not fad diets, although weight loss and improved health are welcome by-products. Rather, the new style of French cooking is a common-sense yet exciting approach to cooking and eating healthfully, in keeping with our contemporary way of life. The object is to eat very well—and you will if you follow these simple procedures.

2.
Equipment and Staples

Since MINCEUR CUISINE is an extension of LA GRANDE CUISINE, you don't have to rush out and buy a lot of new equipment or kitchen utensils, but can use what you already have. Just as imagination is a prime ingredient in adapting your own recipes to this exciting new concept of cookery, it is equally important in adapting your existing kitchen equipment to the new French style of cooking.

EQUIPMENT

You will particularly need an efficient pot for steaming foods, and for cooking AU SEC or ÉTUVER À SEC (which calls for cooking without added water, in tightly closed containers). For either process, any pot of the right size, with a tightly closing cover, will do. To convert another type of pot into a steamer, you will need a metal trivet, a footed vegetable steamer and/or footed metal rack so that the platter of food does not touch the level of water at the base of the pot. Our preferences are listed here.

Primary Utensils:
A 5-quart enamel metal, or glass casserole, with cover
A large and small enamel iron pot with cover; and especially
    one 5-quart size; glass and acceptable ceramic cookware
    should be available for use in microwave ovens
A 5-quart Dutch oven; and/or
A Chinese three-tier steamer with cover

Secondary Utensils:
A 4-quart, or larger, pressure cooker
A 3-quart unglazed clay casserole, with cover
A fish poacher large enough for a three-pound fish
A slow-cooking crockery pot with low and high adjustments

Basic Kitchen Equipment:
Mixing bowls, preferably ceramic or glass for marinades
Charlotte or soufflé molds, both 2-quart and 6-ounce sizes
    (for individual servings)

4

Baking dishes and pie plates, preferably glass

Sharp knives, since, like Chinese cooking, MINCEUR CUISINE largely utilizes cubed and diced meats and vegetables

Electric blender, vegetable mill, and/or mortar and pestle

Cylindrical-type cheese grater for soft cheese (FROMAGE BLANC), such as a Mouli cheese grater, the "Much Better" cheese grater from Switzerland, or your favorite

An all-purpose grater, preferably flat, for grating vegetables

A vegetable peeler, preferably with a swivel blade

A sieve, preferably the CHINOIS type: conical in shape, like the Chinese hat it is named after. A wooden pestle is helpful in pressing foods through the sieve

Measuring cups, preferably, 1-, 2-, and 4-cup sizes

Measuring spoons

Wooden ladles and spatulas, but metal ones will do

A heatproof pad, such as "Flame Tamer," if you have an electric range

An aluminum, legged trivet for converting standard pots to steamers, or a BAIN-MARIE (see Chapter 11, Les Tours de Main, page 237)

FOOD ITEMS

You will want to stock up on, or determine the best sources of supply for, the freshest vegetables and fruits; but don't be timid about using frozen or freeze-dried items when the fresh ones are not easily available at their peak flavor.

You will want to keep on hand a supply of fresh lemons, oranges, apples, and pears. Orange, grapefruit, and lemon juices should also be handy—preferably fresh, but reconstituted juices are acceptable. The following list includes additional ingredients you will wish to keep on hand.

Staples:

Bottled, canned, or freeze-dried green peppercorns are used frequently in MINCEUR recipes

Pepper mill with black peppercorns, and/or ground pepper, both black and white

Salt, preferably coarse kosher, or sea salt

Herbs and spices, fresh, dried, or freeze-dried. I like to grind whole spices such as allspice, coriander, and peppercorns, just before using.

Shallots, raisins, and Indian or pine nuts (PIGNOLI)

Your favorite cookware spray

Plastic Brown-In-Bags, large size, for cooking EN VESSIE

FROMAGE BLANC, such as Iceland cheese, ricotta cheese, yoghurt, or farmer cheese (available in supermarkets)

Armagnac or brandy, Calvados or applejack, white port wine or sherry, and white wine or dry vermouth

Dried seaweed, or laver, found in most Oriental shops

These, then, are the essentials that should be present in most reasonably equipped kitchens as a matter of course; an occasional, atypical item, like dried seaweed, can be obtained from the sources indicated at the end of the book, or from a nearby Oriental food market.

Of course, as you proceed with the preparation of MIN-CEUR recipes in this book, there will be other items you will need for specific dishes, or those you might wish to add to your inventory of kitchen equipment. To assist you in this regard, in Chapter 3, I have selected suggested MINCEUR menus for your first weekend of cooking in the new French Style. These recipes will introduce you to the basic premises, principles and cooking processes (and hence, the necessary equipment) that may not previously have been totally familiar or available to you. Your list of staples, recipe ingredients, cookware, and utensils will grow according to

6

the requirements of each dish. This introduction to MINCEUR recipes will permit you to gradually add to your cooking BAT-TERIE. In this way, you will be building up your kitchen tools of the trade, as well as your larder of staples, both slowly and sensibly.

Since the manufacturer, the design, and the cost range you choose for a particular item are matters of preference, I will leave those decisions to you. May I caution you, how-ever, that there are many alternative uses for each particular item; to impulsively buy something like a French MANDOLINE, when less expensive and more efficient slicing devices are available, is less sensible than purchasing those items you will utilize a great deal—especially if they are time-savers—such as a blender, an electric mixer, a pressure cooker, or even a good pair of kitchen shears.

Avoid expensive and unnecessary items, unless budget and storage are not problems for you, or unless you simply want to use them as part of your kitchen décor. I have doz-ens upon dozens of antique kitchen utensils, most of which are interesting and decorative; however, I refuse to have anything in my kitchen—decorative, new, antique, or whatever—that I cannot use regularly. You will find that there are hundreds of really practical and time-saving items that are both pretty to look at and practical at the same time.

Remember, you can use your imagination in adapting your current BATTERIE DE CUISINE to the new style of French cooking, just as you will later be using it in creating your own MINCEUR recipes.

3.
The First Weekend

Since it's only natural, I assume you've already thumbed through this book and familiarized yourself with its basic approach. However, as we've already discussed, there are basic principles and premises essential to MINCEUR CUISINE and somewhat different cooking processes which may not be familiar to every reader. I would like to suggest, therefore, that before you prepare any of the MINCEUR recipes in this book at random, as you might ordinarily do with conventional recipes, you plan a MINCEUR weekend—a weekend devoted to initiating yourself into this exciting and stimulating approach to hundreds of delicious dishes, with their fascinating blend of flavors that I myself have found so satisfying. Perhaps you would like to share this experience with a friend or a member of your family, who, like you, would enjoy the sense of discovery and fun new cooking experiences afford. On the other hand, there are advantages, and possibly fewer distractions, if you work alone and surprise your friends or family with a delicious meal À LA MINCEUR.

You probably will find that many of the new techniques you will be using are similar to those you are already familiar with, or are beginning to develop on your own. Most of you, as I did, will sense a certain DÉJÀ VU, or will find, perhaps, many of your original ideas or intuitions about cookery confirmed.

The initial recipes presented in this chapter have been carefully selected for two main purposes. First, they are intended to convince you that MINCEUR dishes can be delicious and attractively presented as well as healthful, and at the same time fun to make. Second, each of the recipes utilizes at least one fundamental technique of preparation and a specific cooking process that will assist you in understanding not only that particular recipe, but also the overall approach to the new French style of cooking.

8

Select at least one recipe in each technique category, and add others according to your own preferences and the amount of food you wish to prepare for the first weekend. In the event that you would like to prepare additional meals, you may freeze them for future use. Although I suggest a preferred recipe in each category, there are sufficient alternate choices for you to devise your first MINCEUR menus to suit your own tastes and household needs.

To facilitate preparation, make a shopping list for each of the recipes you plan to use for the first weekend. This will help you to gradually build up your larder to the point where you won't have to go out on special shopping expeditions every time you attempt a MINCEUR recipe. With each shopping list, you should also indicate the staples you wish to have on hand, as well as basic kitchen equipment and utensils that you will need to prepare each specific MINCEUR recipe.

MINCEUR COOKING PROCESSES

Au sec (Étuver à sec) AU SEC means "dry," and this process involves cooking food without added water, using only the natural moisture of the ingredients, in tightly covered containers. The preferred MINCEUR recipe is BLANQUETTE DE VEAU (Steamed Veal with Cheese Sauce), page 20. The alternate MINCEUR recipes are ROSÉE DE FRUITS (Morning Dew Vegetables), page 27; and MARMELADE D'OIGNONS AUX PRUNEAUX (Violet Onion Marmalade), page 29.

Steaming This is an economical method of cooking food, either on a rack above boiling water, which the food must never touch; or in a tiered steamer; or in a steamer with a perforated base placed over any suitable cooking pan. In every case, there must be adequate water so that it will not boil away entirely during the steaming process. The steaming utensil must also have a tightly closing cover. The preferred MINCEUR recipe is SEA BASS AU VARECH (Sea Bass Steamed with Seaweed), page 13. The alternate MINCEUR recipe is NAKYPLYAK (Wedgwood Blue Cabbage in a Mold of Leaves), page 32–33.

Sautéing Most people believe that this process has to be done with fat or oil; the word sauté, however, is derived from the French SAUTER, to jump, which refers to the movements of the food when cooked in a pan over high heat. In our MINCEUR concept, sautéing is achieved by adding minimal amounts of water, stock, or broth, and/or white wine or dry vermouth while cooking. The preferred MINCEUR recipe is SALSA DI POMIDORO (Tomato Sauce Minceur), page 16–17. The alternate MINCEUR recipes are MOUSSAKA IN A MOLD, page 30–31, and NAKYPLYAK (Wedgewood Blue Cabbage in a Mold of Leaves), page 32–33.

9

En vessie **(Cooking in a Bag)**	This is a technique, used by the French and other Europeans, of steaming food in its own juices. The process utilizes the membranous bags or the bladders of animals; since these bladders are expensive and, in addition, cannot always be obtained legally because of the rulings of some health departments, we will use plastic Brown-In-Bags, which are easy to obtain, inexpensive, and more than satisfactory for this cooking process. The preferred MINCEUR recipe is POULE AU POT (Roast Chicken in a Bag), page 24–25. The alternate MINCEUR recipe is AGNELLO IN VESCICA CON GINEPRO (Lamb in the Bag with Juniper Berries), page 14.
Puréeing	This is the preparation of cooked vegetables, fruits, meat, or fish into a smooth consistency by mashing, sieving, or using mechanical blenders. It is used for specific MINCEUR dishes and desserts, and purées are used in place of wheat flour, cream, butter and/or egg yolks to thicken sauces. The preferred MINCEUR recipe is ÉPINARDS AUX POIRES (Spinach and Pear Purée), page 19. The alternate MINCEUR recipes are SALSA DI POMIDORO (Tomato Sauce Minceur), page 16–17; FRUIT MOUSSE, page 15; and GUACAMOLE (Avocado Purée), page 23.
Browning Meats	A process similar to searing, the intent of this is to seal in the natural juices, rather than to have them escape into the cooking liquid. This is accomplished over high heat on top of the range, or in a very hot oven. In MINCEUR cooking, fats or oils are not necessary when browning meats; instead, the meat is dipped briefly in cold water, then drained but not patted dry. The moisture prevents the meat from sticking to the pan or grill, and the process is completed when the surfaces of the meat turn a deep brown color. The preferred MINCEUR recipe is SLOTTSSTEK (Swedish Pot Roast), page 34. The alternate MINCEUR recipe is COSTATA DI MANZO ALLA PIZZAIOLA (Steak with Tomatoes and Oregano), page 35.
Cooking in a Mold	A mold is generally a container that shapes chopped, ground, or puréed foods into a specifically desired form. In cooking, whether on top of the range or in an oven, the mold and its contents are placed in a pan with water reaching approximately halfway up the depth of the mold. The actual cooking process is a form of steaming. The preferred MINCEUR recipe is MOUSSAKA IN A MOLD, page 30–31. The alternate MINCEUR recipes are NAKYPLYAK (Wedgwood Blue Cabbage in a Mold of Leaves), page 32–33; and FRUIT MOUSSE, page 15.
Reduction	From the French RÉDUIRE, this is a process of reducing liquids, such as stocks and sauces, by boiling them down, allowing evaporation to thicken the stock or sauce, and to intensify the flavors. The preferred MINCEUR recipe is POULE AU POT (Roast Chicken in a Bag), page 24–25. The alternate

MINCEUR recipe is SALSA DI POMIDORO (Tomato Sauce Minceur), page 16–17.

<table>
<tr><td>Garnishing and
Presentation</td><td>Decorative edibles added to a dish improve its appearance and presentation and enhance, rather than mask, the inherent flavors and textures of the basic ingredients. Garnishing is an integral part of every dish prepared in MINCEUR CUISINE; an entire section, **The Art of Garnishing,** Chapter 4, is devoted to this subject.</td></tr>
</table>

Depending upon your own preferences and schedule, you may devise your own MINCEUR menus for your first weekend; be sure to include at least one of the preferred or alternate dishes in each category, as I have selected these recipes to assist you in understanding the basic cooking processes. If you prefer, you may use any of the suggested MINCEUR menus that follow as a guide for your first weekend, or you may modify them as you choose. A recipe for each dish included in the menus will be found on the following pages. In addition, there are suggestions for garnishing, and you are invited to try the Bonus Ideas that follow each recipe.

Minceur Menu #1:
   Appetizer: Sea Bass Steamed with Seaweed
   Main Dish: Roast Chicken in a Bag
   Alternate Main Dish: Lamb in the Bag with
       Juniper Berries
   Accoutrement: Violet Onion Marmalade
   Dessert: Fresh Fruit Mousse

Minceur Menu #2:
   Appetizer: Pimientos and Anchovies
   Main Dish: Steamed Veal with Cheese Sauce
   Accoutrement: Morning Dew Vegetables/Medley Sauce
   Dessert: Whitecap Omelet with Fruit

Minceur Menu #3:
   Appetizer: Italian Potato Gnocchi/Tomato
       Sauce Minceur
   Main Dish: Moussaka in a Mold
   Alternate Main Dish: Wedgwood Blue Cabbage
       in a Mold of Leaves
   Accoutrement: Marinated String Bean Salad
   Dessert: Oranges Grand Marnier

Minceur Menu #4:
   Appetizer: Guacamole Salad
   Main Dish: Swedish Pot Roast
   Alternate Main Dish: Steak with Tomatoes and Oregano
   Accoutrement: Spinach and Pear Purée
   Dessert: Bahamian Banana Soup

11

SEA BASS AU VARECH Sea Bass Steamed with Seaweed

FRENCH

1 whole sea bass, cleaned and gills removed, but not scaled •
2 pounds fresh, wet seaweed, or 10 sheets of dried laver (edible seaweed), available in Oriental markets •

Sauce Vierge:
1/4 cup fish stock, or fresh or bottled clam juice •
Juice of half a lemon •
1 cup peeled and seeded tomato, cut into bits •
1/2 teaspoon tarragon •
1/2 teaspoon crushed coriander seeds •
1/2 teaspoon chervil •
1 teaspoon fresh parsley, chopped •

A delicate luncheon dish or appetizer borrowed from Chinese cuisine. It is easy to make and can be ready in a matter of minutes. The freshness of the fish is essential, so if market conditions dictate selecting a fresh, clear-eyed sea bass of larger weight, or two smaller ones, select whichever is the freshest. The sauce can be prepared while the fish is steaming. Serve on a colorful fan of fresh or canned asparagus garnished with bits of pimiento, parsley, or watercress.

YIELD: Four servings

1. Use a heatproof platter and any efficient steaming vessel, such as a Chinese steamer or a tightly covered casserole. You'll also need a fish rack or footed vegetable steamer to raise the platter above the level of the water in the bottom of the vessel.

2. Soak the laver briefly in enough warm water to cover for approximately 10 to 15 minutes. Place half the seaweed or laver on the platter, add the rinsed fish and cover with the balance of the seaweed. Add water to the bottom of the Chinese steamer; or, if using a casserole, use about 1/2 inch water. Put the rack and platter in place and cover the vessel. Bring the water to a boil. Steam for 8 to 10 minutes, or until the fish is tender but not overcooked.

3. While fish is steaming, combine the ingredients for the sauce and set aside in a warm place.

4. Remove the platter of fish from the steaming vessel and discard the seaweed. Skin and bone the fish, and serve with the sauce spooned over each serving. Garnish with chopped parsley.

BONUS IDEAS: Although the basic recipe is delightful as is, you may wish to substitute 3 tablespoons of oil for the lemon juice and the fish stock, and to add one crushed garlic clove.

For those who would like to serve this dish with cooked rice, try roasting two sheets of unsoaked dried laver, crushed, in a hot skillet for several minutes; sprinkle over the rice.

I find the addition of salt or pepper unnecessary to the basic recipe, but these can be added to taste, either to the fish or to the sauce.

13

AGNELLO IN VESCICA CON
GINEPRO Lamb in the Bag with Juniper Berries

ITALIAN

**4 pound leg of lamb,
butt-end preferred** •
**1/2 teaspoon rosemary,
dried** •
**1/8 teaspoon
sage leaves, dried** •
1 clove garlic, peeled •
**2 tablespoons
diced carrots** •
**2 tablespoons
diced celery** •
**2 tablespoons
green onions (scallions),
white part only
sliced into
1/4-inch lengths** •
1 cup white wine •
**1 tablespoon whole
juniper berries** •
1/2 teaspoon coarse salt •
6 twists of pepper mill •
Cookware spray •
**Reynolds Brown-In-Bag
(14- by 20-inch size)** •

The distinctive flavor of juniper berries augments this richly flavored lamb dish, which has the additional advantage of requiring little attention once it's in the oven. After serving, I like to reserve one cup of the cooked lamb for Moussaka in a Mold, another favorite dish.
YIELD: Four to six servings

1. Trim the lamb of all excess fat and pierce the meat with a dozen or more deep slits to accept the herb paste. In a mortar, grind the rosemary, sage, and garlic with a little water, and insert the paste into the slits with the tip of a knife.

2. Preheat oven to 350°F. Apply cookware spray to the inside of a large 14-inch cooking bag and the inside of a deep baking dish. Place the carrots, celery, and green onions in the bag, and add the lamb and the balance of the ingredients. Puff the bag, tie the top, and puncture several holes in the top of the bag to allow the steam to escape.

3. Turn the oven heat down to 175°; place the bag in the baking dish and bake for approximately 1-3/4 hours. Cut away the top of the bag so that the roast is exposed but the cooking juices remain at the base of the bag. Increase the oven heat to 400° and cook 15 minutes longer, until the roast is richly brown and fork-tender.

4. Remove the roast from the baking dish and discard the balance of the roasting bag, maintaining the cooking liquor in the dish. Cover the roast with aluminum foil, and put it in a warm place.

5. To prepare the sauce, remove as much fat as you can from the cooking liquor with a skimming utensil. If you have time, place the liquid in a pie plate and place in a freezer for about 10 minutes, to facilitate skimming off the excess fat. After skimming, reheat the cooking liquor and put into a sauceboat.

6. Remove aluminum foil from the lamb and place on a large, warmed platter. Garnish and serve with the sauce separately.

BONUS IDEAS: Both for attractiveness and taste, I like to glaze pearl onions in the sauce and place them in a ring around the roast on the platter, with sprigs of parsley.

An excellent accoutrement is INSALATA DI ARANCE, or Italian Orange Salad (page 23).

* FRUIT MOUSSE

INTERNATIONAL

2 cups crushed
fresh or frozen fruit:
peaches, nectarines,
apricots, strawberries,
raspberries,
and/or bananas •
1/8 teaspoon salt •
2 tablespoons
lemon juice •
2 egg whites,
beaten until peaks form •

An easy-to-make and refreshing dessert that you can vary to your taste, depending upon which fresh fruits are readily available and at a peak flavor. You can also prepare this anytime you wish using frozen peaches, strawberries, or raspberries, either singly or combined.
YIELD: Eight servings

Combine all ingredients and mix well, then whisk briefly or purée 30 seconds in an electric blender. Pour the purée into a large mold, or eight 3- or 4-inch molds or custard cups. Garnish with slices of additional fruit, or diced bits of the fresh fruits used in preparing the mousse. Chill before serving.

BONUS IDEAS: Other possibilities for garnishing include mandarin orange sections, sliced kumquats, or mint leaves. Powdered almonds can be dusted over the top of the dish. If frozen, defrost before garnishing.

PEPERONI E ACCUIGHE Pimientos and Anchovies

ITALIAN

3 or 4 whole canned
or bottled pimientos,
drained •
4 to 6 flat
anchovy filets, drained •
8 capers,
preserved in vinegar,
drained •
1 sprig fresh parsley •

An instant minor masterpiece. This is one of my favorite "emergency" appetizers, also good as a salad. I keep the required canned ingredients on hand, ready to whip this up at a moment's notice. Another bonus: the three major ingredients provide an ideal combination of taste, color, and texture. Excellent for company, for a special accent to a meal, or simply as an exotic snack.
YIELD: One serving

On each dish, place the pimientos spread open with the glossy side up. Pat the anchovies dry and lay them in crisscross patterns over the pimientos. Sprinkle on the capers, complementing the color pattern of the dish. Chill before serving with a sprig of parsley.

BONUS IDEAS: Traditionally, additional wine vinegar and/or a dash of olive oil is added to this dish, but I find these additions unnecessary. Other possible additions include thinly sliced onion or minced garlic or perhaps marinated mushrooms or black olives. For my taste, however, the sprig of parsley, whole or chopped, is far more delicate and satisfying as a complement to the basic ingredients.

Broiled sweet peppers or Italian style canned roasted peppers are often used with this dish, but I find the taste is more overpowering than that of the pimientos.

You may wish to add marinated artichoke hearts and green or black olives.

* SALSA DI POMIDORO Tomato Sauce
Minceur

ITALIAN

1 35-ounce can
(1000 grams) or
2 16-ounce cans Italian
style plum tomatoes ·
1 clove garlic,
skewered
with a toothpick ·
2 medium onions,
peeled and chopped ·
1 medium carrot,
scraped and grated ·
1 tablespoon each,
water and dry vermouth ·
1 teaspoon coarse salt ·
4 twists of pepper mill ·
1/4 teaspoon each,
thyme and oregano, dried ·
1/4 cup boiling water ·
Cookware spray ·

Wonderfully versatile, this sauce is derived from the Italian MARINARA or fisherman's sauce. It is a gentle complement to the flavors of fish and seafood, and is also delightful as a topping to such dishes as MOUSSAKA (page 30–31), stuffed cabbage, or meat loaf. And if meat is added with the optional red wine during its preparation, it becomes BOLOGNESE SAUCE—an ideal sauce for pasta, and many other dishes that require a rich tomato sauce. It freezes well, so keep extra quantities in reserve for future use.
YIELD: One quart

1. To prepare the MARINARA version, apply cookware spray to a heavy saucepan. Sauté the garlic, onions, and carrots, adding the water and dry vermouth. Cover, and cook over medium heat until the onions turn translucent. Add the balance of the ingredients, bring to a boil, and simmer, uncovered, over low heat for 30 minutes. During the simmering, the sauce should "shudder" gently, with an occasional air bubble breaking through to the surface.

2. Discard the garlic, strain the sauce through a sieve, and serve hot.

**Optional for the
Bolognese Sauce:**
1 pound ground
lean beef ·
1/4 cup red wine ·
2 tablespoons
tomato paste, canned ·
5 grains ground nutmeg ·

BONUS IDEA: You can prepare the MINCEUR version of BOLOGNESE SAUCE by using the optional ingredients and varying the above cooking instructions as follows:
1. Begin by applying cookware spray to the saucepan, then brown the ground beef with the garlic and dry vermouth, separating the beef with a wooden spoon. After several minutes, when the beef has lost its pink color, add the red wine, and simmer for 5 minutes. Remove the cooked beef with a slotted spoon, and set aside. Leave the garlic in the pan.

2. Proceed with step 1 above for preparing the MARINARA version. After sautéing the carrots and onions, add the tomato paste as well as the balance of the ingredients for MARINARA sauce to the mixture. Bring to a boil, then simmer

16

gently, permitting the sauce to "shudder" for 30 minutes. Discard the garlic and sieve the sauce.

3. Return the strained sauce to the pan, and add the reserved cooked meat and the nutmeg. Simmer for at least 15 minutes longer, but this sauce improves if it simmers up to several hours; boiling water should be added when necessary. Serve hot.

ADDITIONAL BONUS IDEAS: To prepare an enriched Bolognese Sauce or spaghetti sauce, try adding 2 stalks of celery, chopped, and 1/2 green pepper, diced, when sautéing the onion and carrot mixture; 2 bay leaves will add extra flavor to the sauce.

Also, many Italians insist on using a combination of meats, such as 1/2 pound lean beef, and 1/4 pound each of veal and lean pork, individually ground, then combined.

During the last 15 minutes of simmering the Bolognese Sauce, 1/4 pound of sliced mushrooms can be added, with a suspicion of nutmeg, about 5 grains. If you desire a thinner sauce, add an extra 1/4 cup of boiling water to the tomato mixture before simmering.

BAHAMIAN BANANA SOUP

BAHAMIAN

5 medium, very ripe bananas, peeled ·
1 quart skimmed milk, chilled ·
1/4 teaspoon salt ·
1 tablespoon grated orange rind, or 1/2 teaspoon dried orange peel ·
1/4 teaspoon arrowroot or cornstarch ·
Cinnamon powder or ground nutmeg to taste ·

Suitable either as an appetizer or a dessert, this is a refreshing way to begin or end a pleasant meal.
YIELD: Four to six servings

1. Mash the bananas, and in an electric blender, blend all of the ingredients with the exception of the arrowroot and cinnamon. Make a paste of the arrowroot and a little warm water, and add to the blended mixture.

2. Pour the mixture into a saucepan, and cook over medium heat for about 10 minutes, until it thickens. Press through a sieve, and beat the mixture, or place in an electric blender for 30 seconds, until fluffy. Serve chilled, garnished with the cinnamon or nutmeg.

BONUS IDEAS: You can add a diced banana to the blended mixture for extra texture.

Depending on whether you use it as an appetizer or a dessert, you will find this dish lends itself to creative garnishing. Try slices or bits of mandarin oranges, kumquats, whole or sliced maraschino cherries, additional sliced bananas, and/or mint leaves.

ÉPINARDS AUX POIRES Spinach and Pear Purée

FRENCH

10 ounces spinach, fresh or frozen •
1 or 2 large pears, about 3/4 pound •
1/2 teaspoon salt •
1 tablespoon water •
Cookware spray •

A surprisingly harmonious blend of flavors, this purée is a delicate accompaniment to most entrées. So simple to prepare it can be made while the main dish is cooking.
YIELD: Four to six servings

1. Remove the stems and hard ribs of the spinach, wash thoroughly, but do not drain. Remove the core from the unpeeled pear, and cut into 2-inch cubes. Apply the cookware spray to two saucepans. Shake off the excess moisture from the spinach, but do not pat dry, then place it with the salt in one of the saucepans. Cover, and cook AU SEC, over medium heat, for about 7 minutes, shaking the pan occasionally. If frozen spinach is used, defrost and cook, also for 7 minutes, following directions on package.'

2. Place the cubes of pear, with 1 tablespoon of water, into the second saucepan; cover, and cook AU SEC, over medium heat, for about 7 minutes, until AL DENTE. Do not overcook either the vegetable or the fruit.

3. With a slotted spoon, remove the spinach and place with the pears into an electric blender. Blend for about 30 seconds, until foamy and soufflé-like in texture. Serve immediately.

BONUS IDEAS: Frozen spinach can be used most satisfactorily, but there is no substitute for a mature pear at the peak of its flavor, so select the best pears you can find.

In all AU SEC cooking, if you want to improve the seal between the pot and its cover, wet a sheet of paper towel and place it under the cover, cover the pot, then fold the edges of the wet paper back over the top of the cover.

BLANQUETTE DE VEAU Steamed Veal
with Cheese Sauce

FRENCH

1 pound lean veal
stew meat, cut into
1-inch cubes ·
3 carrots, scraped,
and cut on the bias into
1/2-inch slices ·
16 small mushrooms ·
1 slice celery root
(knob celery), or the base
of a head of celery,
sliced 1-inch thick
and pierced
with 1 whole clove ·
4 sprigs fresh parsley ·
1/2 bunch watercress ·
1 bay leaf ·
1/2 teaspoon salt ·
freshly ground pepper
to taste ·
1/2 teaspoon thyme ·
1/4 cup chicken broth,
if needed ·
4 tablespoons
grated cheese—dry ricotta
or Iceland cheese,
or combination of both ·
Juice of half a lemon ·
Cookware spray ·

This dish improves on the customary use of aromatic vegetables by permitting the juice of the steamed veal to add to the flavor of the vegetables. I have found that placing the veal on a footed vegetable steamer over the bed of vegetables, in a tightly closed, heavy casserole, is the best method. However, the veal can also be placed in a strainer over the moist vegetables.

YIELD: Four servings

1. Apply cookware spray to the inside of the casserole, and arrange the rinsed and moist vegetables over the bottom of the pot, beginning with a layer of carrots and mushrooms, then the celery root, parsley, and finally the watercress and bay leaf.

2. Sprinkle the veal with salt, pepper, and thyme; place on the footed steamer, or in a strainer, directly over the bed of vegetables. No additional liquid is necessary if the vegetables are sufficiently moist; otherwise add 1 tablespoon of water. Cover tightly and cook over medium-low heat until the meat is fork-tender—about 1-1/4 hours. In the early stages of cooking, shuffle the pot occasionally.

3. When the veal is fork-tender, remove the vegetables to a covered serving dish, top with the cooked veal, and set aside in a warm place.

4. There should be sufficient cooking liquor left in the pot for the sauce. If necessary, add up to 1/4 cup chicken broth. Blend the grated cheese with the lemon juice and whisk lightly. Add this cheese mixture to the pot of cooking liquid and stir over low heat. Pour over the meat and vegetables and serve.

BONUS IDEAS: I like the texture of the cooked vegetables with the veal. However, occasionally you may wish to remove the vegetables, garnish using some of them, and blend the rest into a purée before serving.

VIOLET ONION MARMALADE (page 29) is an excellent accompaniment to this dish.

MARINATED STRING BEAN SALAD

ITALIAN

**1/2 pound fresh
or frozen
whole string beans ·
2 russet potatoes,
peeled and thinly sliced ·
3 twists of pepper mill ·
1/8 teaspoon
coarse salt ·
1 onion, thinly sliced ·
2 tablespoons
tarragon vinegar ·
1 clove garlic,
minced (optional) ·
Cookware spray ·**

Another versatile, easy-to-make appetizer, salad, or accoutrement to many meals. It is both light and satisfying and lends itself to creative presentation.
YIELD: Four to six servings

1. Trim the ends and any strings from the beans and chill in cold water until ready to use. Peel and thinly slice the potatoes; add to the cold water to avoid discoloration.

2. Apply cookware spray to a heavy saucepan. Drain the beans but do not shake off the moisture, or pat dry. Place the beans, then the potatoes, with salt and pepper in the pan. Cook AU SEC, tightly covered, 15 minutes, shuffling the pan occasionally. If other than new potatoes are used, precook the sliced potatoes for 5 minutes before adding the beans. The vegetables should be cooked AL DENTE, pleasantly crisp. Adjust the cooking to your taste, but do not overcook.

3. Remove the vegetables and dip into cold water; drain, and place in a mixing bowl. Add the sliced onion, the tarragon vinegar and, if you choose, the minced garlic. Blend the ingredients well, being careful not to break the potato slices.

4. Chill the mixture in the freezer for 15 minutes before serving. If you prepare this dish sufficiently in advance, simply place in the refrigerator to chill.

5. Arrange the string beans in attractive patterns, placing them in parallel groups over a bed of the potato slices. Place the onion slices in the center, ring with pimiento strips, and sprinkle minced parsley over the surface.

BONUS IDEAS: A dash of olive oil is optional, as is the minced garlic. I find that neither is essential to the innate quality of this refreshing dish.

There are many garnishing possibilities: consider sliced stuffed olives, a sprinkling of chopped blanched almonds, a cherry tomato, or whatever suits your fancy.

The vegetables can be cooked in a microwave oven in 6 to 8 minutes, 5 minutes longer if other than new potatoes are used, covered with wax paper; or, in an oven at 200°F. for about 15 minutes, or until the moisture is absorbed and the vegetables are AL DENTE.

ORANGES GRAND MARNIER

INTERNATIONAL

4 navel oranges •
4 tablespoons
orange juice (optional) •
1 teaspoon lemon juice •
Grand Marnier or
Cointreau,
sprinkled to taste •

A perfect finale to any meal, this dessert offers an interesting blend of flavors—the natural essence of the oranges sparked delicately with the orange-based liqueur. I like to serve this in clear, glass dessert dishes, or in stemmed wine glasses; another, more unusual, way I serve it is arranged in antique, clear glass finger bowls.

YIELD: Four to six servings

1. Remove the zest (rind) of the oranges with a potato peeler or sharp knife, discarding all traces of bitter white pith. Cut the zest of one orange into julienne strips about 1-1/2 inches long, reserving the rest for other use. Place the strips in a saucepan with water to cover and parboil for about 5 minutes to remove any bitterness. Rinse in cold water, drain, and set aside.

2. Separate the sections of the oranges, discarding any pits and the interior white membranes (see page 241). Place the sections in a bowl with any of the natural juices you have been able to reserve; otherwise add 4 or more tablespoons of orange juice. Add the parboiled zest of orange, and the lemon juice; mix carefully with the orange sections so as not to break them. Sprinkle with the Grand Marnier to taste, and chill before serving.

BONUS IDEAS: This colorful dessert needs little in the way of garnishing other than a possible mint leaf for accent.

If you prefer to eliminate the touch of Grand Marnier or other liqueur, substitute 1 tablespoon of honey—although the fresh orange flavor alone is so satisfying that you can do without the honey as well.

In Italy, there are two interesting variations of this recipe that you might like to try. The first is ARANCE ALLA MARSALA, or ORANGES WITH MARSALA. Combine 1/2 cup water, 2 tablespoons Marsala, the juice of 1/2 lemon, and 2 tablespoons of honey; bring the mixture to a boil over low heat, stirring frequently. Add the strips of parboiled zest, and simmer until the mixture is reduced by about a third. Set aside and let it cool. Then, instead of dividing the oranges into sections, separate them in halves, lengthwise, and remove all pits and bitter white membranes. Join the halves again, and hold them together with attractive skewers or toothpicks. Arrange the oranges in one large, or several individual, glass bowls, and add the reserved natural juices, or 4 or more tablespoons of extra orange juice as necessary. Spoon the cooked sauce over the oranges, and garnish each one with a pleasant arrangement of the caramelized strips of orange zest.

The second variation is a delightful accoutrement to any meal: INSALATA DI ARANCE, or ITALIAN ORANGE SALAD. Peel the oranges, remove all bitter white membranes, and divide the oranges into sections; or cut them into very thin slices, reserving the natural juices, and set aside. Meanwhile, peel and thinly slice 1 small Bermuda onion; separate the rings and place in a sieve in cold water for 5 minutes. Pat the onion rings dry, and place in a bowl with 1/4 cup of dry sherry; marinate them for 2 hours. In another bowl, blend the juice of 1/2 lemon, 2 tablespoons of safflower, corn, or preferably walnut oil, 1/8 teaspoon of ground white pepper, 2 tablespoons of anise liqueur or Pernod, and 2 tablespoons of the sherry marinade from the onions. Whisk well, and let the mixture stand, until the onions have been completely marinated. Arrange watercress in a glass bowl, then make patterns of the orange slices covered with the drained onion rings. Shake the dressing well in a jar, or whisk until well blended, and pour over the salad. Toss the salad well before serving.

GUACAMOLE Avocado Purée

MEXICAN

1 large,
very ripe avocado •
2 tablespoons
fresh lemon or lime juice •
3 tablespoons onion,
diced •
2 cloves garlic,
minced •
1 medium ripe tomato,
peeled and diced •
1/4 teaspoon
Tabasco sauce,
or 1 serrano
or jalapeño, chopped •
Pinch of salt (optional) •

A refreshing and popular party dip with a piquant flavor. You can serve this with chilled CRUDITÉS, which are raw vegetables such as celery stalks, carrot strips, cucumber and scallions—or with crackers.

YIELD: Ten to twelve servings

Cut the avocado in half, remove the pit, and scoop out the flesh with a spoon, adding the lemon or lime juice immediately to avoid discoloration. In a mixing bowl, mash the flesh with the prongs of a fork, stir in all the other ingredients and blend together. Chill and serve.

BONUS IDEAS: You can also use GUACAMOLE as a salad serving 3 or 4, by placing the purée on a bed of lettuce leaves and garnishing each plate with chilled raisins and other strips of CRUDITÉS. Depending on taste, chopped coriander leaves may be added to the purée, or served as garnish.

POULE AU POT Roast Chicken in a Bag

FRENCH

**2 chickens,
3 pounds each ·
2 green apples,
one cored and cut into
1/2-inch cubes,
the other sliced ·
1 large ripe pear,
cored and cut
into 1/2-inch cubes ·
1/4 cup pine nuts ·
2 chicken livers,
cut into small pieces ·
2 stalks celery,
scraped and cubed ·
1/2 cup raisins ·
1/2 teaspoon salt ·
20 green peppercorns,
crushed ·
2 tablespoons
fresh parsley, chopped ·
1/4 teaspoon thyme ·
freshly ground pepper
to taste ·
1 egg white ·
2 tablespoons Calvados
or applejack ·
1/2 cup apple cider—
unpasteurized if possible ·
1/2 cup grapefruit juice ·
1/4 teaspoon chervil,
dried ·
1/8 teaspoon tarragon,
dried ·
Cookware spray ·
Reynolds Brown-In-Bag
(14- by 20-inch size) ·**

The first time I made this dish I prepared one chicken for three members of my family; it proved so delicious that I was criticized for not making more. Since then, I generally prepare two chickens as part of the basic recipe and find it just as easy to prepare the stuffing for four, six, or even eight chickens at the same time, freezing what I wish to reserve for future use. A special caution, however: be certain to puncture the roasting bag before you start cooking, or you will find that the end result may prove more explosive than you intended!

YIELD: Six to eight servings

1. Preheat oven to 350°F. Remove fat from the cavity of each chicken; remove the wingtips, and discard. Puff the raisins by placing them in warm water for about 20 minutes.

2. To prepare the stuffing, place the apple and pear cubes in a mixing bowl, reserving the sliced apples. Add 10 crushed green peppercorns, black pepper, salt, pine nuts, chicken livers, celery, and drained raisins. Sprinkle the parsley and thyme over the mixture, and blend.

3. Lightly whisk the egg white until frothy and blend it into the stuffing mixture. Stuff each chicken and skewer or sew the cavities closed.

4. Apply cookware spray to the inside of a large roasting bag, such as Reynolds Brown-In-Bag. Add the chickens, side by side, and breast side up. Puff the bag, and tie at the top. Be certain to puncture the bag at the top with several holes to allow the steam to escape.

5. Apply cookware spray to the inside of a deep baking dish. Place the bag with the chickens in the dish. Place in the preheated oven with the top of the bag extended vertically. Bake for 1-1/2 hours until tender, but still firm. Cut away the top of the bag, so that the breasts of the chicken are exposed but the cooking juices are maintained at the base of the bag. Increase the oven heat to 400°F. and cook for 10 minutes longer.

6. Remove the chicken from the oven, and cut away and remove the balance of the roasting bag so that the cooking liquor flows into the deep baking dish. Place a serving platter, arranged with thin slices of green apple, in the oven and keep at warming temperature.

7. Meanwhile, using kitchen shears, cut the chicken into serving sections; remove the backbone and any other unwanted sections of the bone structure. Place serving por-

tions of the chicken on the warmed platter and cover with the warmed sliced apples. Keep the food warm until the sauce is prepared, approximately 5 minutes, for best results.

8. To prepare the sauce, bring the cooking liquor in the baking dish to a boil, and begin reducing. Meanwhile, heat the Calvados to the boiling point, and set it to flame. Add the flaming Calvados, the apple cider, and grapefruit juice to the liquor and continue to reduce the sauce to half. Add the remaining peppercorns, tarragon, and chervil, and stir constantly over medium heat for approximately 5 minutes.

9. Pour the finished sauce over the apple slices and chicken, garnish with parsley and cherry tomatoes, and serve.

BONUS IDEAS: Violet Onion Marmalade (page 29) is an ideal accompaniment to this dish. As a side dish, try Rosée de Fruits (page 27) with Medley Sauce (page 31).

* GNOCCHI ALLA PIEDMONTESE
Italian Potato Gnocchi

ITALIAN

**1-1/2 pounds
boiling potatoes,
preferably small, old,
and floury, unpeeled ·
6 to 8 ounces
sweet rice flour
or potato starch ·
1 tablespoon
coarse salt ·
1 tablespoon oil,
optional ·
2/3 cup grated
Parmesan cheese ·**

These light and fluffy potato dumplings are an Italian specialty, and virtually every Italian cook will boast that he or she can make the "best you've ever tasted." GNOCCHI ALLA ROMANA are prepared with semolina flour, GNOCCHI VERDI (page 76-77), with spinach and ricotta—a memorable variation. Once you get the knack of making GNOCCHI, their preparation will seem easy; you will find yourself making a large batch and freezing the extras for future use. In all cases, however, be sure that the sauce you will be using to top this dish is ready before you start cooking the GNOCCHI.

YIELD: Four to six servings

1. Place the potatoes in 4 quarts of water without salt; cover and bring to a boil, then cook about 30 minutes for smaller potatoes, or until tender. To avoid waterlogging, do not puncture the potatoes too often while testing for doneness. Drain; peel while still hot but comfortable to handle. Rice or mash the potatoes into a purée while still warm.

2. Add 4 ounces of the potato starch to the potatoes, flouring your hands to protect them from the heat of the potatoes, and knead the mixture in the shortest possible time to achieve a smooth, homogeneous mixture. While kneading, add additional flour as necessary but in small quantities.

3. Flour a pastry board, or hard surface, and using a quarter of the mixture at a time, shape it into sausage-like rolls 1/2 inch thick, then cut each roll into pieces 3/4 inch long. Sprinkle a bit of flour to coat a grater, preferably one that has a grating side curved into a semi-circle. Roll each cut piece gently over the floured grater so that it is scored with the grater's teeth; this adds to the lightness of the GNOCCHI.

4. Fill a large pan with 4 quarts of salted water, bring to a boil, and gently drop about 20 GNOCCHI into the water at a time. (This will prevent their sticking together.) A tablespoon of oil can be added to prevent sticking. Cook for about 5 minutes, at which point the cooked GNOCCHI will rise to the surface. Remove the GNOCCHI with a slotted spoon (do not use a colander) and place them in a warm serving bowl or platter. Season them with a spoonful of the sauce you are using, but do not stir. Repeat the cooking process until all the GNOCCHI are done. Spread the rest of the sauce over them, and sprinkle with the grated Parmesan cheese, or serve the cheese separately at the table.

BONUS IDEAS: GNOCCHI are excellent with TOMATO SAUCE MINCEUR (page 16–17), preferably the Bolognese version.

The preparation of GNOCCHI sounds far more complicated than it actually is. You can buy frozen GNOCCHI in many Italian markets, but I do want to encourage you to make your own as this is far less expensive and certainly more fun.

GNOCCHI are an excellent accompaniment to many meat dishes such as LAMB IN THE BAG WITH JUNIPER BERRIES (page 14); in this case, use the sauce derived from the dish for the GNOCCHI.

Other memorable variations in serving GNOCCHI include using PESTO (page 126–27), or GORGONZOLA CHEESE SAUCE (page 133) in place of tomato sauce.

ROSÉE DE FRUITS Morning Dew Vegetables

FRENCH

3 carrots, scraped and sliced diagonally •
2 stalks celery, scraped and cut into 1/2-inch slices •
2 tomatoes cut into quarters or sixths, depending on size •
1/2 pound string beans (remove strings and julienne into 2- or 3-inch lengths) •
1/4 teaspoon coarse salt •
10 green peppercorns, crushed •
5 twists of pepper mill •
5 sprigs fresh parsley •
1 mint leaf •
Cookware spray •

Ideally, this dish should be prepared from fresh garden vegetables and cooked AL DENTE to maintain the natural blend of flavors. Since we live in a practical world, however, use the freshest vegetables you can, but cook them as little as possible—so that they are still pleasantly crisp.
YIELD: Four servings

1. Wash the vegetables and shake off the excess water. Place all the ingredients except the mint leaf in a tightly covered heavy pot to which cookware spray has been applied. If necessary, add 1 tablespoon additional water. Cook AU SEC over low heat for approximately 20 minutes, shuffling the pot occasionally and checking periodically to determine when the vegetables are AL DENTE. Cool and serve with reserved sauce from BLANQUETTE DE VEAU (page 20), MEDLEY SAUCE (page 31), or VINAIGRETTE MINCEUR (page 135).

BONUS IDEAS: This dish is so naturally attractive it doesn't need special garnishing, although you may wish to add a fresh mint leaf and a ring of sliced almonds to each serving.

An excellent accompaniment to BLANQUETTE DE VEAU, especially if you serve the aromatic vegetables of that dish puréed, which permits utilizing the same sauce for both; it is also a delightful adjunct to most meat dishes. You can experiment with reserved sauces from other dishes as well or quickly prepare a special MEDLEY SAUCE.

If you prefer using a pressure cooker, cook for approximately 3 to 4 minutes after the valve begins functioning.

WHITECAP OMELET WITH FRUIT

AMERICAN

4 egg whites ·
**Salt and freshly ground
pepper to taste** ·
**1/8 teaspoon basil,
dried** ·
**4 tablespoons
skim-milk ricotta,
cottage, or cream cheese** ·
**1 tablespoon
polyunsaturated margarine
(optional)** ·
Cookware spray ·

This is a pleasant American variation of the Italian FRITTATA, made with egg whites and delicate ricotta cheese. It's amazingly good as a hearty pick-me-up breakfast, a light luncheon dish, a dessert, or an evening snack—any time you're looking for something light, special, and different.
YIELD: Two servings

1. Separate the egg whites from the yolks. If not using the "bonus" concept, reserve the egg yolks. Add the salt and pepper to the egg whites and beat or whisk for about 1 minute until they are foamy. Add the basil.

2. Apply cookware spray to a skillet. If using margarine, heat until melted. Add half of the egg white mixture and cook over medium heat until it is the consistency of a paper-thin FRITTATA or crêpe. Turn the thin omelet over and spread with half the ricotta cheese in a thin layer to cover the entire omelet.

3. Cook several minutes longer until the underside of the omelet is cooked and the ricotta is warm. If the "bonus" concept is used, add half the egg yolk (beaten) on top of the cheese and cook until the yolk reaches the consistency you prefer. In either case, garnish the omelet with parsley, tomato bits, relishes—or whatever suits your fancy—and serve. Repeat with the balance of the ingredients to form your second omelet.

BONUS IDEAS: Of course, you can extend this pleasant dish to a larger number of servings by using 2 egg whites and 2 tablespoons of ricotta per person.

I have tried it with and without the addition of the egg yolks and find that the whitecap version, using egg whites alone, is more interesting; so did the originator of this recipe when he first permitted me to adapt it to a MINCEUR CUISINE version.

Some of the garnishing variations I have enjoyed are fresh tomato bits, parsley, mushrooms, and diced artichoke bottoms.

As a dessert, try adding apple butter, sliced apples or apple pie filling, chopped pineapple, chutney, or mandarin oranges—it's simply a matter of your creativity and your taste. Add a dash of cinnamon or nutmeg when you feel it is appropriate.

* MARMELADE D'OIGNONS AUX PRUNEAUX Violet Onion Marmalade

FRENCH

6 large violet onions, often referred to as red or purple— about 2 pounds •
3/4 cup raisins •
12 fresh plums— about 2-1/2 pounds •
3 slices each, fresh lemon and orange •
2 whole cloves, crushed •
Cookware spray •

Although this tangy marmalade takes about two hours to prepare, which is about the length of time it takes for the onions to caramelize, you will find it will become one of your favorites. Besides being an excellent accompaniment for veal and poultry dishes, the marmalade freezes well and makes a marvelous gift. Try designing your own labels and making larger quantities for special occasions.

YIELD: About one quart

1. Peel and slice the onions. Puff the raisins by soaking them in 1/2 cup of warm water for 20 minutes. Apply cookware spray to a deep, heavy skillet. Do not add any liquid.

2. Place the sliced onions in the skillet and cover tightly. Cook over moderate-to-low heat, stirring and shuffling the pot occasionally to avoid burning. After about an hour, remove the cover and continue cooking until the onions are caramelized—about one hour more.

3. Meanwhile, split the plums and remove the pits. Combine the plums, raisins, lemon and orange slices, and the crushed cloves. Cook about 1 hour in 1 cup water until the plums are tender.

4. Add the stewed fruits to the caramelized onions in the skillet, blend, and cook for an additional 10 minutes. Cool and serve at room temperature.

BONUS IDEAS: The marmalade can be attractively served over a bed of fresh or stewed orange slices. For freezing, I use small glass jars, leaving a little space for expansion, and top the marmalade with an orange or lemon slice before capping.

Since the length of time for caramelizing the onions is a major factor, I often double the recipe, using 3 crushed cloves; or triple the recipe, using 4 crushed cloves.

* MOUSSAKA IN A MOLD

GREEK

4 eggplants,
totaling
about 3-1/2 pounds •
1 cup cooked lamb,
diced •
4 tablespoons oil •
5 tablespoons water •
1 tablespoon lemon juice •
1/2 onion, diced •
1 clove garlic, minced •
1/2 cup mushrooms,
sliced lengthwise •
1/4 cup white wine,
dry vermouth, or consommé •
2 tomatoes diced,
or 1-1/2 cups canned
Italian style plum tomatoes •
3 tablespoons parsley,
chopped •
1 teaspoon coarse salt •
3 twists of pepper mill •
2 egg whites •
Cookware spray •

For those who like the combination of eggplant and lamb, this will become a family favorite and a tasty conversation piece at parties. You can use the purple eggplant or the pearl-white eggplant that can be found in Chinese markets. Both make decorative centerpieces when the unmolded MOUSSAKA is garnished with tomato sauce and other colorful edibles.

YIELD: Six to eight servings

1. Precook lamb in the oven at 350°F. with condiments of your choice, or use lamb reserved from an earlier meal. Dice 1 cup of lamb and set aside.

2. Cut 2-1/2 pounds of eggplants (or 2 or 3 large ones) in half lengthwise. Carefully separate the pulp from the skins so that the skins are not damaged. Do not remove the pulp. Score the pulp with a sharp knife in a crisscross pattern. Cook in a skillet, pulp-side down, with 2 tablespoons of polyunsaturated oil for 3 minutes. Add the water and lemon juice, cover, and steam for approximately 7 minutes over medium heat. Place the pulp in a mixing bowl and reserve the skins.

3. Cut the balance of the eggplants, unpeeled, into round slices, 1/4 inch thick, and brown in remaining oil for approximately 5 minutes. Cover and steam for 5 minutes longer. Combine with the pulp in the mixing bowl.

4. Preheat oven to 350°F. Apply cookware spray to a skillet and sauté the onions until translucent, adding a little water if necessary. Add garlic and mushrooms. Meanwhile combine the cooked eggplant with the wine or consommé, the diced lamb bits and the tomatoes, parsley, pepper, and salt. Stir this mixture into the skillet and continue to sauté until the lamb is warm. Whisk the egg whites until they foam and add to the mixture in the skillet after removing it from the stove.

5. Apply cookware spray to a 1-1/2 quart soufflé dish, charlotte mold, or ovenproof glass bowl. Arrange the eggplant skins with the colored side against the walls of the mold. Cover the inside of the mold completely, extending the edges of the skins over the top rim of the mold as much as possible to serve later as a cover for the contents. Place the cooked mixture into the mold, within the skins, and press into the mold firmly. Cut a circle of aluminum foil slightly smaller in diameter than the size of the mold and place over the top of the mixture. Turn the extended edges of the skins over to cover the top of the foil and the mixture.

6. Place the mold in a pan of water about 1/2 the depth of the mold and bake in the oven for about 2 hours. (If you are planning to freeze this dish for future use, remove the mold from the oven after 1 hour; cool it and then freeze.) Once cooked, remove the mold from the oven and let it cool for at least 15 minutes before unmolding. Carefully remove the circle of foil and turn the mold over onto a warm platter. Serve with hot TOMATO SAUCE MINCEUR (page 16–17) and garnishes of your choice.

BONUS IDEAS: If food has been frozen, thaw and then cook for 1-1/2 hours.

This stunning dish lends itself to decoration. Garnish with watercress, ring with red cherry tomatoes, spread the top with a few spoonfuls of tomato sauce, and decorate with fresh basil or mint leaves.

Remember that you can save a step if you reserve 1 cup of cooked lamb from a previous meal.

SAUCE MÉLANGE Medley Sauce

FRENCH

1/2 cup reserved cooking liquor, preferably from Steamed Veal with Cheese Sauce •
1 tablespoon Armagnac brandy •
1-1/2 tablespoons Iceland cheese, grated •
1/2 tablespoon Parmesan cheese, grated •
2 shallots, minced •
1/8 teaspoon each, dried thyme, parsley, and tarragon •
1 tablespoon lemon juice •

An imaginative sauce for vegetable dishes whenever you would like a variation from vinaigrette sauce. This sauce is based on reserved cooking liquors from steamed dishes you have previously prepared, especially STEAMED VEAL WITH CHEESE SAUCE (page 20). A superb accompaniment to MORNING DEW VEGETABLES (page 27).
YIELD: Four servings

Pour the cooking liquor into a pan, bring to a boil, and cook for 5 minutes over high heat to reduce the liquid. Heat the Armagnac, set aflame, and add to the cooking liquid. Blend the grated cheeses, mix with the lemon juice, and whisk into a foam. Add the cheese mixture and the balance of the ingredients to the cooking liquid, reduce the heat, and simmer for 3 minutes; serve.

In the event that suitable cooking liquids are not easily available, you can utilize chicken or beef broth, or consommé, delicately flavored with your favorite bottled meat bases, such as Valentine's, Bovril or B-V.

NAKYPLYAK Wedgwood Blue Cabbage in a
Mold of Leaves

UKRAINIAN

1 medium head of
green cabbage,
or preferably a mixture
of leaves from both
green and purple cabbages ·
1 tablespoon grated onion ·
1 tablespoon water ·
1 tablespoon white wine,
or dry vermouth ·
1/2 pound
chicken breasts, minced ·
4 egg whites ·
1/2 teaspoon coarse salt ·
4 twists of pepper mill ·
1/4 cup soft bread crumbs ·
1 3-foot length
of cheesecloth ·
Cookware spray ·

Aromatics for Steaming:
2 carrots, scraped
and cut lengthwise into
3-inch strips ·
2 celery stalks,
scraped and cut
into 1-inch slices ·
1 small onion,
peeled,
with 1 clove inserted ·
1 bay leaf ·
4 sprigs parsley ·
1/4 teaspoon thyme ·

This impressive Ukrainian specialty is simple and fun to make, and has proved to be an effective conversation piece. I like to use both green and purple cabbage combined, which creates an interesting color variation. You can make it equally well with green cabbage alone. Many Russians cherish using a special mold with the impression of a cabbage so that when this dish is unmolded, it looks like a head of cabbage. I find it more fun and impressive to use the actual outer leaves of the cabbage, presenting a more realistic and attractive cooked head of cabbage to my guests.
YIELD: Six servings

1. Remove the outer leaves of both heads of cabbage for use as a mold. You will have 4 large leaves from the green cabbage and 5 smaller leaves, about 3 inches wide, from the purple head of cabbage. Be careful not to tear the leaves.

2. Place the cabbage leaves in a large pot of water and bring to a boil, uncovered. Remove the leaves as soon as the water has boiled; drain them and let cool. The purple cabbage will leave an attractive color in the cooking water. Reserve the pot of cooking liquor.

3. Cut the remaining heads of cabbage into quarter sections. Remove and discard the core and the hard, center ribs of each cabbage leaf. Shred the cabbage as you would for cole slaw. Bring the pot of cooking liquor to a boil again, and cook the shredded cabbage, uncovered, for about 10 minutes, until it is cooked but still crisp. Drain immediately and set aside to cool. Now you will find that the purple cabbage has turned to a refreshing Wedgwood blue color.

4. Once cooled, squeeze all the moisture out of the cooked shredded cabbage, and chop finely or put it through a grinder. Apply cookware spray to a skillet, add 1 tablespoon of water and begin sautéing the tablespoon of grated onion; add the dry vermouth and continue cooking until onion is translucent. Add the onion to the ground cabbage, and blend in the minced chicken. Whisk the egg whites until fluffy; add the salt, pepper, and soft bread crumbs and combine this with the cabbage mixture.

5. Spread cheesecloth, or a cotton towel, in warm water. Squeeze the cloth dry and double at its widest width; spread onto a counter surface. Apply cookware spray to the cloth and arrange the purple cabbage leaves to form a petal-like base for the larger green leaves. Arrange the green leaves to

create a round, hollow shape. Spoon the ground cabbage mixture into the hollow of the leaves, so that when you lift the edges of the cheesecloth you have formed a realistic impression of a full head of cabbage. Tie the ends of the cloth together, leaving sufficient room for the contents to expand.

6. For cooking, you need a large pot and two racks for steaming. A metal trivet, inverted ovenproof dishes or blocks of wood can be used to elevate the racks. Place the aromatic herbs and vegetables, wrapped in cheesecloth if necessary, on a small rack, over sufficient water for steaming. Place the cloth containing the stuffed cabbage on a second rack, higher than the first. Cover the pot, using damp paper towels between the pot and cover for extra sealing if necessary, and steam for about 1 hour.

7. Lift the cloth-covered cabbage mixture out of the steamer, drain well, and place on a platter. Untie or cut away the cloth. Then turn over once more so that the base of the cabbage form is at the bottom of the platter. Garnish the platter with cooked potato slices, watercress, basil, or mint leaves and serve with Tomato Sauce (page 16–17) or Mushroom Sauce (page 114). I like to alternate a ring of sautéed mushroom buttons and pearl onions around the base of the stuffed cabbage head, as part of my presentation.

BONUS IDEAS: In Russian, NAKYPLYAK refers to the puffing of the cabbage while cooking. If you prefer to use a large mold instead of the cabbage leaves, you can eliminate the aromatic herbs and vegetables, which contribute to the cooking and flavoring of the leaves. Apply cookware spray to the inside of the mold and sprinkle wheat germ, or bread crumbs, inside the mold. Fill the mold about two-thirds full with the cabbage mixture, to allow for expansion. Cover the mold with tinfoil and set it on the second layer of a steamer or simply on a rack in a large pot.

Add enough boiling water to the pot to reach halfway up the mold on its rack. Cover the pot tightly, using the damp-paper-towel technique if necessary, and steam for about 1 hour. Unmold, garnish, and serve as indicated previously.

Excellent variations you will enjoy: substitute 1/2 pound of filet of veal cutlets for the chicken breasts, or, for an extra bonus, use veal brains or one set of sweetbreads. In the case of the latter, press through a sieve before combining with the ground cabbage.

SLOTTSSTEK Swedish Pot Roast

SWEDISH

4 pounds
rump beef roast •
1 teaspoon salt •
6 to 8 twists of
pepper mill •
1-1/4 cups
beef bouillon,
or canned consommé •
2 medium onions,
chopped •
4 anchovy filets,
chopped •
6 black peppercorns
and 6 green peppercorns •
8 allspice berries,
or 1/2 teaspoon
ground allspice •
1 bay leaf •
2 tablespoons vinegar •
1 tablespoon molasses •
1 teaspoon arrowroot,
or cornstarch •
Juice of half a lemon •
4 tablespoons
fromage blanc
(Iceland cheese),
grated, or
1/2 cup plain yoghurt •
Cookware spray •

Here is a hearty family meal that is simple to prepare and that requires very little attention during the cooking process. You and your guests will find SLOTTSSTEK not only satisfying but memorable: its interesting aroma will permeate the kitchen, eliciting comments and questions, and generally creating a mood of happy anticipation.

YIELD: Six to eight servings

1. Apply cookware spray to a pressure cooker, or large heavy pot. Trim all excess fat from the beef roast, and dip it briefly in cold water. Drain, but do not pat dry, and rub all surfaces with the salt and ground pepper. Place the beef roast in the cooker or standard pot and brown on all sides over high heat.

2. Add the bouillon, onions, anchovies, peppercorns, allspice, bay leaf, vinegar, and molasses. Reduce the heat to medium, cover and cook in the pressure cooker for 20 to 25 minutes after the valve is engaged. If a standard pot is used, cook on the top of the range or in an oven at 350°F. for about 2 hours, or until meat is fork-tender.

3. Remove the meat, cover with aluminum foil, and set aside in a warm place. Strain the sauce and return the liquid to the pot, reserving the mixture of onions and seasonings. Dilute the arrowroot with 2 tablespoons of the liquid. Blend the lemon juice with the FROMAGE BLANC or yoghurt; stir in the arrowroot mixture, then add the entire mixture to the liquid in the pot. Cook over low heat, stirring constantly, until the sauce thickens, but do not permit it to boil. Slice the pot roast and serve with the yoghurt sauce and, as a relish, the reserved onion and seasoning mixture.

BONUS IDEAS: If you prefer to use a slow-cooking crockery pot, cover and cook over low heat 6 to 8 hours, then proceed with step 3 of the recipe.

Garnish with watercress, or parsley and strips of pimiento.

An excellent accompaniment is ROAST POTATOES A LA CABAÑA (page 111).

34

COSTATA DI MANZO ALLA
PIZZAIOLA Steak with Tomatoes and Oregano

ITALIAN

2 cross-ribs beef, each
weighing 3/4 pound ·
1/2 teaspoon coarse salt ·
6 twists of pepper mill ·
1 clove garlic ·
1/2 tablespoon each,
olive and corn oil ·
1-1/2 pounds
fresh tomatoes;
or 1 16-ounce
can of Italian style
plum tomatoes ·
1/4 cup white wine,
or dry vermouth ·
2 or 3 sprigs
fresh oregano or
2 teaspoons, dried ·
Cookware spray ·

We tend to think that gourmet dishes take a great deal of time and attention; but this one is so simple and satisfying, I am sure it will become one of your own easy-to-make favorites. Perfect for busy homemakers who can simply thaw a frozen steak and draw on the family larder for all the other ingredients necessary for this special dish. If at all possible, however, do use fresh sprigs of oregano.

YIELD: Four servings

1. Cover the steaks with waxed paper, and pound them with a mallet or the side of a cleaver until very thin. Discard any excess fat, skin, and sinews. Discard the wax paper, and dip the steaks briefly into cold water; drain, but do not pat dry. Season both sides of each steak with salt and pepper, pressing the seasonings into the meat with the side of a knife.

2. Apply cookware spray to a large skillet, and brown the steaks on both sides over high heat. Remove the steaks, place them between two heated plates, and set aside in a warm place. Mash the garlic by pressing it with the side of a knife; add it with the oil to the pan and reduce the heat to medium. When the garlic has turned golden brown, remove it and discard. Core the tomatoes and cut into quarters or eighths, depending on size, and add them with the wine to the skillet. Cook over a high heat for 3 minutes, stirring constantly.

3. Place the reserved steaks with their natural juices back into the pan, and sprinkle the oregano over them. Stir so that the steaks are covered with the sauce and absorb its flavors. Tightly close the lid, and remove the skillet from the stove. Let it stand for 5 minutes, before serving.

BONUS IDEAS: The Neapolitans always use wine, although it is optional in other regions of Italy; also, they would never consider making this dish in Naples without fresh oregano, and plenty of it—but it can be done. Fresh oregano, like fresh parsley, tarragon, basil, and coriander, can be frozen and used as needed (see page 245).

As an accompaniment, try serving MARINATED STRING BEAN SALAD (page 21), or ITALIAN ORANGE SALAD (page 23).

4.
The Art of Garnishing

As we have indicated previously, MINCEUR CUISINE and the
new French style of cooking places considerable emphasis
on the imaginative garnishing of each dish, which is generally presented on a large platter in an attractive composition
of textures, colors, and shapes. Confucius, who considered
well-prepared food an art form, recommended this concept
centuries ago. Besides the blending of tastes and textures to
achieve a marriage of flavors, he advocated that a dish please
the eye and stimulate the visual senses as well. Chinese
cuisine has been true to this tenet up to the present day. A
simple example can be found in one of our family's favorite
Chinese recipes for chicken and peppers. The dish is made
with diced bits of red and green fresh peppers, though as a
matter of taste and texture, two fresh peppers of the same
color could be used. The combination of the red and green,
however, remarkably enhances the visual appeal of the dish.

All of us are familiar with sophisticated or, more often,
simple everyday ways of presenting a dish so that it is more
visually attractive. Saffron, for instance, is added to rice
more for its color than its nutritional value. Each of us has
favorite or traditional combinations of edibles for garnishing
certain meals. Turkey is often served with an appetizingly
rich-red cranberry sauce, a sunset-orange touch of cooked
yams, or an accent of fresh, green sprigs of parsley. Another
favorite is baked ham that has been attractively scored in a
crisscross pattern, decorated with whole cloves, glazed, and
garnished with slices of golden pineapple and brilliant, red
maraschino cherries.

Over the centuries every major cuisine has incorporated
some visual appeal in order to enhance the appreciation of
its special dishes. However—with the exception of Chinese
and Japanese cooks, who float beautiful Picasso-like edibles

36

in attractive colors and shapes in their soups—our tendency has been to dress up and decorate the surroundings of our dishes rather than to truly coordinate and make satisfying compositions of their actual ingredients. As we have mentioned earlier, Charlemagne had flowers and petals strewn on holiday tables, and Catherine de Medici, with Renaissance finesse, dressed her table gloriously with gold and silver masterpieces and fine glassware. Subsequent master chefs of LA GRANDE CUISINE, many of whom had some architectural training or interest, applied their artistic bent to PIÈCES MONTÉES—meticulously detailed, but hardly edible, representations of famous buildings and other objects. The famous chef Auguste Escoffier was photographed, posing most proudly, in front of one such masterpiece, an exquisite sugar model of the world-famous Grosvenor House in London. Antonin Carême, whom many consider to be the founder of LA GRANDE CUISINE, once wrote: "The fine arts are five in number, to wit: painting, sculpture, poetry, music, architecture—whose main branch is confectionery."

In fact, the European emphasis on sauces and garnishes was designed more to mask the inherent taste and essence of ingredients than to enhance and complement them. For years, I found that in French cuisine string beans were dark and limp, although covered with a delightful sauce, whereas the Chinese, with their concept of suiting the cooking process to the ingredient, seemed to bring out the beautiful, natural colors of their vegetables.

The tendency among international chefs, then, has been to focus on the surrounding decorations, as opposed to the incorporation of decorative elements into the actual dish. Table settings could prove enchanting with fine tablecloths, gold or silver eating utensils, candlesticks, decorative glassware, flowers, bowls of fruits and nuts, and so on. Even today, one need only check most of the advertisements and illustrated cookbooks available to realize that all the pretty pictures focus more on the décor of the table rather than on the creative garnishing of the food. A major function of the advertising agencies is to dress up their clients' food products to make them more appealing and increase sales. In many cases, this is done by surrounding the food with attractive and eye-catching paraphernalia of table décor.

I am reminded of when I worked as an associate to Russel Wright, the famous industrial designer who specialized in designing functional and attractive items for the table as well as for the home. The constant demand by advertising and promotional firms for exciting table items to be photographed with their clients' food products was so great that Russel set up a "library" of items that could be loaned out for photographic sessions. Platters, dishes, eat-

37

ing utensils, vases, tablecloths, and all decorative table accessories were available in a variety of colors, shapes, and designs, and were checked in and out in much the same way as a library handles its books.

Instead of emphasizing table décor, we will explore the art of garnishing, which places the prime emphasis on the creative and attractive composition of edible ingredients in terms of their textures, colors, and shapes as well as in terms of a harmonious blending of tastes. Like artists, we have a huge palette of colors provided by nature, which we can utilize as creatively as we choose. On the following pages we will list an initial color palette of edible ingredients for garnishing your dishes. You can add to or adapt these ingredients according to your own artistic bent and preferences.

Before we get to the actual garnishing techniques, however, I would like to explore some additional factors that can influence your own personal approach to the art of garnishing. In addition to your use of colors, your concept of forms and shapes, and of the dish as a whole, will be important. For example, Salvador Dali has illustrated and co-authored a cookbook called LES DINERS DE GALA, with recipes by his wife and famous chefs. Even if you haven't had an opportunity to examine this book, you can probably imagine the exotic garnishing concepts created by this unusual and flamboyant artist.

For example, a platter of cauliflower with Roquefort cheese is shown with a golden cheese sauce layered like strips of spaghetti, surrounded by large cauliflower florets. This part is not unusual; however, the dish is then topped with a gold-filigreed, glass-heeled lady's evening slipper, which is filled with more of the spaghetti-like sauce and topped with another cauliflower floret, arranged to suggest a pompom for the slipper. Other illustrations in the book indicate original and, let us say, interesting concepts of garnishing; but in general I found that many of the garnishes were created more for purely visual effect (one I thought rather bizarre) and less for the enhancement of the basic ingredients. One wonders how tempted a diner would be to actually eat some of these forbidding creations. I find this approach to be the very antithesis of effective garnishing.

I still remember Russel Wright's basic tenet of good design: GOOD DESIGN SUGGESTS THE MOOD OF ITS USE. In other words, an elaborate, finely made doorknob that one is not sure how to operate or how to grasp may be exciting to look at, but must, as good design, be considered a failure. A coffee cup with a handle that is imaginative but uncomfortable to hold is equally a failure. I have a pen made in Europe that is very expensive and exquisitely tooled. It is a polished metal tube so masterfully constructed that, when closed, it suggests an abstract work of art and stimulates a great deal of conversation. Yet, I am constantly disturbed by the pen because it suggests to me the tubular case for a thermometer. Although it is beautifully made, as a pen, again, I must label it a design failure. The mood it suggests is not consistent with its function. In garnishing, therefore, the end result must be honest and satisfying in order to truly enhance the basic ingredients so that they satisfy our visual sense as well as our palate.

Perhaps one reason that most of us have not investigated this aspect of cooking before is that, in the past, it has been considered a luxury, indulged in only by those who could afford domestic help to direct or assist in the kitchen. The great chefs of the past, after all, had at their beck and call numerous assistants rushing around and performing time-consuming tasks.

These head chefs were often dictatorial, and there are many stories of how difficult an apprenticeship in the kitchen could be. Paul Bocuse, who served his apprenticeship under the fabled Fernand Point in the Michelin-starred Pyramide Restaurant in Vienne, was recently interviewed by NEWSWEEK magazine. "Above all," NEWSWEEK reported, "Bocuse keenly admired the autocratic chef's imperiousness. 'Point was tough, a little mean,' Bocuse now recalls rather fondly. 'Some of that certainly rubbed off on me.'"

There are similar stories concerning Carême and Escoffier, both of whom ended up becoming as autocratic as the head chefs under whom they served their apprenticeships. Even today, the chefs of the new wave of French cooking, including Bocuse and Michel Guérard, have large kitchen staffs and delegate tasks that are presumably carried out only under their strict eye and personal supervision. However, the results can be less than would be expected if they handled these tasks themselves.

I am reliably informed that, when a well-known magazine published its article on Guérard and MINCEUR CUISINE, Guérard sent several assistants to New York to adapt his recipes to American standards. One of the recipes was for a tomato tart, with cooked spinach layered on the bottom and top of a tomato mixture in a 4-inch mold. A friend who tried this particular recipe, which calls for 4-1/4 pounds of spinach to fill six molds, asked me if I had ever tried washing that much spinach in my own kitchen. And how, he asked, could one possibly use that much spinach to line six 4-inch molds? He claimed that he had almost two pounds of spinach left over.

In our own American culture, during the Victorian and pre-World War I periods, when wealthier families and the comfortable middle class had live-in domestic help, cookbooks were aimed at the head cook and at the lady of the house, who—like the gourmet wives in Confucius' time—planned the menus. These volumes included many references to setting the table for various types of meals—again the tablecloth, the candlesticks, the glassware. And occasionally there were suggestions for garnishing a PIÈCE DE RÉSISTANCE. One example I chanced upon was a turn-of-the-century masterpiece, a frozen plum pudding garnished with colorful green holly, including the brilliant red berries and all the spikes that are characteristic of this plant.

Of course, the color of shiny holly leaves and the contrasting berries (which I believe are poisonous) can be attractive. However, to serve the pudding, the hostess—while chatting amiably—would first have to remove the top garnish of holly and place it as decorously as possible, with its messy pudding residue, onto a separate dish. Then, she would have to hold her arms well over the serving platter to avoid the prickly leaves still ringing the pudding at the bottom. Without such precautions, she could easily scratch her bare hand or tear the lace ruffles off the sleeve ends of her dress.

I trust that now you can understand why our approach will be to honestly and creatively garnish our cooked dishes so that they will appeal to the eye as well as to taste, so that the entire dish will be harmonious—a marriage or blending of tastes, colors, textures, and shapes—a satisfying unit in its own right.

In our approach to the art of garnishing, we will establish an initial palette of edible ingredients varying in texture, size, shape, and taste, and we will utilize them much as a creative artist would utilize the elements of his palette. We will use our own good judgment and creative abilities to complement our basic, cooked dishes. Besides realizing that the red of cranberry is a colorful complement to turkey, we will also take into consideration that its taste is harmonious with the main ingredient of the dish.

All of us know at least one fine cook who takes pride in his or her cooking and presents each dish with great aplomb and appeal. More often than not this takes place in baking, where attractive decoration has been accepted for some time as an integral and appealing part of the overall product. In fact, in my own home, we have taken the art of garnishing for granted. I have discovered, however, that many of us need direction before we can incorporate specific concepts of our own.

Perhaps if I give you some indication of the influences I have found valuable, it may help you to remember and realize similar experiences in your own life. First of all, there is always the influence of the distinctive cooks we knew in our childhood. Although I was an active boy who rarely thought of the kitchen except as a haven of special goodies, I do remember my mother's cooking and that of some of her neighbors. It was my father, however, who initiated my interest in garnishing; he was a creative artist in the kitchen. In his youth, he had been apprenticed to a butcher and had eventually organized his own trucking firm specializing in supplying general stores and butcher shops. He never lost his skill with a knife.

I first learned to appreciate his cutting prowess when he tackled tomatoes, onions, and other vegetables, which he sliced with great relish until there was an impressive pile of perfect and thinly-cut slices ready for him to arrange on a platter. This memory is probably one reason I like the preparations required by Chinese cuisine, with its emphasis on the cutting, chopping, slicing, and mincing of ingredients. I find, incidentally, that I prefer doing these cutting tasks by hand rather than by using many of the old or new mechanical marvels, ranging from the famous French MANDOLINE to the currently popular Cuisinart cutter-blender. Generally, with a good, sharp knife I can cut more efficiently, and can more easily adapt the cutting thickness to my needs, in less time than I could with mechanical assistance, considering the time needed to assemble the machine, prepare the food for it, and then clean the machine afterwards. In addition, I frankly enjoy what has been called the therapeutic value of the cutting and chopping activity in the kitchen.

My father had a special talent for assembling and decorating each dish he prepared, especially platters of cold cuts and dishes of antipasto; every item contributed to the artistic presentation of the dish. In fact, he even added a slice of a fresh peach to a glass of red wine, which not only enhanced the flavor but was also an attractive garnish.

Years later, during my twin careers as an executive with major design firms and as a playwright, I was fortunate to meet outstanding designers, decorators, architects, and creative personalities. I was greatly influenced, as I have mentioned previously, by Russel Wright, whose whole life was bound to the investigation of and solutions to the problems of harmony of color, shape, and form (in terms of the essential parameters of use). I'm reminded of an experiment he conducted at the New York World's Fair in the late 1930's concerning the visual effect of various dishes. He carefully prepared a series of commonly acceptable foods and placed them on plates varying in color from stark white through the spectrum to a forbidding black. He discovered that the identical foods had less appeal when placed on some of the brighter-colored plates than when they were

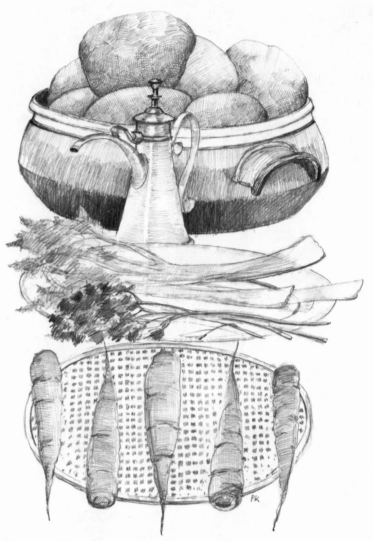

served on plates with neutral colors. In addition, Russel prepared plates of foods with unexpected color combinations, such as green mashed potatoes, orange meat, blue peas, etc., which he accomplished with special lighting effects. As one might guess, visitors to the Fair turned away from the unusual and unfamiliar colorations and preferred those with which they were comfortable and which suggested freshness, attractiveness, and a pleasant taste.

I relate this incident to caution that everything worth doing is not necessarily worth overdoing. The palette of edible garnishes we will be exploring is so vast that one must be careful to avoid destroying or masking the essential nature and appeal of the basic ingredients. Remember that an artist does not begin by mixing and spreading every color variation onto his palette each time he paints. Of the edible shapes and colors that appeal to you, select a sufficient but limited number for each occasion; you do not have to use all of them at once, although you can add items or vary them for special effects whenever you desire.

In our household, we have always taken great pleasure both in preparing a delightful dish and presenting it with flair but not ostentation. My wife has developed her own palette of colors and ingredients and even her own "trademark"— the use of baked and stewed fruits as garnishes. Although the same edible ingredients are available to every family member, each one has expressed individuality in selecting and using the ingredients, just as an artist does. After all, musicians have only eight notes to work with—and with these few have pleased our ears for centuries with infinite variations of melodies and rhythms.

The initial list of edible garnishes is intentionally as large as possible in order to permit each of you to select the items you prefer for a personal palette. I am sure that each of you can add to this initial list and make substitutions as you see fit. If black truffles are too expensive, black olives can be equally effective. One is reluctant to open a can of lichee nuts when only one or two may be required for garnishing, so feel free to substitute a refreshing fruit of the color, shape, and texture you find appealing—a few white grapes, half a cooked pear, or whatever satisfies your creative and practical instincts.

Here then is an initial palette of edibles in varying colors, textures, and shapes, which you can adapt to your own personal preferences.

INITIAL PALETTE OF COLORFUL EDIBLES

As an amateur painter and former student of fine arts, I know that there is no agreement among well-known artists about the placement of colors on the artist's palette or the number of color variations they will utilize. Depending on the subject to be painted, some artists use as few as six colors, others many more. To assure success, most advocate placing the right color in the right place on the palette. Generally, they begin with the reds and oranges and proceed clockwise to the yellows, greens, blues, browns, and eventually, to the blacks and whites.

As students of the art of garnishing, we have at our disposal the enormous palette provided by nature itself—a palette we will arrange and use as deliberately as the artists do theirs. We will begin arranging our palette with the whites, a color predominant in the edibles provided by nature. We will then progress through the generally standard palette of colors, ending with the black edibles. Of course you can add to each color category any special favorite garnishing edible you may wish to use.

Whites: almonds, peeled
apple, peeled
asparagus, white
banana, peeled
cauliflower
chestnuts
coconut, pieces or shredded
cottage cheese
cream
cucumber, peeled
eggplant, Oriental white
egg white, hard-boiled
endive
fennel, white part
horseradish
leeks, white part
lichee nuts, fresh
   or canned
onion, pearl
parsnip
pear, peeled
pine nuts
potato, peeled
rice
ricotta
salsify, or oyster plant
scallions, white part
sour cream
truffles, white
turnip
white cheese, hard
yoghurt

Reds: banana, red
beets
bell pepper
caviar, red
cayenne
chilies, red
cranberries
ginger, red
horseradish, red
kidney beans
lobster, cooked
olives, red
paprika
pepper, red
pimiento
pistachio nuts
plum sauce
radishes, red
raspberries
rhubarb
russet potato, unpeeled
shrimp, cooked
spiced apple
strawberries
Tabasco, red
tomato, tomato sauce, or
   catsup
watermelon meat

Oranges: apricot
canteloupe
carrot
Cheddar cheese
duck sauce, Chinese
egg yolk, hard-boiled
kumquat
mandarin orange
nasturtium
orange
peach
pumpkin
red pepper, roasted
rutabaga
smoked salmon
squash
tangerine
tiger lily, dried

Yellows: apple, golden
aspic with chicken stock
banana, cooked
celery, cooked
cheese, yellow
endive, fennel, cooked
grapes, yellow
lemon
pasta, cooked
pepper, golden
pineapple
raisins, golden
saffron rice
squash, yellow

44

Greens: apples, green
artichoke, bottom and heart
asparagus, green
avocado
basil
broccoli
broccoli rabe
Brussels sprouts
capers
coriander
cucumber
dandelion greens
dill
escarole
green cabbage
green onion
lettuce
lime
melon, honeydew
mint
mustard greens
okra
olives, green
oregano
parsley
pepper, green
peppercorns, green
pickles and gherkins
sorrel
spinach
string beans
tarragon
thyme
tomato, green
watercress
zucchini

Blues and Purples: blueberries
broccoli, purple
cabbage, purple
grapes, blue-black
grapes, purple
lingonberries
onion, violet or purple
plum

Browns: anchovy
bran, toasted
bread crumbs, toasted
chestnuts, unshelled
chutney
cinnamon
dates and figs
eggplant, cooked
lentils
maple syrup
meat, cooked
mushroom
nutmeg
nuts—walnuts and
  cashews
potato, unpeeled
prunes, cooked
soy sauce

Dark Blues and Blacks: caviar, black
grapes, blue-black
olives, black
peppercorns, black
plums
poppy seeds, black
prunes
truffles, black

CUTTING AND SHAPING TERMS

In the art of garnishing, the shapes and textures of the edibles used are as important as their color. Here, then, are a number of possibilities for working with the shaping of edible forms to realize maximum garnishing effects.

Allumettes Generally refers to strips of puff pastry cut 1/4 of an inch thick and about 3 inches long, and then filled with different mixtures.

45

Brunoise	Diced rectangular-shaped vegetables about 1/8 inch wide and 1/2 inch square.
Jardinière	Similar to MACÉDOINE but varying from 2 to 3 inches in length or diameter.
Julienne	Vegetables or meat shredded or cut into thin strips, about 3 inches long. Named after chef Jean Julienne of France, who came into prominence a century or more ago.
Macédoine	Usually diced pieces of fruits or vegetables, but can refer to balls or lozenge-shapes as well; these are generally larger than PRINTANIER, averaging 1/4 inch in length or diameter.
Mirepoix	About the same size as BRUNOISE, but this generally refers to diced fish, meat, or poultry mixed with ham, mushrooms, or truffles.
Noisette	Refers to potatoes scooped out to look like hazelnuts about 1/2 inch in size. The term also refers to a round of meat about 3 ounces in weight cut from the filet.
Parisienne	Vegetables, which generally include potatoes, cut at least 1 inch in diameter, the slices often cut at a 45° angle.
Printanier	Cutting vegetables into fine strips about 1 inch long for use as garnish for soups; usually associated with fresh and tender spring vegetables, such as new carrots and turnips. String beans, however, are cut into the shapes of lozenges, or 1-inch strips with ends cut diagonally.
Salpicon	About the same size as BRUNOISE but this generally refers to diced fish, meat, or poultry mixed with ham, mushrooms, or truffles.
Scoops	Rounds of vegetables or fruits formed into ball-like shapes, about 3/8 to 1/4 inch in diameter.

SPECIAL CUTTING AND SHAPING TECHNIQUES

Anvil, or T-shaped Mushrooms	Slice the mushrooms vertically, from stem, and sprinkle with lemon juice to avoid discoloration. Particularly adaptable to Oriental dishes and to serving raw in salads.
Carrot Curls	Using a potato peeler or swivel-type parer, cut the carrot in long, bold strokes, from the tip to the thicker base. Roll up the cut curls, secure with a toothpick, and place in iced water until firm. Once firm, remove the toothpicks.
Carrot Sticks	These delicate, long strips of rectangular-shaped carrots are easily made if the curved edges of the carrot are cut away, producing a long rectangular center. Split this centerpiece lengthwise, and continue splitting each piece until you have thin, uniformly-sized carrot sticks.

Chrysanthemum Roots	It is traditional for the Japanese to "half-cut" small roots such as turnips, or large-sized radishes, into flower-like garnishes. Pare the root, and line up two chopsticks, barbecue skewers, or even pencils, one to either side of the root. Make thin slices down to the level of the chopsticks, which prevents cutting too far down through the base. Turn the root 90 degrees, and make thin cross-cutting slices, again down to the level of the chopsticks. Place in iced water to cover, until the sliced top of the root opens into the shape of a chrysanthemum flower.
Cucumber Boat	Slice a cucumber lengthwise about 1/3 from the top. Scoop out the cucumber pulp and reserve for other use. Fill the scooped-out cucumber boat with colorful edibles or relishes to garnish main-course dishes.
Fluted Lemons	Cut off the tip of each end of the lemon, and using a lemon stripper, paring knife or potato peeler, make bold cuts vertically, gouging out strips about 1/8 inch wide. Reserve these long thin strips of rind for other use, leaving alternating stripes of white and yellow around the lemon.
Fluted Mushrooms	This attractive garnish is easier to make than to describe. Using a lemon stripper, curved grapefruit knife, or the tip of a paring knife, flute the mushroom by gouging out thin strips nearly to the top of the cap. Keep rotating the mushroom, gouging out additional thin curved strips until you have fluted the entire mushroom with curving lines. Sprinkle with lemon juice to avoid discoloration.
Fluted Oranges	Using a lemon stripper or paring knife, make bold cuts vertically, fluting the orange in the manner described in instructions for fluting lemons. The removed strips of zest can be crisscrossed for garnishing effects and topped with an edible of contrasting color, such as parsley. The strips can also be tied into simple attractive knots. Once the orange has been fluted, you can turn it on its side and slice it, making thin slices with fluted edges; these can then be used as garnish—either whole, in halves, or in quarters.
Fruit Halves	Peel and cut in halves cored pears, peaches, and/or apricots. Bake until cooked but still crisp and tender, and fill the cavities with mint jelly relishes, or any other complementary edibles.
Green Vegetable Shavings	Using long, green vegetables such as green beans or asparagus, shave off thin strips with a sharp knife, as you might in sharpening a pencil, and use to sprinkle over foods for a pleasant contrast of color or texture.
Mushroom Caps	Remove the stems from large mushroom caps and fill with complementary edibles for garnish. An excellent way to serve snails is in sautéed mushroom caps.

Nature's Own Molds Many other edibles in interesting colors and shapes can make attractive and practical containers for special dishes. Eggplants, melons, and members of the squash family are all admirable. With a sharp knife, remove a small portion of the stem end making V-shaped cuts, as for sawtooth cups. Reserve the cap. If the mold is simply being used as a container, remove the pulp. (In the case of CHINESE WINTER MELON SOUP, page 92–93, do not scoop out the pulp, since you will want to steam the entire melon filled with broth and other ingredients; the pulp will be scooped out when serving.) Cabbage and other leaves can also be used to form a mold, as we have already seen with WEDGWOOD BLUE CABBAGE IN A MOLD OF LEAVES (page 32–33).

48

Orange or Lemon Baskets	Starting at the stem end, and cutting about a third through the orange, make two slices about a quarter inch apart—which is the width of the handle to the basket you are creating. Now cross-cut the sides of the orange, about a third down from the top, so that the two wedges can be removed, leaving the basket handle. Using a sharp, pointed knife, remove the flesh from the basket handle, being careful not to cut through the rind that forms the handle. At this stage, you can leave the flesh of the fruit in the base of the basket. If you wish, make V-shaped cuts along the top diameter of the basket for a sawtooth effect as described in producing sawtooth cups. You can achieve the effect of a multi-pointed star by laying sections of the same fruit, or a contrasting one, into the V-shaped grooves, having them come to a point at the center of the basket. Or, if you prefer, you can scoop out the flesh from the basket and refill it with relishes or other edibles of a contrasting color. A final pleasant touch is to carefully pierce a small hole in the top center of the basket handle and insert a fresh leaf from the garden.
Orange Maypole	This is an extremely long string of the zest, consisting preferably of one unbroken peel from each orange. Cut it starting from the top, immediately below the navel; continuing to within one inch of the base. An effective garnish is to leave the long strip attached to the orange. The long strips are also effective as "maypoles" encircling roasted poultry, or as a topping to gelatin salads.
Petals	Run the prongs of a fork across the length of a carrot, cucumber, or radish, or cut V-shaped grooves of about 1/8 inch into the sides of the vegetables. If you leave the peel on the cucumber, you will get a pleasant contrast when you cut slices crosswise, about 1/8 inch thick, to form flowerlike petals. The radish petals can be stacked on one another, and accented with parsley or small strips of carrot for an additional flowerlike effect.
	NOTE: Always place in iced water and refrigerate until ready for use.
Radish Flowers	Cut off the root end of a red radish; place on its side; with a sharp knife make thin crisscross slices cutting almost but not completely through the back end of the radish. Place in cold water; this will encourage the cut radishes to curl into flower shapes.
Sawtooth Cups	Attractive containers, made usually from the rinds of citrus fruits and filled with puréed foods or diced fruit. Using an orange, or any hard-shelled citrus fruit, insert the tip of a sharp knife halfway through the fruit on an angle, near its center. Move the knife up and then, on a 45° angle, down,

making a V-cut, and repeat until you have a circle of V-cuts around the orange. Separate the sawtooth halves, remove the pulp, and fill attractively as you choose. The same procedure can be used with hard-boiled eggs that have been chilled; these can be refilled with deviled egg mixture, or used for garnish.

Scallion Brushes A mandatory garnish for Peking Duck, but one that can also be used effectively for many other dishes. Cut off the root and the green outer leaves and discard, reserving about 3 inches of the firm white part of the scallion. Make 4 crisscross cuts on each end about 3/4 inch deep and place in iced water to curl the outer ends.

Scoring Crisscross cuts, which generally form a diamond pattern. In both occidental and Oriental dishes, baked hams and some cuts of meat are scored for eye appeal, as well as for tenderizing purposes. Scoring can be used for decorative effect also on hard shelled melons and other members of the squash family, producing a geometric or basket-weave pattern.

Tomato Rose Peel a long single strip from a firm fresh tomato with a sharp knife, as you might peel an orange skin. Turn the strip in the palm of your hand until it is coiled to form the impression of a rose flower. Place in iced water, still coiled, to firm up the tomato rose. For additional accent you can fill the spaces between the inner petals with appropriate thick dressings, especially herbed cottage cheese, ricotta, creamed blue cheese or Gorgonzola.

TEXTURE AND FLAVOR

Now that we have explored the many contributions that color and shape can make to the technique of garnishing, let's investigate the remaining factors important to MINCEUR cooking: texture and flavor.

As always, in considering the whole matter of garnishing, it's well to keep in mind the Chinese, who, as we have seen, pride themselves in attractive presentation of food and in judiciously harmonizing the basic elements of flavor, color, texture, and shape. In considering flavor, the aroma of a dish is also implied since this appeals to the senses, just as the other elements appeal to the eye. Keep in mind, too, that in MINCEUR CUISINE our aim is to enhance, rather than mask, the inherent qualities of the basic ingredients. As a guide to our garnishing approach, perhaps it would be helpful if we broadly categorize the basic types of dishes we will be preparing.

Category I Dishes in which the basic ingredient is predominant in flavor, with only a delicate accent, at most, to bring out its inherent quality. A very simple example would be a slice of melon, sprinkled with a few drops of lemon or lime juice. This category includes most of the seafood that can be eaten uncooked, such as clams, oysters, and mussels. A prime example is TRUITE AU BLEU, blue trout—a dish that gets its name from the fact that the trout is killed immediately before boiling, which causes it to turn blue. Here the emphasis is on the inherent taste of the fresh trout, which is delicately accented by the COURT-BOUILLON in which it is boiled and the optional addition of a hollandaise sauce.

Category II   Dishes that still involve a basic, major ingredient, but in which the preparation and garnish can produce an additional flavor desired by the cook. Category II applies to many French dishes in which a distinctively strong sauce is used, such as a SAUCE BÉARNAISE with CHÂTEAUBRIAND, a prized part of the beef filet. Italian SCALLOPINI of veal with Marsala sauce is another example, as are any of the Indian chicken or lamb dishes to which piquant curries are added. Among Chinese dishes, Sweet and Sour Fish and Peking Duck fall into this category.

Category III   This category includes the widest range of dishes that you will be considering—those that involve two or more basic ingredients that blend together in pleasant harmony, and which, through cooking, are transformed into a distinct, new flavor. An example is the famous French soup, POT-AU-FEU, which is made with a blend of beef, chicken, and vegetables. PAELLA, with its combination of seafood, chicken, vegetables, and saffron rice, is still another of the many examples we could mention.

As these broad categories suggest, it is particularly in Category III that we will be able to exercise our garnishing techniques most creatively. Here we can most effectively influence the new over-all flavor of our MINCEUR dishes by introducing elements that contrast with but nonetheless emphasize the harmony of our basic ingredients. Some of these contrasts include: sweetness versus saltiness; smoothness versus crunchiness; large-sized ingredients versus minuscule ones; hot foods versus cold ones; and formal shapes versus irregular and/or natural forms.

But perhaps a cautionary note is in order here. We must not go overboard, and must not pursue the art of garnishing like a child with a whole new set of toys. Keep in mind that artists, in using their palettes of colors, are extremely careful to introduce a clear, primary, or basic statement—perhaps amplified with specific and well-chosen accents. They know that they can confuse the finished painting if it is cluttered with too many distracting or conflicting elements. Similarly, I would encourage you to begin with a relatively small palette of colorful edibles, and a modest assortment of texture, shapes, and forms—knowing that you can always add to or change the ingredients whenever you wish. As a guide, each of the MINCEUR recipes in this book has one or more garnishing suggestions that may prove helpful in assisting you to establish your initial palette of edibles for garnishing.

I have often heard the expression, "Anything worth doing, is worth overdoing!" When it comes to the art of garnishing, however, I prefer to subscribe to the motto of the architect Ludwig Mies Van der Rohe, one of the titans of modern architecture. He said, quite profoundly, but simply: "Less is more!"

Now that you have experienced your "first weekend" and understand the principles and techniques of the art of garnishing MINCEUR dishes, I welcome you to enjoy the remaining MINCEUR recipes on the following pages.

5.
Main Dishes First

I have often wondered why virtually every cookbook I own, or have perused, always begins with recipes for appetizers and hors d'oeuvres, and then proceeds with recipes for main dishes, ending with desserts and beverages. I suspect this has been due to the influence of standard restaurant menus, for the restaurants obviously assume that patrons will select their appetizers first, then their main dish and possible accoutrements. Once this part of the meal is consumed, the diner can decide which dessert he will have, if any. But I can't conceive of many people planning a meal by selecting the appetizer first. Certainly, we all have favorites in this category, but it makes little sense to expect any good cook to say, "First I'll serve my pâté flavored with orange zest, then—let me see—perhaps fish, or maybe lamb would go well with the pâté, and then maybe. . . ." Hardly likely! I find most cooks, including myself, plan their meals around a particular main dish—the heart of the meal. We are more inclined to say, "Spring lamb is in season and a particularly good buy right now. I think I'll prepare a ROAST OF LAMB IN THE BAG WITH JUNIPER BERRIES, and as an accompaniment MORNING DEW VEGETABLES, or perhaps, ITALIAN ORANGE SALAD, and then as an appetizer. . . ."

With this approach in mind, I am presenting MINCEUR CUISINE recipes for the main dishes first. Now that you have had an opportunity to try your first weekend of cooking in the new French style, and have learned to implement the specific processes and techniques of cooking À LA MINCEUR, you are invited to explore the wide variety of main dishes offered in this chapter, whether your preference is for meat, poultry, seafood, or game. You are now prepared to cook these main dishes and, as an integral part of their presentation, to garnish them attractively. Then, of course, you can proceed to determine which accoutrements you will use as side dishes, which appetizer will precede the main course; and which dessert will follow.

TA BIN LO Hong Kong Hot Pot

CHINESE

**10 cups chicken stock
or canned consommé ·
1 whole chicken breast ·
1/2 pound top sirloin or
filet of beef ·
1/2 pound lean pork ·
1/2 pound filet of sole
or halibut ·
12 Chinese Stuffed
Bean Curds ·
15 large shrimp ·
12 shucked oysters
or clams ·
1 pound Boston or
Chinese lettuce ·
1 pound fresh spinach or
Chinese celery cabbage ·
1/2 pound snow peas,
bamboo shoots, or
mushrooms ·
1 egg per serving or
1/4 cup sherry or
4 ounces of
cellophane noodles,
optional ·**

Preferred for entertaining during the cold winter months, this is essentially a Cantonese version of the traditional Hot Pot. Each region of China has its own variation of ingredients, which are cooked individually at the table by each diner. Although the ingredients vary, they are generally equally divided among the three main categories of thinly sliced meat or poultry, fish or other seafood, and vegetables. The Hong Kong version includes Chinese Stuffed Bean Curds as well. Since only small quantities of each ingredient are used, this is not necessarily an expensive meal to prepare. I have always found it to be very easy to make, requiring only the initial preparation of the broth and the ingredients—for each participant will cook his own portion at the table. Dipping sauces (see Bonus Ideas below), which I prefer to limit to 4 varieties, are also used. Based on my own experience, I suggest that no more than 10 diners share this unusual meal. As each cooks the provided ingredients, the simmering broth is continuously enriched and, as a finale, the broth itself is sipped by all.

YIELD: Eight to ten servings

1. Prepare the chicken stock (page 117). Bone and skin the chicken breast (see page 238) and place the trimmed meat, chicken, and fish filets in the freezer for half an hour to facilitate slicing later. Prepare the table, protecting it from scorching (page 240), with the following: a traditional brass hot pot, or any chafing dish substitute (see Bonus Ideas below), chopsticks, and fondue forks or the traditional long-handled wire mesh strainers used for cooking morsels of food at the table. Arrange platters or a series of bowls to hold the raw ingredients around the hot pot. Select the dipping sauces (see Bonus Ideas below) you will serve and provide the number of small relish-sized individual dishes you will require, usually 2 for each dip.

2. Prepare the Chinese Stuffed Bean Curds, but do not add the sherry or cook them since they will be cooked at the table, as will be all of the other ingredients of the meal. Remove the ingredients from the freezer, and with a sharp knife, slice the meat, chicken, and fish as thinly as possible, about 3 inches long and 1 inch wide to accommodate the chopsticks. The shrimp, oysters, or clams are served whole, or cut in halves, depending on their size. Wash and drain the vegetables, removing any hard ribs or wilted leaves as necessary. Cut the leaves in half if they are too large. If mushrooms are used, slice them thinly into T shapes (page 46). Place the sherry, if used, in a small pitcher. The optional fresh eggs can be placed in baskets or bowls for easy access. Arrange the table simply, emphasizing not only the variety of colorful ingredients but also the equipment and paraphernalia for cooking and eating.

3. Just before your guests arrive, transfer the boiling broth to the hot pot or chafing dish, filling it to about half of its capacity and permitting it to continue simmering over medium heat. Your hot pot is ready, awaiting only the diners who will select the food, cook it to their own taste in the simmering broth, and dip the morsels into one of the dipping sauces. I find it helpful to briefly explain the process to my guests, and to have someone already familiar with the hot pot technique demonstrate how it is done; or you can demonstrate it. Point out that the meats should be cooked, dipped into one of the sauces, and eaten first, then the fish and seafood, followed by the vegetables. The concept is to enrich the broth while each morsel is being cooked with the natural juices of the ingredients; and that at the end of the meal the enriched broth will be consumed with any of the options you select (see Bonus Ideas below). Prepare to add extra broth to the hot pot during the meal, as necessary.

4. There are several acceptable approaches to the preparation of the enriched broth. I prefer the traditional method in which each diner lines the mesh cooking strainer with lettuce leaves to form a cup. Then a raw egg is broken into the lettuce cup and cooked in the hot broth until the egg is poached to taste. The cooked egg is then transferred to the diner's individual bowl, over which the enriched broth is ladled. This is fun to do and not particularly difficult, provided the lettuce forms a proper cup. If the mesh strainers are not available, or if you find this method too troublesome, each diner can crack a raw egg into their individual bowl. Hot enriched broth is then ladled into the bowl and the egg stirred with chopsticks while it is being cooked by the hot broth. Generally the Hong Kong Pot does not utilize sherry, which should be left out of the recipe for Chinese Stuffed Bean Curds, on the assumption that the wine is inconsistent with the flavors of the various other ingredients that enrich the broth. In some regions of China, however, sherry is added to the enriched broth before serving it at the end of the meal. Another possibility is to provide 4 ounces of cellophane noodles that have been previously soaked in warm water to cover, drained, and cut into 8-inch lengths. After all of the other ingredients have been consumed, the cellophane noodles and any of the raw ingredients that remain (you may have to provide additional vegetables) are cooked in the enriched hot broth for about 2 minutes, then ladled into each individual bowl, to climax a memorable meal.

BONUS IDEAS: If using a charcoal-burning hot pot, be sure to see page 240. Other possibilities that can be used successfully for a hot pot include an electric pan or casserole (set at 300°F.), a chafing dish, or any heatproof earthenware casserole over an electric or alcohol burner or hibachi.

Other ingredients or ideas that can be added or substituted for those in the recipe include: dressing strips of beef by dipping them into a mixture of lightly beaten egg whites, to which pepper, salt, and soy sauce have been added to taste; draining them and adding a pinch or two of waterchestnut flour or corn starch. Thinly sliced chicken livers or gizzards, a particular Chinese specialty, may also be used. Filets of any white-fleshed fish may be substituted for the sole or halibut, and thinly sliced scallops, abalone, or bite sizes of cleaned squid are often included. Among the vegetables, parboiled waterchestnuts, broccoli florets, watercress and 1-inch cubes of bean curd are also possibilities.

Garnishes are hardly required, but you might consider accenting the food platters with scallion brushes (see page 50), bamboo trees or tomato roses (see page 50).

Rice may be served with the meal, and even a crisp salad. After this meal, dessert is generally an anticlimax.

Dipping sauces, however, are essential; out of the following, 4 should be provided:

GEONG OHO CHEUNG, or Ginger-Vinegar Dipping Sauce

Blend 1 tablespooon minced fresh ginger and 1 teaspoon each of chopped scallions and honey into 3 tablespoons of malt vinegar. Add 1/2 teaspoon of PLUM SAUCE (page 138) and a dash each of salt, ground white pepper, and Tabasco. Blend thoroughly and serve. Particularly good with poultry and duck.

GEONG SEUNG TOW CHEUNG, or Ginger-Garlic Dipping Sauce

Cut 5 slices of fresh ginger into thin strips and cut 3 scallions into 2-inch length strips. Mash and mince 2 cloves of garlic; sauté the ginger, scallions, and garlic in 2 tablespoons of concentrated chicken broth until they are soft. Remove from the heat and add 1 tablespoon of corn oil and transfer the sauce to serving dishes, adding a sprinkle of salt and soy sauce to taste.

KARE JUIP CHEUNG, or Chinese Red Dipping Sauce

Apply cookware spray to a saucepan; sauté 1/2 minced onion in 1 tablespoon of chicken broth until the onion is translucent. Dissolve 1 tablespoon of cornstarch in 1 cup of broth and add 4 tablespoons of tomato paste or catsup, a dash of Tabasco or several bits of chili pepper, 1/8 teaspoon of salt to taste, and 1 tablespoon of honey (optional). Blend the mixture with the onions, and serve. This is a mildly hot sauce, excellent with seafood, particularly shrimp.

KAR LAI CHEUNG, or Chinese Curry Dipping Sauce

A spicier version of the CHINESE RED DIPPING SAUCE, used with seafood; made by substituting 2 tablespoons of curry powder for the tomato paste or catsup, and using the optional honey called for in the previous recipe.

CHI MA CHEUNG, or Chinese Sesame-Soy Dipping Sauce

Blend thoroughly 1 tablespoon sesame oil with 1/4 cup of soy sauce, and serve as a dip for cooked poultry, or as a sauce over meat.

GEONG LA SZECHEUNG, or Chinese Ginger-Chili Dipping Sauce

Finely shred 2 thin slices of fresh ginger and the white part of 4 scallions and place in a heatproof bowl with 1/2 teaspoon honey. In a saucepan, heat 1/4 cup double strength chicken broth or corn oil until it begins to bubble. Remove from the heat and add 1/2 teaspoon of bits of chili peppers or 1/4 teaspoon of Tabasco. Pour the hot mixture into the bowl with the ginger and permit to cool. Serve as a dipping sauce for cooked poultry or ladle it over meat.

HO YAU, or Chinese Oyster Sauce

This popular sauce is commercially prepared and available at most Chinese markets. It can be made at home, however, by grinding 2 cups of raw oysters, adding enough water to cover, and bringing the mixture to a boil. Lower the heat and simmer for 30 minutes. Strain and combine the liquid with 3 tablespoons of soy sauce; bottle and store without refrigeration. This is an excellent dipping sauce for poultry or beef and may be used sparingly over meats, vegetables, and some seafoods instead of soy sauce.

Other dipping sauces you may consider for your hot pot are PLUM SAUCE (page 138) and CHINESE SWEET AND SOUR SAUCE (page 139).

LINGUA CON SALSA VERDE Tongue
with Green Sauce

ITALIAN

1 precooked
calf or beef tongue,
about 2 pounds ·
1 large onion,
cut in quarters ·
3 stalks celery,
chopped ·
3 carrots,
coarsely chopped ·
1 clove garlic, mashed ·
Salt to taste ·

Salsa Verde:
4 tablespoons
chopped parsley ·
4 tablespoons
fresh basil leaves,
minced ·
5 blades fresh chives ·
3 tablespoons capers ·
3 tablespoons
bread crumbs or
wheat germ ·
1 teaspoon
lemon zest, minced ·
1/2 clove garlic,
mashed ·
2 scallions,
white part only,
shredded ·
1 pimiento, chopped ·
2 flat anchovies ·
1 tablespoon vinegar ·
3 tablespoons oil,
preferably olive ·
Salt and freshly
ground pepper to taste ·

An exciting meal by itself, or as part of a buffet, whether it is served hot or cold. I've cooked many a calf and beef tongue from scratch, which for me takes too many hours. Now I insist on using a beef tongue under 3 pounds in weight, for ideal flavor and texture, and on one that has been precooked, so that it requires boiling for only 15 minutes before serving. If you insist on doing it the hard way, consult the Bonus Ideas below for a number of alternate cooking methods. In any case, the sauce is an orchestrated masterpiece of blended flavors.

YIELD: Six to eight servings

1. Place in a saucepan the onion, celery, carrots, garlic, and salt with water to cover and bring to a boil. Add the precooked beef tongue, in its unbroken plastic sac, to the boiling water and continue boiling for about 15 minutes, or until tender. Test for doneness with a fork. Remove the tongue, cut away the sac, and drain well.

2. Meanwhile, place all of the ingredients for the green sauce in an electric blender and blend at medium speed for about 1 minute, or until you have a smooth purée. If you have prepared the tongue in advance, reheat it by steaming for about 7 minutes until heated through. Cut into slices, and serve covered with the green sauce.

BONUS IDEAS: If starting from scratch, boil the tongue with water to cover for about 2-1/2 hours, or until tender. Drain and remove the outer skin. Cut into slices and serve with the sauce. The European method for preparing tongue is to cook it in boiling water for about 5 minutes, draining it and then removing the skin, which will have turned white. The skinned tongue is then soaked in running water for 3 or more hours; it is returned to a pan with fresh water to cover; the onion, celery, garlic, and salt are added, brought to a boil, and permitted to simmer over low heat for about 4 hours or until tender.

A wonderful way to serve this dish cold is as LINGUA IN GELATINA (BEEF TONGUE IN ASPIC): After the tongue is cooked, remove the pot from the heat and let the tongue cool in the water. Meanwhile, prepare the aspic by adding 1-1/2 tablespoons of gelatin powder to 2 cups of beef broth or consommé and bring to a boil. Add 1/2 cup of white wine, 1 tablespoon of Madeira or 1 teaspoon of Worcestershire sauce, 1 tablespoon of honey, and salt to taste. Place a 1/2-inch layer of the aspic in a mold, and chill in the refrigerator or freezer until it is about to set. Add garnishes of any of the cooked vegetables used in preparing the tongue, and 1/4 cup, or more, of chopped gherkins. Place the tongue into the mold, and pour in the balance of the aspic to cover. Chill until set. Serve, unmolded, on a bed of lettuce, garnished with parsley, watercress, bits of pimiento, and lemon slices. Serve with the GREEN SAUCE (SALSA VERDE), HORSERADISH SAUCE (page 107), BONUS MAYONNAISE (page 124) or PIQUANT GREEN ANCHOVY SAUCE (page 131).

* CYNTHIA'S SHEPHERD'S PIE

BRITISH

3 cups cooked beef, cut into 1/2-inch cubes, or 2 pounds ground beef ·
2 onions finely chopped ·
1/3 cup each, chopped celery and pepper ·
1 carrot, julienned ·
1 tomato, chopped ·
1/8 teaspoon crushed red bell pepper or Tabasco ·
1-1/4 cups reserved beef gravy or beef consommé ·
1/4 teaspoon paprika ·
2-1/2 cups mashed potatoes, about 5 potatoes ·
Salt and pepper to taste ·
Cookware spray ·

In Britain it is traditional to reserve some of the cooked meat from a Sunday roast, in anticipation of preparing the dish later in the week. Many believe a true shepherd's pie is made only with cooked beef; others insist it must be made with cooked lamb or mutton. You can try it either way or even use ground lean meat as the basic ingredient.
YIELD: Six servings

1. Apply cookware spray to a skillet and heat the beef—which has been trimmed of all excess fat—over medium heat. If using uncooked ground beef, sauté it until it loses its pink color, stirring occasionally with a wooden spoon. Add all of the ingredients except the reserved gravy, the mashed potatoes, paprika, and the seasonings; simmer 5 minutes. Add the reserved gravy or consommé and simmer 10 minutes longer.

2. Meanwhile, boil the potatoes until cooked; peel and mash. Apply cookware spray to a casserole and fill with the cooked meat mixture, reserving 1/2 cup of the cooking liquid; blend the liquid with the mashed potatoes. Cover the meat with the potato mixture and spread until it is smooth. Sprinkle the layer of potatoes with paprika and cook in an oven preheated to 375°F. for about 30 minutes, or until the topping is puffed or bubbling. If not sufficiently browned, place under the broiler for a few moments. Let the pie settle about 5 minutes, then serve.

BONUS IDEAS: Most of your favorite vegetables—especially mixed vegetables, mushrooms, peas, and (instead of mashed potatoes) puréed cauliflower—can be added to or substituted for other ingredients. One tablespoon of beef base such as B-V or Bovril can be added to the gravy if necessary. Parsley, sliced mushrooms, and minced cooked carrots are suitable for garnishing.

* JARRET DE VEAU OSSO BUCO

Leg of Veal—Osso Buco

FRENCH

3-1/2 pounds
veal shanks,
cut in pieces
osso buco style,
about 12 pieces •
2 large onions,
peeled and diced •
1/2 teaspoon salt,
optional •
Freshly ground pepper
to taste •
24 green peppercorns,
crushed •
1/2 cup white wine,
or dry vermouth •
2 cups orange juice •
1/2 cup lemon juice •
4 dozen
small white onions,
fresh or frozen •
2-1/2 dozen
baby carrots,
fresh or frozen •
1 dozen mushrooms,
sliced lengthwise •
1/2 pound peas,
fresh or frozen •
1 clove garlic, minced •
5 sprigs fresh parsley •
1 teaspoon chives •
1 teaspoon tarragon •
6 white peppercorns •
2 tablespoons water •
1/4 cup white port wine •
2 oranges
and 2 lemons, sliced •
Cookware spray •

An unusual party dish that assures compliments and contented guests. Except for the marinating preparation the night before, this is a very easy dish to prepare and lends itself admirably to the use of frozen vegetables if fresh vegetables at peak flavor are not readily available.

YIELD: Twelve servings

1. Apply cookware spray to a heavy skillet, and cook the diced onions with up to 1 tablespoon of water as necessary until translucent. Add the veal, 1/4 teaspoon salt, and freshly ground pepper, and cook over moderate heat until the surface of the meat begins to lose its pink color. Add 12 crushed green peppercorns and the white wine. Continue cooking until the meat is no longer pink. Use more white wine if necessary to keep the meat moist.

2. Place the contents of the skillet into a large ceramic, glass, or plastic container and add the orange and lemon juices. Blend well and place in the refrigerator to marinate for at least 12 hours.

3. When ready to cook, apply cookware spray to a heavy casserole. Using a slotted spoon, transfer the veal and cooked onions to the casserole, and discard the marinade. Add the white onions, carrots, mushrooms, peas, garlic, parsley, chives, and tarragon. Add 1/4 teaspoon of salt if desired, the white peppercorns and 6 crushed green peppercorns. Add the 2 tablespoons of water, unless frozen vegetables are used, in which case no additional water is needed.

4. Cover the casserole tightly and cook over medium heat for about 1 hour, or until the meat is fork-tender. Shuffle the pot occasionally and stir the contents to avoid burning, adding a little water as necesary.

5. Remove the cooked contents and put in a covered serving dish in a warm place, maintaining the cooked liquor in the original cooking vessel. Boil the liquor to reduce to about one-half, and add the white port wine and the remaining 6 crushed green peppercorns. Stir to blend.

6. Decorate the veal with the slices of orange and lemon and spoon the sauce over it before serving.

BONUS IDEAS: For a dinner party, SEA BASS STEAMED WITH SEAWEED and served with SAUCE VIERGE (page 13) can be used as an appetizer or first course. An excellent accompaniment would be the VIOLET ONION MARMALADE (page 29), preferably served at room temperature.

* CHARTREUSE NAVARIN
PRINTANIER Mold of Lamb with Spring
Vegetables

FRENCH

**2 pounds lean lamb,
cut into 1-inch cubes ·
2 cups chicken stock
or canned consommé ·
1 pound string beans,
as uniform in size
as possible ·
2 large carrots ·
2 medium zucchini ·
2 medium summer squash ·
1/4 cup fresh or
frozen green peas ·
1-1/2 cups
mashed potatoes ·
6 large green
cabbage leaves ·
1/2 cup fresh or
frozen artichoke hearts ·
1/2 cup fresh or
frozen cauliflower
florets ·
Salt and freshly
ground pepper to taste ·
1 tablespoon
polyunsaturated margarine ·
1/4 cup melted
polyunsaturated margarine ·
Cookware spray**

This is probably one of the most spectacular dishes you will ever present at your table. It takes a little time to prepare, but at the same time will stimulate your creative possibilities when you attempt your own version of this dish. I always make several portions simultaneously, since it freezes extremely well, an occasionally I will omit the cubes of lamb in order to create a satisfying dish for our vegetarian friends. But the vegetarian version can, of course, be enjoyed by all. In fact, this dish is so attractive that I use an ovenproof glass mold so that it can be admired even before it is unmolded.

YIELD: Six to eight servings

1. Apply cookware spray to a skillet, and brown the cubes of lamb that have previously been dipped in water and drained but not patted dry. Place the lamb in a saucepan with the 2 cups of stock and simmer over low heat for about 1 hour. Meanwhile, trim the ends of the string beans, scrape the carrots and cut them into thin sticks, about the same length as the beans. Both should be slightly longer than the depth of your mold. Slice the zucchini and squash, unpeeled, into thin even slices. Moisten the balance of the vegetables in cold water, drain but do not pat dry, and separately, cook each of them covered, AU SEC, for about 5 minutes. Drain the vegetables, season to taste, and set aside to cool.

2. Apply cookware spray to a deep mold with a 6-inch diameter; rub the bottom and sides with the tablespoon of margarine. Arrange the peas in a single circular border around the circumference of the bottom of the mold; the peas should be held firmly in place by the margarine. Arrange the slices of squash in an outer circle bordering on the ring of peas. Fill the uncovered base of the mold with a dozen cubes of drained lamb, then cover with a smaller ring of sliced zucchini, until the entire base of the mold has been covered. Begin to alternate the string beans and the carrot sticks around the circular border of the mold, standing them upright and resting on the ring of peas. The inside of the mold should now be completely covered with the several rings of peas, squash, and zucchini, covering the bottom; and there should be an alternating fence-like effect of upright string beans and carrot sticks covering the inside border. Using scissors, trim the top ends of the carrots and beans so that they are even with the rim of the mold. Using a spatula, spread a layer of mashed potatoes covering the bottom and sides of the mold, further anchoring the patterns of vegetables in place. Layer half of the cabbage leaves over the potatoes, pressing them down firmly.

3. Preheat your oven to 350°F. Drain the remaining lamb cubes, reserving the stock, and arrange them in a layer over the cabbage, to cover completely. Now place an outer border of artichoke hearts over the meat cubes, and fill the center with the cauliflower florets. Cover these with a final layer of zucchini and squash in overlapping circles as in the very first layer. Pour the melted margarine and 2 tablespoons of the cooking broth from the lamb into the mold. Cover the top of the mold completely with the balance of the cabbage leaves, and add a final layer of the mashed potatoes overall. Place the mold in a roasting pan, add water to 1/2 the height of the mold, and bake for 20 minutes. Remove the mold from the oven, cover with foil, and let it set for 10 minutes before turning it out on a serving platter.

BONUS IDEAS: The combination of vegetables provides the garnish for this dish, but in addition you can circle it with a border of watercress. If you want to prepare the recipe vegetarian style, omit the lamb cubes. If you freeze this dish, cover the mold with aluminum foil and freeze in an airtight plastic freezer bag. Thaw thoroughly and reheat in an oven at 350°F. before serving hot. Other ingredients you may wish to consider include grapes, instead of the ring of peas; Brussels sprouts, instead of the artichokes; and snow peas, instead of the string beans. If you like, you may add 1/4 cup of Parmesan cheese to the mixture after pouring in the melted margarine.

POULET À LA CHINOISE Monique's
Chinese Chicken

FRENCH/ CHINESE

1 3- to 4-pound chicken ·
3 or more pounds of coarse salt ·
1 lemon, cut in half ·

This is one of the most unusual, yet one of the simplest, recipes I know for preparing chicken. It was given to me by a French friend whose family has passed it down for generations, and who has always assumed it was of Chinese origin. The recipe calls for a great deal of salt in which the chicken is encased; during baking the salt hardens into a shell that has to be broken, before serving, so that the chicken can be extracted. The process is a conversation piece, but more importantly the results are a savory dish. The recipe originally called for a French cast-iron COCOTTE, but an ovenproof oval casserole or Roman clay casserole works equally well.

YIELD: Four servings

1. Rinse the chicken, pat it dry, and remove any excess fat from the cavity and other areas. Rub the inside of the cavity with the lemon halves. Pour a layer of salt about 1 inch thick into the bottom of the casserole. (If using the clay casserole, it must be presoaked for 15 minutes.) Place the chicken on the layer of salt, breast side up, and pour additional salt over it until it is completely covered with about a 1-inch layer. It is not necessary to close the cavity of the chicken, but don't force the salt into the cavity. At the same time, don't be concerned if some of the salt gets inside.

2. Cover the casserole tightly, using aluminum foil between the cover and lid to improve the seal if necessary. Place the chicken in an oven set at 475°F.—which hasn't been preheated—and cook for 1-1/4 hours. Remove from the oven, and turn onto a work counter. With a heavy sharp knife, make a hole in the hardened salt shell, then pull it away from the chicken. A kitchen mallet can also be used to break the shell. Brush off any particles of salt, and serve your delicious chicken SUPERBEMENT DORÉ ET SALÉ JUSTE À POINT—beautifully golden in color and perfectly salted.

BONUS IDEAS: Since you will probably want to share with your guests the unveiling of the chicken from its hardened salt shell, I suggest you have a warm platter ready with the garnishes you plan to use. Once the cooked chicken has been brushed of excess salt particles, place it on the serving platter, and carve at the table. Or, if you prefer, you can carve beforehand, and place the serving pieces on the garnished platter.

The original recipe called for up to 6 pounds of salt, depending on the size of the casserole. I have found that about 3, and rarely more than 4, pounds of salt are required. Of course, the salt is discarded after the chicken has been cooked.

✳ CROWN ROAST OF LAMB

BRITISH

1 or more
racks of 16 ribs
of spring lamb prepared
in a crown shape •
2 tablespoons
polyunsaturated margarine,
melted •
2 egg whites •
1/2 pound Boudin Blanc
(page 96–97) •
2 small
onions, minced •
2 stalks celery, minced •
1 clove garlic, mashed •
1 tablespoon
white wine or
chicken broth •
3/4 cup
soft bread crumbs •
3 tablespoons
fresh parsley, chopped •
2 tablespoons
fresh chives, chopped •
1/2 teaspoon each thyme,
rosemary, and salt •
1/2 teaspoon salt •
8 twists of pepper mill •
1/4 cup white wine
or chicken broth •
Aluminum foil •
Cookware spray •

Besides being a delicious and satisfying dish, this traditional British specialty is most impressive when presented at the table. You will want a whole loin of 16 ribs, or 2 or more racks shaped into a "crown." Your butcher will do this for you; he should also grind the unused lamb for part of your stuffing, and supply you with paper frills for garnishing each rib bone. As you will see in the Bonus Ideas that follow, however, there are a number of other garnishing possibilities you will want to consider. The center of the crown is generally filled with stuffing, which will give you an opportunity to use some of your reserved Boudin Blanc (page 96–97), as well as other possibilities.

YIELD: Eight servings

1. The butcher will have prepared the crown roast, removed the backbone to facilitate carving, and filled the center with ground lamb. Remove the ground lamb and set aside in a mixing bowl. Place the meat in a roasting pan and brush the surfaces with the melted margarine. Cut 3-inch squares of aluminum foil and cover the end of each rib to prevent charring. Whisk the egg whites for about 1 minute until foamy, crumble the pre-soaked Boudin Blanc sausage meat, and set aside.

2. Apply cookware spray to a skillet and sauté the onions, celery, and garlic in the tablespoon of wine or broth for about 5 minutes until the onions are translucent. Combine the onion mixture with the reserved ground lamb, crumbled sausage meat, and egg whites; add all of the other ingredients except the 1/4 cup wine or broth. Stir the mixture well, then gradually add the wine or broth to moisten the stuffing. Spoon the mixture into the center of the roast and cover with a circle of aluminum foil in order to maintain moisture.

3. Preheat the oven to 350°F. and roast the lamb for about 3 hours, or until fork tender. Transfer to a hot platter, remove the foil, add the paper frills, and garnish. Serve the roast with its own strained pan juices.

BONUS IDEAS: The center can be garnished with your favorite vegetables, especially cooked peas, pearl onions, and sliced mushrooms. Garnish the platter with mushroom caps, spiced apple rings, citrus fruit baskets filled with mint sauce or jelly, and watercress, parsley, or mint leaves. Instead of the paper frills, try placing cherry tomatoes on the end of each rib or on alternating ribs for a different garnishing effect.

CÔTELETTES DE PORC MARINÉES AVEC SAUCE PIQUANT Marinated Pork Chops with Piquant Sauce

FRENCH

**4 large loin pork chops ·
3/4 cups corn oil ·
2 bay leaves ·
2 cloves ·
1/8 teaspoon each,
salt and pepper ·
1/2 cup Sauce Piquante
(page 123) or see
Bonus Ideas ·
Cookware spray ·**

Except for the length of time it takes to marinate the chops, this is a relatively simple way of preparing pork to achieve a most satisfying and flavorsome meal.

YIELD: Four servings

1. Combine the oil, bay leaves, cloves, and salt and pepper in a ceramic or glass bowl. Trim all excess fat from the pork chops, place them in the marinade; refrigerate, covered, for at least 2, and preferably 3, days. Turn the chops in the marinade several times each day.

2. When ready to cook, drain the chops. Apply cookware spray to a skillet and cook the chops with 3 tablespoons of the marinade over low medium heat for 25 minutes, until tender and thoroughly done. Serve with heated SAUCE PIQUANTE.

BONUS IDEAS: As accompaniment, try stewed fruits, VIOLET ONION MARMALADE (page 29) or ITALIAN ORANGE SALAD (page 23).

You can prepare a piquant sauce specifically for this dish, by applying cookware spray to a saucepan and melting in it 2 tablespoons of polyunsaturated margarine. Stir in 1 tablespoon of potato flour or cornstarch to make a ROUX. When blended, add 5 chopped shallots or scallions, 3/4 cup of water and stir with a wooden spoon over medium heat for 5 minutes. Add 3 tablespoons of good white wine or dry vermouth, or 1 tablespoon of lemon juice or vinegar; reduce the heat and simmer for about 20 minutes. Skim off the fat, strain and add two chopped gherkins before serving.

BORJUPAPRIKÁS Veal Goulash

HUNGARIAN

2 pounds boneless veal, cut into 1-1/2-inch cubes •
1 tablespoon paprika, or more to taste •
1-1/2 teaspoons coarse salt •
2 cups thinly sliced onions •
1 tablespoon beef broth or dry vermouth •
1 cup peeled and cubed tomatoes, or 1 large whole tomato •
1 cup Minceur Tomato Sauce (page 16–17), or canned sauce •
2 tablespoons plain yoghurt or sour cream •
1/2 teaspoon fresh lemon juice •
Cookware spray •

A traditional veal dish that has earned its reputation as an international favorite. I find that one of its secrets is to permit the flavor of the paprika to permeate the meat before cooking.

YIELD: Six servings

1. Sprinkle the veal cubes with a mixture of paprika and salt and let it stand at least 10 minutes. Apply cookware spray to a heavy saucepan and sauté the onions with the broth or dry vermouth until they are translucent. I generally add the whole fresh tomato at this point, gradually rotating it, which facilitates peeling. Peel and cube the tomato, and set aside. Alternatively, use the cup of cubed tomatoes in step 2.

2. Add the veal and cook over medium heat until it loses its pink color, stirring with a wooden spoon. Add the tomato sauce and reserved tomato cubes, cover, and reduce the heat to simmer until the veal is tender, about 1 hour. Turn off the heat, and stir in the yoghurt combined with the lemon juice. Serve over rice or noodles.

BONUS IDEAS: Instead of the tomato sauce, you can substitute 1/3 cup of beef broth or consommé. Also, you can cook the goulash in your microwave oven: first sauté the onions, uncovered, for 3 minutes, in a 2-quart casserole. Add all of the ingredients except the yoghurt and lemon juice; place in the microwave oven and cook, covered, for 25 minutes, or until the veal is tender. Remove; let it set for 5 minutes, then stir in the yoghurt and lemon juice and serve.

If using a pressure cooker, first sauté the onions, then the veal; and add all of the ingredients except the yoghurt and juice. Cook at 15 pounds pressure for about 15 minutes, or until tender; then add the yoghurt combination. I have also made this goulash in a clay pot casserole, which is always soaked first—top and bottom—for 15 minutes in cold water. After the onions and meat have been sautéed in a skillet, they are transferred to the clay pot with all of the other ingredients, except, of course, the yoghurt mixture. Set in an oven at 450°F. and cook for about 40 minutes, or until the veal is tender.

I find that veal cubes don't particularly lend themselves to being cooked in a slow-cooking crock pot, but this dish does work in a crock pot if you substitute beef cubes for the veal. Combine all of the ingredients except the yoghurt mixture and add 1 minced clove of garlic and 1 tablespoon of honey. Cover and cook on low for 9 hours, stir the mixture well, and then cook on high for 10 minutes longer. Let the goulash set for 15 minutes, then add the yoghurt mixture and serve.

POLLO EN ESCABECHE Portuguese
Marinated Chicken

PORTUGUESE

1 3-pound chicken •
2 tablespoons
chicken broth or
dry vermouth •
2 cups white wine
or dry vermouth •
2 tablespoons
lemon or lime juice •
2 tablespoons vinegar •
2 bay leaves •
5 each,
whole black and
green peppercorns •
5 juniper berries •
1/2 teaspoon coarse salt •
1 orange or 1 lemon sliced •
Cookware spray •

An every-season specialty you will enjoy. It may be served either hot or, during the summer months, chilled in its own aspic. This dish is simple to make but extremely rewarding because of the memorable blend of the marinade and the garnish of sliced citrus fruits.
YIELD: Four servings

1. Remove excess fat from the cavity of the chicken. Apply cookware spray to a large skillet; dip the chicken quickly in water, drain, but do not pat dry. Brown the chicken on all sides over high heat, with the broth or vermouth; set aside.

2. Preheat your oven to 350°F. In a saucepan, combine all of the other ingredients except the slices of orange or lemon. Simmer over medium heat until the mixture begins to bubble, about 10 minutes. Apply cookware spray to a deep casserole, and place the chicken into it breast side up. Pour the marinade over the chicken, cover the casserole tightly, and bake for 1 hour, or until fork-tender. Cut the chicken into serving pieces, and garnish with the slices of orange or lemon, or a combination of both. Serve hot. If serving cold, allow the chicken to cool in the marinade, then cut into serving pieces, and chill in the refrigerator overnight with the sauce, which will become an aspic; before serving add the garnish of sliced oranges or lemons.

BONUS IDEAS: You can prepare this dish in a Roman clay casserole, in a slow-cooking crockery pot, or in a microwave oven. Presoak the clay casserole for 15 minutes in cold water, then brown the chicken and place with the marinade in the casserole and cook in an oven set at 450°F. 50 minutes, or until fork-tender. Or brown the chicken as called for in step 1, and cook, covered with wax paper, in the microwave oven for 25 minutes. If using a crock pot, cut the chicken into quarters or serving pieces and brown the chicken, then cook with the marinade on low heat for 3 to 4 hours.

POULET SAUTÉ À LA MARENGO
Chicken Marengo

FRENCH

1 3-pound chicken, quartered or cut into serving pieces ·
1 thinly sliced onion ·
1 clove garlic, minced ·
1 tablespoon dry vermouth ·
1/2 cup white wine or sherry ·
1/2 cup chicken stock or canned consommé ·
3 tomatoes, peeled and seeded; or a 1-pound can of Italian style plum tomatoes ·
1 tablespoon tomato paste ·
1/2 bay leaf ·
1/4 teaspoon dried basil ·
1/2 teaspoon salt ·
3 sprigs fresh parsley or 1/4 teaspoon dried ·
20 pearl onions ·
1/2 pound sliced mushrooms ·
1/2 cup pitted black olives ·
1 tablespoon Armagnac or other brandy ·
2 tablespoons chopped fresh parsley ·
Cookware spray ·

This is the now-famous dish Napoleon's chef is reported to have created in 1800, after the Battle of Marengo, from the immediate ingredients available to him; it can be made either with chicken or with veal (see Bonus Ideas below).

YIELD: Four to six servings

1. Apply cookware spray to a large heavy skillet and sauté the sliced onions and the garlic in the vermouth until translucent. Remove the onions and garlic with a slotted spoon and set aside. Dip the chicken parts into cold water, drain but do not pat dry; brown over high heat in the same skillet in which the onions and garlic were cooked.

2. Add the wine, chicken stock, tomatoes and the paste, the bay leaf, basil, salt, and the sprigs of parsley; simmer for 30 minutes. Meanwhile apply cookware spray to a casserole and warm in an oven at 200°F. When the chicken is cooked, transfer it to the warm casserole. Strain the sauce and reduce it over high heat for about 7 minutes. Add the pearl onions and mushrooms to the sauce and cook over medium heat for 5 minutes.

3. Transfer the cooked onions and mushrooms to the casserole; add the black olives, arrange the chicken parts, and garnish for serving. Sprinkle Armagnac over the chicken, add the sauce and heat in an oven at 350°F. for half an hour. Garnish with parsley, serve with rice and green salad.

BONUS IDEAS: Instead of chicken you can use 1-1/2 pounds of lean veal, cut into 1/2-inch cubes, for VEAL MARENGO (SAUTÉ DE VEAU MARENGO). If planning to serve a party of 8, increase the quantity of veal to 2-1/2 pounds and use 2 chickens or 16 serving pieces of chicken comprised of 2 breasts, halved, and 4 each of legs and thighs.

* DAD'S DUBLIN STEW

IRISH

YIELD: Six servings

1-3/4 pounds lean lamb or mutton, cut into 1-1/2-inch cubes •
2-1/2 pounds potatoes, peeled and sliced into 1/8-inch thickness •
1 cup onions, thinly sliced •
Salt and freshly ground pepper to taste •
1 bay leaf •
1 teaspoon fresh thyme or 1/2 teaspoon dried •
1 cup boiling water •
1 cup boiling chicken broth or dry vermouth •
3 tablespoons finely chopped parsley •
Cookware spray •

1. Apply cookware spray to a heavy pan or Dutch oven and arrange a layer of 1/3 of the sliced potatoes. Cover with a layer of the lamb cubes, followed by a layer of the sliced onions. Sprinkle a third of the seasonings over the onions; then repeat the layers of potatoes, meat, onions, and seasoning until all of these ingredients are used. The top layer should be onions.

2. Add the boiling water and broth, and the balance of the ingredients except the parsley. Bring the contents to a boil, cover tightly, and simmer over low heat, shuffling the pot occasionally, for about 2-1/2 hours, or until the meat is tender. Serve hot sprinkled with parsley.

BONUS IDEAS: You may also cook the lamb stew in a covered casserole in a preheated oven set at 350°F. for about 1-1/2 hours, or until done. If using a microwave oven, place the contents in a non-metal casserole and cook, uncovered, for 5 minutes, then shuffle the casserole. Cover, and continue to cook for about 25 minutes until the meat is tender. A slow cooking crock pot will require about 10 hours on low heat before the meat and other ingredients are tender.

DOLMA Baked Apples Stuffed with Veal

MIDDLE EASTERN

4 large apples •
1/2 pound lean veal cut into 1/2-inch cubes •
1 cup chicken broth or consommé •
Salt to taste •
4 cloves •
1 teaspoon honey •
2 ounces unsweetened wheat germ •
1 tablespoon polyunsaturated margarine •
Cookware spray •

A memorable and satisfying luncheon dish, side dish, or hearty dessert, the filling of which can be varied to suit your own preferences—and still prove to be a sure-fire conversation piece.

YIELD: Four servings

Preheat the oven to 375°F. Slice off the top of each apple and carefully remove the core. In a saucepan over medium heat, cook the cubes of veal with the broth for 7 minutes; drain, and mince the cooked veal. Fill each apple with one quarter of the minced veal, 1 clove, and salt to taste. Place the apples in an ovenproof dish to which cookware spray has been applied. Pour the honey over the minced meat and into each apple, and sprinkle with the wheat germ. Top with a dot of the margarine, and bake for 1 hour, or until the apples are soft. Serve hot, or at room temperature.

BONUS IDEAS: You can substitute 1 whole chicken breast or a pair of sweetbreads for the veal. If using sweetbreads, soak them in cold water for 45 minutes, then cook in the broth for 15 minutes until they turn white. Remove all covering tissues and press through a sieve to mince. Large pears may be substituted for the apples for a pleasant flavor variation.

* HONG SIU CHU YUK Red-Simmered Pork

CHINESE

3 pounds lean pork, preferably butt ·
2 cups water ·
3 slices ginger root, minced ·
6 tablespoons soy sauce ·
1 tablespoon sherry ·
1 teaspoon coarse salt ·
3 teaspoons honey ·

This is a delightful blend of harmonious flavors, which is achieved by a relatively long period of simmering or braising—in contrast to the very short periods of cooking time required by most Chinese dishes. Try reserving the sauce, once this dish is cooked, and creating your own "perpetual" CHINESE MASTER SAUCE (page 134–35). "Red-simmering," so-called because of the reddish color of the sauce, can be accomplished on top of the range, in an oven or microwave oven, as well as in a pressure cooker or slow-cooking pot.

YIELD: Six servings

1. Cut the pork into 1-1/2-inch cubes. Place in a heavy pan or casserole with water to cover and bring quickly to a boil over high heat. After 5 minutes, remove the meat and rinse with cold water, discarding the cooking water. Return the meat to the pan; add the 2 cups of water and all of the other ingredients except the honey; simmer over low heat, covered, for 1 hour.

2. Add the honey, and turn the meat several times; then continue to cook over low heat for 30 minutes. Serve the meat either hot or cold with CHINESE DIPPING SAUCES, reserving the sauce for future use, or as a starter for your own CHINESE MASTER SAUCE. The sauce should be strained, skimmed and refrigerated. (See page 134–35).

BONUS IDEAS: I prefer the red-simmered pork served as I have indicated above with suitable accoutrements. However, the more authentic version calls for adding 1 pound dried Chinese squid, which has been cut lengthwise, scored on its inside with a sharp knife, and soaked in warm water for 24 hours. One-quarter cup of Chinese lily buds, soaked in warm water for 1 hour, are another authentic touch. If you decide to use these ingredients, add the squid after the other ingredients have simmered 1/2 hour in step 1; and add the soaked lily buds with the honey in step 2.

MOULES À LA MARINIÈRE Mussels
Fisherman Style

FRENCH

2 quarts mussels •
1 large onion, diced •
3 sprigs parsley
1 bay leaf •
4 twists of pepper mill •
1/2 teaspoon
dried thyme •
1 cup white wine
or dry vermouth •
2 tablespoons
parsley, chopped •

One of the most memorable meals I have ever had was one my family and I enjoyed at the home of friends in Paris; this dish was served in huge quantities as a first course. That was the first time I learned the trick of eating a mussel by scooping it out of its shell with the empty adjoining shell. All of us had a festive and amusing time developing the knack of scooping—which is really so much easier and more practical than resorting to special forks or other utensils. This dish is also an excellent main course. I rarely make it without at least doubling the recipe so that I can simultaneously prepare another family favorite: MOULES FARCIES, or STUFFED MUSSELS (page 150). I suggest you do the same, since this recipe is the basis of the MOULES FARCIES.

YIELD: Four servings

1. Thoroughly wash, scrub and beard the mussels. Reserving the chopped parsley for garnish, place the onion, parsley sprigs, and seasonings in a heavy pot with cover; then add the mussels, the wine, and pepper. Close the cover of the pot tightly, using wet paper toweling if necessary between pot and cover for a thorough seal. Steam over a low flame for approximately 12 minutes, or until the mussels have opened. Discard any mussels that have remained closed.

2. Add the chopped parsley. Serve hot in a covered tureen, over English muffin or French bread, as desired. Reserve the unused mussels and some of the broth for MOULES FARCIES (page 150).

BONUS IDEAS: I keep a special wire brush with a handle for cleaning mussels, and I pull out or clip the beard as necessary. Soaking mussels in cold water beforehand is helpful in cleaning, and some recipes call for sprinkling flour in the water to tempt the mussels to open, thereby assisting the cleaning process. Some theorize that the flour also serves to fatten the mussel. If you choose this technique, use 1 tablespoon of rice, potato, or gluten flour.

I don't find it necessary, but if you like you can add up to 2 tablespoons of polyunsaturated margarine to the mussels before steaming, and an additional 2 tablespoons, or less, to the tureen before serving.

Arrange the mussels in the tureen, removing the adjoining empty half-shells if desired. As I have mentioned, however, I like to use these empty shells for scooping out the filled ones, Parisian style.

CHICKEN BRAISED WITH PEANUTS

RHODESIAN

YIELD: Four servings

1 3-pound chicken, cut into serving pieces ·
2 cups chicken broth or water ·
2 onions, peeled and sliced ·
2 red chilies or 1/2 teaspoon Tabasco ·
1/2 teaspoon coarse salt or to taste ·
1 cup roasted peanuts, ground ·
1/2 cup diced potatoes (optional) ·
1 orange, sliced ·
1/4 cup shredded unsweetened coconut ·
Cookware spray ·

Apply cookware spray to a large heavy skillet. Dip the chicken pieces in water, drain, but do not pat dry. Brown the chicken over medium heat, then lower the heat and add the chicken broth, onions, chilies, salt, and ground peanuts. Simmer, partially covered, over low heat for 2 hours, or until the chicken is tender and the gravy is quite thick. About 1/2 hour before the chicken is cooked, add the optional diced potatoes. With a slotted spoon remove the chicken pieces to a serving platter and garnish with the sliced orange and shredded coconut, serving the sauce separately. The chicken may be served on a bed of rice, or with the rice served separately.

LANCASHIRE HOT POT

BRITISH

YIELD: Four servings

1-1/2 pounds lean
rib lamb chops ·
3 pounds potatoes,
peeled ·
2 onions, peeled ·
Salt and freshly
ground pepper to taste ·
3 medium carrots,
scraped and sliced
diagonally 1/4-inch thick ·
2 cups chicken stock or
consommé ·
12 shucked oysters
in their own liquor ·
Cookware spray ·

Preheat your oven to 350°F. Trim the excess fat from the chops. Apply cookware spray to an ovenproof earthenware casserole. Slice the potatoes and onions into 1/4-inch thicknesses. Place a layer of the potatoes at the base of the pot, then add a layer of the chops, the seasonings, and the sliced carrots, repeating until all the ingredients are used, ending with a top layer of sliced potatoes. Add the chicken stock. Bake tightly covered for about 2 hours, or until the meat is tender. Meanwhile, in a saucepan heat the shucked oysters in their own liquor. Remove the cover from the casserole, spread the oysters and liquor on top of the mixture and continue baking for about 20 minutes to allow it to brown. Serve hot.

SASATIES South African Kabobs

SOUTH AFRICAN

YIELD: Eight to ten servings

1 leg of lamb,
about 4 pounds ·
3 onions,
coarsely chopped ·
2 tablespoons
beef broth or
dry vermouth ·
2 tablespoons
curry powder ·
1 tablespoon honey ·
1/2 tablespoon
coarse salt ·
4 twists of pepper mill ·
2 cups vinegar ·
1 cup water ·
2 teaspoons orange or
lemon zest, or
1 teaspoon dried ·
Cookware spray ·

Trim the lamb of excess fat, remove the meat from the bone, and cut into 1- to 1-1/2-inch cubes. Season the lamb cubes with salt and pepper and skewer them with presoaked wooden skewers or with metal skewers. Apply cookware spray to a skillet and sauté the onions in 1 tablespoon of the beef broth or dry vermouth until they turn translucent. Dissolve the curry powder in the balance of the beef broth and add to the skillet, cooking over low heat 3 minutes longer. Place the balance of the ingredients into an earthenware or glass bowl, and blend in the onion and curry mixture. Add the skewers of lamb and marinate overnight, turning them occasionally. Drain the lamb well, and broil or barbecue until tender. Serve with rice and CURRY SAUCE (page 138).

POULET AVEC SAUCE AU CHAMPAGNE Chicken with Champagne Sauce

FRENCH

8 serving pieces of chicken, consisting of legs, thighs, and breasts ·
4 shallots, fresh or freeze-dried ·
2 tablespoons dry vermouth ·
2 tablespoons polyunsaturated margarine ·
3/4 cup Sauce Béchamel (page 125) ·
1 tablespoon cornstarch or arrowroot ·
1/4 cup brandy ·
1/3 cup white port wine ·
1/2 cup dry champagne ·
1 cup chicken broth or canned consommé ·
1/2 cup evaporated skimmed milk ·
Salt and pepper to taste ·
1/2 pound sliced mushrooms ·
Cookware spray ·

The sauce is somewhat thinner in texture than you might expect, but its flavor combination is most satisfying. The sauce also can be made in advance and kept warm until ready for use. Don't put off making this dish until you have leftover champagne on hand; use the small quantity called for in the recipe and drink the rest with the meal.
YIELD: Six to eight servings

1. Apply cookware spray to a large skillet and sauté the shallots with 1 tablespoon of the dry vermouth for 3 minutes. Dip the chicken pieces in cold water, drain but do not pat dry. Place the chicken in the skillet with seasonings to taste and brown lightly; then add 1 tablespoon of the margarine; cover, and simmer for 25 minutes. Shuffle the pot and turn the chicken pieces occasionally.

2. Meanwhile heat the BÉCHAMEL SAUCE. In another saucepan, blend the cornstarch with 1/2 tablespoon of melted margarine and cook about 4 minutes to make a ROUX. Add the heated BÉCHAMEL SAUCE and simmer, stirring constantly, for 10 minutes until it thickens.

3. Remove the cooked chicken to a warm platter and cover with aluminum foil. Add the brandy to the pan over medium heat and scrape with a spatula to deglaze. Add the white port wine and the champagne, and bring to a boil. At the boiling point, ignite the mixture and, after the flame has been spent, simmer for an additional 15 minutes. Stir in the BÉCHAMEL SAUCE, the chicken broth, and the evaporated skimmed milk. Cook over high heat 15 minutes longer, stirring constantly, to reduce the sauce. Add the chicken and simmer for 10 minutes, turning the pieces occasionally so they absorb the sauce. Meanwhile, sauté the sliced mushrooms with the reserved tablespoon of dry vermouth, about 3 minutes.

4. Transfer the cooked chicken pieces to a warm serving platter, and add the sautéed mushrooms. If the sauce is still too thin, increase the heat and reduce it further to the desired consistency. Strain the sauce over the chicken, garnish, and serve.

* GNOCCHI VERDI Green Dumplings

ITALIAN

2 pounds
unpeeled potatoes,
boiled, or
3-3/4 cups
mashed potatoes ·
2 whole or 4 halved
breasts of chicken ·
1-1/2 cups
chicken broth or
consommé ·
1/2 pound
fresh spinach or
1 10-ounce package
frozen spinach ·
1/2 teaspoon
coarse salt or to taste ·
4 egg whites ·
1/4 cup dry skimmed
milk cottage cheese
or part-skim ricotta ·
4 drops
fresh lemon juice ·
3/4 cup potato or
rice flour ·
1/8 teaspoon grated
or ground nutmeg ·
2 twists of
pepper mill (optional) ·
2 tablespoons
fresh parsley, chopped ·
1/4 cup grated
Parmesan cheese ·
Ground pepper to taste ·
Cookware spray ·

These delicate green dumplings are particular favorites of mine; they can be graced with a number of sauces, each of which creates a completely different and succulent dish. My favorite sauce with GNOCCHI VERDI is Gorgonzola sauce, but others may better suit your own taste preferences. (See Bonus Ideas below.) Since they freeze well, you can make as many as you like, reserving portions in the freezer for the future.

YIELD Six to eight servings

1. Boil the potatoes in their jackets, without salt, in 4 quarts of water to cover for about 30 minutes, depending on the size of the potatoes. Avoid over-puncturing to test for doneness or you will waterlog the potatoes. Drain, then peel the potatoes while still hot but comfortable to handle, sprinkling your hands with flour if necessary to avoid scorching them. Rice or mash the potatoes with a fork while still warm.

2. Meanwhile boil the chicken breasts in the broth for 7 minutes, or until tender; remove, drain, pat dry, then bone and finely grind the breasts. Set aside while you prepare the spinach. Discard the stems, hard ribs, and any wilted leaves of the fresh spinach; wash thoroughly, drain, but do not pat dry. Cook the moist spinach with 1/2 teaspoon of salt AU SEC for 15 minutes or until tender, adding 1 tablespoon of broth if necessary. If frozen spinach is used, thaw and cook with the salt for 5 minutes, uncovered.

3. Whisk the egg whites for 1 minute until foamy, then, with a wooden spoon, blend them into the spinach mixture with the dry cottage cheese, the lemon juice, and the flour; add the balance of the ingredients, except the Parmesan cheese and chopped parsley, and blend thoroughly once again. Adjust the salt to taste. Dust your hands and a mixing board with flour and knead the mixture to the consistency of pie dough, adding more flour or sprinkles of water as necessary. Cover with a clean cloth and let the dough set for about 15 minutes, then knead for a few more minutes.

4. Cut the dough into pieces about the size of an egg, and with the palms of your hands roll out 1/2-inch-thick rolls in the shape of long bread sticks. Cut the thin rolls into 1/2- to 3/4-inch lengths. Flour the surface of a grater with a curved semicircular cutting edge and roll each dumpling across the grater so that it is scored with the impression of the teeth of the grater. This adds lightness and helps the sauce to adhere to the cooked GNOCCHI.

5. Preheat your oven to 350°F. Apply cookware spray to a 2-quart ovenproof casserole, layer the bottom with the sauce you are using, and cover with a layer of GNOCCHI. Sprinkle with grated cheese and season to taste. Beginning and ending with the sauce, make as many layers as you can until all of the ingredients have been used. Sprinkle the chopped parsley over the top, if parsley is consistent with the sauce you are using; cover and bake for 30 minutes or until the GNOCCHI are tender.

BONUS IDEAS: Gnocchi Verdi lend themselves to a variety of sauces such as MINCEUR TOMATO SAUCE (page 16–17), BOLOGNESE SAUCE (page 16–17), PESTO (page 16–17), GORGONZOLA SAUCE (page 133) or GUIDO'S WALNUT SAUCE (page 140). If you are using one of the tomato sauces, try topping each serving with 1 tablespoon of ricotta or blending the cheese into the sauce. You can also serve GNOCCHI VERDI IN BRODO, GREEN DUMPLINGS IN BROTH, by cooking the GNOCCHI in about 8 cups of boiling chicken or beef broth for several minutes until the broth returns to the boiling point. With a slotted spoon, remove the cooked GNOCCHI and serve covered with the hot broth and sprinkled with grated Parmesan cheese.

CREAMY STEAK

ZAMBIAN YIELD: Four servings

2 pounds lean beef steak •
2 tablespoons cornstarch or waterchestnut flour •
Salt and freshly ground pepper to taste •
4 onions, peeled and sliced •
2 tablespoons beef broth or dry vermouth •
3/4 cup skimmed milk •
1/4 cup evaporated skimmed milk •
Cookware spray •

Preheat your oven to 350°F. Cut the trimmed steak into 1-inch squares and roll in a combination of the cornstarch and seasonings. Apply cookware spray to a skillet, and sauté the onions in 1 tablespoon of the beef broth until they turn translucent. Add the balance of the broth and brown the beef over high heat, stirring constantly, adding some of the milk as necessary. Continue stirring while adding the balance of the milk until the sauce becomes thickened. Apply cookware spray to an ovenproof casserole, transfer the steak covered with the sauce, and bake for about 1-1/2 hours, or until tender. Serve hot.

POULET VIVANDIÈRE Stuffed Chicken with Apples and Calvados

FRENCH

1 3-pound chicken •
3 or 4 links of
1 lemon •
Boudin Blanc (page 96–97) •
3 tablespoons of
Calvados or applejack •
6 tablespoons apple cider,
preferably unpasteurized •
2 large green or
golden apples,
thinly sliced •
4 tablespoons water •
1 teaspoon honey •
1 pinch each,
powdered cinnamon
and salt •
Cookware spray •

This recipe was originally featured by Escoffier and combines a number of special ingredients which, during the cooking process, blend into an unusual flavor. It is a simple dish to make and one you will enjoy preparing—especially if you have reserved BOUDIN BLANC (page 96–97) in the freezer. YIELD: Four to six servings

1. Set your oven at 350°F. Cut the lemon in half and rub the cavity of the chicken, before stuffing with the precooked BOUDIN BLANC (page 96–97). Secure the cavity and truss the chicken. Apply cookware spray to a roasting pan or casserole and place the chicken in it, breast side up. Bake the chicken for about 1 hour, or until fork-tender. Remove from the oven.

2. Untruss the chicken and place the pan with the chicken on top of the range. In a saucepan heat the Calvados, set it aflame, and pour over the chicken and into the sauce. When it stops flaming, pour the apple cider into the sauce; simmer for about 10 minutes. Meanwhile, combine the sliced apples and the balance of the ingredients in another saucepan and simmer gently, covered, for about 10 minutes. Place the chicken on a platter; carve at the table, or cut beforehand into serving pieces. Spoon some of the sauce over the chicken, garnish with some of the apples and other garnishes of your choice. Serve the balance of the sauce and the apples separately.

BONUS IDEAS: You can prepare this dish with a turkey or with cornish hens, adjusting the amount of stuffing you will use. The BOUDIN BLANC can be combined with the stuffing for ROAST CHICKEN IN A BAG (page 24–25), and can be cooked as well in a Brown-In-Bag in the same manner. If cooking in a microwave oven, cover the leg and wing tips with aluminum foil, and place the chicken breast-side down in a glass casserole. Cover with a sheet of wax paper and cook for 15 minutes, basting occasionally. Turn the chicken breast-side up and cook 10 minutes longer. Remove from the oven and insert thermometer, which should read about 185°F. when the chicken is cooked. Wrap in foil, and proceed with preparing the spiced apple mixture and heating the Calvados. Unwrap the chicken, and pour the ignited Calvados, then the cider, over the chicken. Return to the oven along with the apple mixture, which should be placed in a separate glass bowl. Cook for 3 minutes. Serve.

If using a clay pot, presoak the pot, add the stuffed chicken, and place into a cold oven set at 450°F. for 45 minutes. Remove the cover and cook an additional 10 minutes to brown the chicken. Remove from the oven, baste well, then add the ignited Calvados and cider. Return to the oven and cook for 10 minutes more until fork-tender. Meanwhile, prepare the spiced apples, and serve.

* MAMMA ROSA'S SOUPE À LA SANTÉ Mamma Rosa's Health Soup

ITALIAN/ FRENCH

3 quarts water, or 1 quart chicken stock or consommé and 2 quarts water·
2 teaspoons coarse salt·
2 pounds fresh or frozen spinach, chopped·
1 bunch celery, including leaves, chopped·
1 onion, thinly sliced·
4 carrots, thinly diced or grated·
1 pound tomatoes, peeled and quartered, or 1 pound canned Italian style plum tomatoes·
8 white peppercorns, whole·
1 bay leaf·

Meatballs:
1 pound lean ground beef·
3/4 cup uncooked rice·
1 egg white, whisked·
5 twists of pepper mill·
1 tablespoon Parmesan cheese, grated·
3 tablespoons parsley, chopped·

This hearty one-dish meal probably originated in France but now has been absorbed into Italian cuisine. Of course, others claim this chain of events was the other way around. The dish was a favorite of my mother, who was reluctant at first to share the recipe, and only did so after innumerable guests asked for it the moment they tasted this invigorating soup. You may wish to make large quantities, since the soup freezes beautifully and improves with reheating. My mother liked to serve small portions as a first course at festive meals; what was left over was a welcome main dish for the entire family.

YIELD: Eight to ten servings

1. Place the vegetables in a stock pot with the water, chicken stock, and 1 teaspoon coarse salt, the peppercorns and bay leaf. Bring to a boil, cover and simmer over lowered heat for approximately 40 minutes.

2. Meanwhile, prepare meatballs by blending the ground beef with the meatball ingredients and 1 teaspoon coarse salt. Roll into balls 3/4 inch in diameter and add to the soup. Return the soup to a boil, cover and simmer over lowered heat for 1 hour longer; adjust seasonings to taste. Serve hot, sprinkled with Parmesan cheese.

BONUS IDEAS: Like many hearty soups, this one permits the addition of any vegetables you like and have on hand. My mother often added 3/4 pound of diced potatoes, 1/4 pound sliced mushrooms, and sometimes 1/2 pound diced chicken breasts, skinned and boned.

* SOUPE DE POISSON Mediterranean
Fish Soup

FRENCH

3 pounds whole fish
with heads left on:
sea bass, haddock,
red snapper,
cod and/or eel;
or 2 pints fresh
or bottled clam juice ·
Leftover shellfish parts,
if available,
including the shells ·
5 pints water, or 3 pints
if clam juice is used
instead of fish ·
1-1/4 cups onion, minced ·
2 tablespoons water ·
1 tablespoon
dry vermouth ·
1 tablespoon
olive oil (optional) ·
4 cloves garlic, mashed ·
1-1/4 cups Italian style
plum tomatoes, drained ·
3 tablespoons
tomato paste ·
1 pinch saffron ·
1/4 cup fresh or
bottled clam juice ·
6 sprigs parsley ·
1 large leek or
4 scallions, minced ·
1/2 teaspoon basil ·
1/4 teaspoon fennel seed ·
1 teaspoon
fresh orange peel ·
3 twists of pepper mill ·
8 each, white and
green peppercorns ·
2 large white potatoes,
peeled and cut
in quarters ·
Cookware spray ·

For those who find BOUILLABAISSE troublesome to prepare and serve (since it calls for shellfish and many other seafoods), this soup has the same delicious flavor but is strained and thickened into a smooth delight. It is most effective for festive occasions and marvelously enhanced when served with rounds of toast topped with ROUILLE, a specially prepared condiment in the form of a thick sauce (page 130). When fresh or frozen fish is not readily available, this soup can be made easily using fresh or bottled clam juice.
YIELD: Eight to ten servings

1. Apply cookware spray to a saucepan, add 2 tablespoons of water and sauté onions 2 or 3 minutes; add the vermouth and optional oil and sauté until the onions are translucent. With edge of a knife, mash the garlic and add with the tomatoes and tomato paste to the onions. Simmer this mixture over low heat for approximately 5 minutes.

2. Dissolve the saffron with 1 tablespoon of warm water, then fill a large pot with the water and/or clam juice; add the fish and shellfish parts (if these are used instead of clam juice), then the balance of the ingredients except for the potatoes. Cook over medium heat, uncovered, for approximately one-half hour.

3. With a slotted spoon, remove and discard any firm shellfish parts, especially the shells. Reserve 1 to 2 cups fish and shellfish meat in unbroken pieces, then press the extra cooked fish through a sieve. Return the strained soup to the cooking vessel and adjust pepper and saffron seasoning to taste. Add the potato pieces, bring the soup to a boil, then lower the heat to medium and cook for approximately 30 minutes until the potatoes are fork-tender.

4. Remove the cooked potatoes and blend or mash them with several tablespoons of the fish soup. Reserve one-half of the potato purée for the ROUILLE, and blend the balance into the fish soup. Bring the soup to a boil, lower the heat to medium and continue cooking for approximately 15 minutes longer. Cover and let set for 5 minutes. Serve hot with rounds of toast topped with ROUILLE.

BONUS IDEAS: I like to float rounds of toast topped with spoonfuls of ROUILLE (page 130) in each bowl of soup served. In addition I put out a sauceboat of this delightful PIMIENTO AND GARLIC SAUCE for those who want extra toasted rounds or who simply prefer to streak the sauce into their soup bowls.

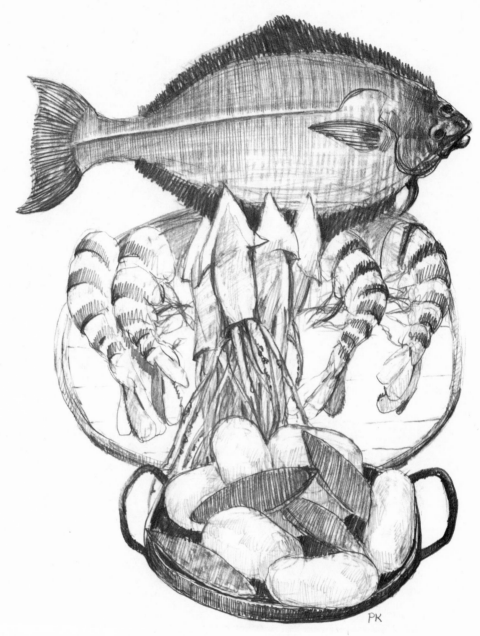

You'll find that you won't need special occasions for
serving this satisfying dish; since you can freeze both the
leftover soup and the ROUILLE, SOUPE DE POISSON can be an
everyday delight. So next time you are preparing fresh lobster or shrimp, consider reserving the remaining shells and
parts for this superb soup, which is, incidentally, equally
successful as a first course or a hearty main-course dish.
The reserved pieces of fish and shellfish meat can also be
used for other dishes such as a refreshing fish salad (page
90), or frozen until required.

81

* HONG SIU GAI Red-Simmered Chicken

CHINESE

1 3-1/2-pound
whole chicken or fowl ·
3 thin slices ginger,
minced ·
2 cloves garlic, mashed ·
1 small onion,
thinly sliced ·
2 scallions,
sliced lengthwise ·
1/4 cup chicken broth
or consommé,
double strength ·
2 star anise cloves ·
1/3 cup soy sauce,
preferably dark ·
1/4 cup sherry
or dry vermouth ·
1 teaspoon sesame oil ·
2 tablespoons wine vinegar ·
2 tablespoons honey ·
8 scallion brushes
(page 50)
for garnish ·
Cookware spray ·

Red-simmering—braising or stewing poultry, meat, or game over low heat—is popular with most Chinese families. The term is derived from the reddish-brown color of the sauce, which after the meal is cooked can be reserved as a starter for CHINESE MASTER SAUCE (page 134–35). Here an advantage is that this process permits you to prepare dishes well in advance, and it can be easily varied by substituting any type of meat you have on hand or prefer (see Bonus Ideas); the sauce also improves with reheating.

YIELD: Four servings

1. Remove and discard any excess fat from the chicken, especially from its cavity. If using fowl, wrap it in aluminum foil and bake in the oven at 450°F. for 15 minutes, then remove and discard the skin and the layer of fat beneath it. Meanwhile, apply cookware spray to a WOK or heavy skillet and sauté the ginger, garlic, onion, and scallions with 1 tablespoon of concentrated broth, which is made either by reducing chicken broth to half its volume over high heat, or simply by adding a bouillon cube to the broth. When the onions are translucent, add 2 additional tablespoons of the concentrated broth and brown the chicken on all sides over high heat, adding additional broth as necessary.

2. Apply cookware spray to a heavy pan or casserole and add the balance of the ingredients except the honey and scallion brushes. Stir the mixture well, then add the browned chicken. Bring the contents to a boil, then reduce the heat and simmer covered for about 1-1/2 hours, or until the chicken is almost tender, turning it at least 4 times during cooking. Add the honey and simmer for about 15 minutes longer, or until the chicken is tender. Drain the chicken and cut it into 2-inch pieces, removing and discarding the bones if you prefer. Serve garnished with the scallion brushes and CHINESE SALT DIPPING SAUCE (see Bonus Ideas below). Strain the sauce in which the chicken has cooked, skim off any fat, and reserve for other red-simmered dishes or as a starter for CHINESE MASTER SAUCE (page 134–35).

BONUS IDEAS: Although the Chinese generally do not use the red sauce with the chicken, preferring instead dipping sauces, you may moisten the chicken with the sauce or ladle it over rice, steamed vegetables, and the chicken before serving. Then add the scallion brush garnish and bits of chopped parsley or additional chopped scallions.

You may also serve any of the CHINESE DIPPING SAUCES; however, CHINESE SALT DIPPING SAUCE or WA YIUM, is preferred with chicken dishes. The sauce is made by blending 2 tablespons of coarse salt with 1/2 teaspoon of ground white pepper dissolved in 2 tablespoons of chicken broth. Add 1/3 cup of corn oil and stir the mixture well, before serving in small individual relish dishes for each diner to use for dipping.

You can use the reserved red sauce or MASTER SAUCE (page 134–35), which can also be frozen for future use, in red-simmering any of the following:

✳ HONG SIU TAI GAI, or Red-simmered Capon

Use roasting chicken or fowl weighing 5 to 6 pounds for six servings. Brown the capon, as called for in the recipe above, using additional concentrated broth as necessary. Use the reserved red sauce, the MASTER SAUCE, or, if this is the starter sauce, use all of the ingredients of the above recipe. Cook the capon covered in a large heavy casserole for 3 hours over low heat, turning the capon every half hour. Adjust the honey and sherry to taste and simmer for 20 minutes longer, until tender. Garnish with 12 scallion brushes and serve as described above.

✳ HONG SIU NU YUK, or Red-simmered Beef

Use 2 pounds of lean shin of beef, or even a tougher beef cut (which will be tenderized while simmering) for four servings. Use the reserved red sauce, the MASTER SAUCE, or use all of the ingredients of the above recipe if this is the starter sauce. Trim the beef of excess fat and dip it into water for a moment, drain but do not pat dry. Proceed to brown the meat over high heat, transfer it to a heavy casserole with the reserved red sauce, and simmer covered over low heat, for about 2-1/2 hours or until tender, turning the meat every half hour. Add the honey and sherry to taste, and simmer for 15 minutes longer. Garnish with 8 scallion brushes and serve as described above.

✳ HONG SIU TO, or Red-simmered Rabbit

Use 5 pounds of fresh or frozen rabbit cut into small pieces for six servings. If frozen, thoroughly thaw before cooking. Wash the rabbit pieces, drain and place the pieces in a heavy casserole but do not brown, since this is not necessary when cooking rabbit in this fashion. Use the reserved red sauce, the MASTER SAUCE, or use all of the ingredients of the above recipe if this is the starter sauce. Cover and simmer over low heat for 3 hours, turning the meat every half hour with a wooden spoon. Add the honey and sherry to taste, and continue to simmer for another hour, or until the meat is tender. Garnish with 12 scallion brushes and serve as described above.

* PETITE MARMITE Savory Soup

FRENCH

2-1/2 quarts water •
**2 pounds chuck beef,
cut into
1-1/4-inch cubes** •
**1 beef knucklebone,
tied in cheesecloth** •
**2 carrots,
scraped and
cut diagonally into
1-inch slices** •
**1 medium onion,
pierced with 1 clove** •
**3 leeks,
white part only,
cut into 1-inch lengths** •
**1 cup chopped cabbage,
blanched (optional)** •

**Bouquet Garni,
tied in cheesecloth,
consisting of:
1 stalk celery,
with leaves** •
1 bay leaf •
**3 sprigs each,
fresh chervil and parsley,
or 1/2 teaspoon each,
dried** •
**2 sprigs fresh thyme,
or 1/4 teaspoon dried** •

This is one of the traditional family dishes of France. It has many variations using different kinds of meat, though beef is used predominantly. MARMITE is the name of the stock pot the soup is cooked in; it can be metal, but an ovenproof earthenware pot is preferred for better flavor. One can either begin the soup in an earthenware MARMITE on top of the stove over a heatproof pad, or in a metal pot, and finish cooking in an earthenware pot in the oven.

YIELD: Six to eight servings

1. To avoid later skimming, place the knucklebone in a stock pot with water to cover and bring to a boil. Discard the water. Drain and pat the knucklebone and tie in cheesecloth.

2. Brown the knucklebone in an oven at 400°F. to insure a richer broth. Place the knucklebone, the beef, and the water in the MARMITE or stock pot, and bring to a boil over medium heat; skim very well.

3. Add the balance of the ingredients and bring the soup to a boil once again. Skim as necessary, although the initial preboiling should minimize the need; cover and cook in the earthenware MARMITE in an oven at 350°F. for approximately 3 hours.

4. Remove the beef, bone, and vegetables and arrange on a serving platter. Strain the bouillon or clarify with egg whites (page 241). You may enjoy serving the clear bouillon with toasted slices of gluten bread sprinkled with Parmesan cheese floating on top, and the meat and vegetables as a side or second dish.

BONUS IDEAS: Grated horseradish or a horseradish sauce is an excellent accompaniment to the meat.

It is also traditional to substitute a hen for other meats, whereby the soup becomes POULE-AU-POT, or CHICKEN IN A POT. To prepare this, wrap the fowl in aluminum foil and bake with the knucklebone at 400°F. for 15 minutes. Before adding the chicken to the water, remove the foil, the chicken skin, and the thick layers of fat that are concentrated under it.

There is one school of thought that recommends discarding the cooked vegetables on the theory that their flavors and nutrients are already in the broth. This school recommends replacing the previously cooked vegetables with a fresh batch and cooking them in the broth for approximately 1/2 hour until fork-tender.

VITELLO TONNATO Cold Veal with
Tuna Sauce

ITALIAN

2 to 2-1/2 pounds leg
or top round of veal,
boned and tied ·
5 flat anchovy filets ·
1 onion,
pierced with 1 clove ·
1 carrot,
cut into 2-inch pieces ·
2 stalks of celery,
julienned ·
4 sprigs of
fresh parsley, or
1 teaspoon dried ·
1 bay leaf ·
1 teaspoon coarse salt ·
1 cup dry white wine,
or dry vermouth ·
1 7-ounce can of tuna
in oil,
preferably olive oil ·
3 tablespoons capers,
finely chopped ·
1/2 cup oil,
preferably olive oil ·
Juice of 1 lemon,
or more to taste ·
Lemon wedges ·

In Italy during the summer months, you will see this delicacy featured on the presentation tables as you enter many restaurants, or in the refrigerated "picture windows" where specialties are often displayed. While it takes time to prepare, you can do so well in advance, since VITELLO TONNATO keeps in the refrigerator for a week or more, and in the long run is very well worth the time and effort. Select the freshest young veal you can find, or cook longer until tender if you must use older veal.

YIELD: Six servings

1. Trim the veal of all excess fat and skin; make 10 slits and insert into the veal 2 of the anchovies, each drained and cut into 10 pieces. Tie the veal loosely and place in a large pot with the onion, carrot, celery, parsley, bay leaf, salt, wine, and enough water to cover. Cover, bring to a boil, then simmer over low heat for 1-1/2 hours or until the veal is tender.

2. When done, untie the veal, and let it cool thoroughly. Meanwhile, prepare the tuna sauce by thoroughly mashing the tuna and the balance of the anchovies with a fork, adding the capers, oil, and lemon juice and blending until smooth—to the consistency of mayonnaise; or you can combine these ingredients in an electric blender until smooth.

3. When the veal is thoroughly cooled, cut it into thin slices. Spread a layer of the tuna sauce on a serving platter, and layer the sliced veal above it, covering this with additional tuna sauce. Repeat this process until all of the sliced veal and tuna sauce have been used, but the topmost layer must be the tuna sauce—to prevent the sliced veal from drying out. Cover with a plastic wrap, and refrigerate for at least 24 hours.

4. Just before serving, sprinkle the top with additional capers, and garnish with the lemon wedges. If properly refrigerated, this dish will last a week or more.

BONUS IDEAS: Many Milanese prepare this dish with mayonnaise, and you may utilize MINCEUR MAYONNAISE (page 124) at room temperature, but the initial simmering of the veal with aromatic vegetables and the wine must still be done. While the meat is cooling, in an electric blender combine the tuna with the balance of the anchovy filets, the olive oil, the capers, and lemon juice and blend for about 15 seconds at high speed until smooth. Transfer and blend into the mayonnaise; then proceed with layering the tuna sauce and slices of veal as described above. If using the mayonnaise you can elect not to refrigerate the dish overnight, but you must thoroughly chill it before serving.

Whenever possible, you should reserve cooking liquors from stewed or other dishes, for use in rice dishes such as RISOTTO ALLA MILANESE (page 200–201). The broth in which this veal has been cooked certainly fits into this category.

BIFTECK AU POIVRE VERT Sirloin Steak
with Green Peppercorn Sauce

FRENCH

1 1-1/2-inch thick
sirloin steak or
1-1/2 pounds rib steak ·
1 tablespoon cognac ·
1 tablespoon each,
crushed green peppercorns
and polyunsaturated
margarine ·
1/4 cup evaporated
skimmed milk ·
1/2 teaspoon prepared
Dijon mustard ·
Cookware spray ·

Here is one of the simplest delicacies I know and one you'll want to make often—steak with a refreshingly different pepper sauce. The green peppercorns can be blended with margarine and rolled into small balls, which then can be frozen and ready for use for this or other meat dishes.
YIELD: Two or more servings

1. Trim the steak of all excess fat, and quickly dip into cold water; drain, but do not pat dry. Apply cookware spray to a skillet, sear the steak on both sides over high heat, and lower the heat to cook as desired, adding a little extra water as necessary. Place the cooked steak on a warm serving platter, while preparing the sauce.

2. Add the cognac to the skillet, and deglaze, stirring with a spatula. Add the crushed peppercorns—combined with the margarine and rolled into a small ball—to the skillet; when melted, add the evaporated skimmed milk. Simmer over low heat and stir until the sauce is blended. Just before serving, add the Dijon mustard, stirring again. Pour the sauce over the steak, cut it into serving pieces, and garnish with watercress and parsley.

BONUS IDEAS: This POIVRE VERT sauce is also excellent with roasted duck. I generally prepare a large quantity of the blended green peppercorns and margarine—in the same proportions as indicated above—roll them into walnut-sized balls, and freeze them individually wrapped in wax paper before placing them in containers.

Another favorite of mine is CALVES LIVER WITH GREEN PEPPERCORNS. The liver should be scored with a crisscross pattern; after dipping quickly in water, draining, but not patting dry, I broil one side of the liver first, then the other, and add one of the reserved frozen peppercorn and margarine balls during cooking. Do not overcook; serve hot.

86

* ZUPPA DI PESCE "Emergency" Bouillabaisse

ITALIAN

1-1/2 pounds halibut, flounder, or any white-flesh fish filets •
1 dozen large fresh shrimp, or frozen shrimp •
1/2 pound fresh cleaned squid, or an 8-ounce can •
1 dozen clams, or a 24-ounce can of clams in the shell •
16 mussels, or an 18-ounce can of mussels on the half-shell •
1/3 cup oil, preferably half olive oil •
1 large clove garlic, peeled and minced •
4 tablespoons fresh parsley, chopped •
1 20-ounce can Italian style plum tomatoes •
1 cup white wine, or dry vermouth •
1/2 cup water •
1/8 teaspoon each salt, ground ginger, and cayenne •
1/4 teaspoon thyme, dried •
1/4 teaspoon each, oregano, basil, dried •
Croutons or toasted gluten bread •

A very simple and thoroughly satisfying dish that is one of my family's "Blizzard Meals." You can make this recipe with fish and seafood freshly purchased at your market, or in an emergency, with frozen or canned ingredients; in either case it's cooked in about a half-hour. This can be a hearty meal, or, in smaller portions, a successful first course.

YIELD: Six to eight servings

1. In a large saucepan, sauté the garlic and half the parsley in the oil for 3 minutes over medium heat. Add all of the other ingredients except the fish and seafood, the basil, oregano, croutons and the reserved parsley. Bring the mixture to a boil, then simmer over medium heat for about 1/2 hour.

2. Add the fish and seafood, the basil, and the oregano; cover and cook a few minutes longer, or until the clam and mussel shells open and the mixture is thoroughly hot. Serve over the croutons or toasted bread, and garnish with the balance of the chopped parsley.

BONUS IDEAS: You can add any additional fish or seafood you like, especially fresh, frozen, or canned lobster that is cooked quickly, just before serving. You can spread a thin coat of polyunsaturated margarine on the toast, or rub it with a cut garlic clove for additional flavor.

Because the fish and seafood require little cooking time, it is recommended that you remove them when reheating this fish soup. Return the fish and seafood to the hot soup just before serving and garnish with the fresh parsley.

FONDUE NEUCHÂTELOISE Swiss
Fondue

SWISS

1-1/2 pounds Fontina, Gruyère, Monterey Jack, Swiss, or Jarlsberg cheese, shredded; or any combination of 2 of those cheeses (6 cups) · 1 clove garlic, slightly mashed · 2 cups Neuchâtel or any dry white wine · 1-1/2 tablespoons cornstarch · 2 tablespoons water · 3 tablespoons kirsch, cognac or rum · Freshly grated pepper or nutmeg to taste · Cookware spray · 1-inch cubes of French bread, gluten bread or whole breadsticks ·

This is undoubtedly the most famous fondue. It can be most easily prepared and it is always successful for a festive evening. There are a number of variations, as you will see in the Bonus Ideas below: a more tangy cheese fondue, as well as beef and vegetable fondues, all of which can be made with equal success.

YIELD: Six servings

1. Apply cookware spray to a chafing dish, electric casserole or skillet, or to any heatproof casserole with a heat source for cooking at the table. Protect your table top from scorching as necessary. Rub the inside of the pot with the garlic, pour in the wine, and heat until it simmers, but do not boil. Blend the shredded cheese with the cornstarch and add gradually to the simmering wine, about a handful at a time, stirring constantly until each portion of the cheese is melted. When all of the cheese is melted, add the water, the kirsch, and the pepper or nutmeg.

2. Keep the fondue simmering, but never boiling, at the table. Provide each diner with a long-handled fork for spearing the cubes of bread, which are then dipped into the melted cheese. Be prepared to add additional wine or water should the fondue become too thick. When all of the melted cheese is consumed, the brown crusted residue in the pot is considered a special delicacy and should be served separately with coffee or wine.

BONUS IDEAS: For a more tangy fondue, you may substitute 2 cups of Gorgonzola or Bleu cheese and blend with 4 cups of other cheese of your choice. To vary the number of servings, reduce or increase the amount of shredded cheese by 1/2 pound, or 2 cups, for every two diners, but do not vary any of the other ingredients except the amount of bread cubes you provide. For example, if serving 4, use 1 pound or 4 cups of cheese.

For BEEF FONDUE, or FONDUE BOURGUIGNON, you will need 2 pounds of filet or sirloin of beef cut into 3/4-inch cubes, 1 cup of corn or olive oil or a combination of both, and 3 tablespoons of polyunsaturated margarine. Arrange the meat cubes on a large platter or individual plates; preheat the oil and margarine in a fondue pot to 375°F. and keep it hot and bubbling so that each diner can spear the meat cube with a long fork and cook it in the bubbling oil mixture for 1 minute or more, depending on desired doneness: 1 minute is rare. The cooked meat is then dipped into 1 of 3 or more of the following dipping sauces, which should be provided at the

table: Béarnaise Sauce (page 51), Horseradish Sauce (page 107), hot Chinese mustard, Piquant Anchovy Sauce (page 131), Barbecue Sauce (page 133) or any suitable minceur sauce for meat (see Chapter 6). Serves 6 with a salad and garlic bread, or serves 12 as an appetizer.

Another favorite of mine is Italian Vegetable Fondue, or Bagna Cauda. For 8 servings you will need a variety of about 8 young and tender vegetables that, with the exception of mushrooms, are chilled in ice water for an hour, drained, patted dry, and attractively arranged on a platter set at the table. Generally the crisp vegetables used include: 3 or 4 stalks of celery, cut into 2-inch pieces; 2 carrots, cut into 2-inch strips; 1 or 2 sweet peppers cut into 1-inch strips; 8 to 10 radishes with root tips trimmed but leaves left on; 8 asparagus stalks, trimmed and peeled; 1/4 pound of button mushrooms wiped with a damp cloth; 1/2 pound of cauliflower or broccoli florets, spinach leaves, and about 8 cherry or small plum tomatoes. These are then individually dipped by each diner into a hot, but never boiling, fondue pot containing a combination of 1/2 cup of polyunsaturated margarine, 1/2 cup of olive or corn oil, 2 teaspoons of minced garlic, and 10 chopped anchovy filets. Serve with breadsticks. If preparing ahead, be sure to keep the platter of vegetables, covered with plastic, in the refrigerator until ready to serve.

BIRYANI AND RICE, Moslem Meat and Rice Casserole

INDIAN/
PAKISTANI

The Biryani:
3 pounds lamb,
cut into 1-1/4-inch cubes;
or a 3-pound
roasting chicken;
or 2-1/2 pounds chicken
legs and breasts ·
10 ounces plain yoghurt ·
2 lemons, juiced ·
6 cloves garlic, minced ·
3 tablespoons oil ·
6 thin slices ginger, minced ·
1 teaspoon each,
ground coriander and
coarse salt ·
1/2 teaspoon each,
ground cloves and cinnamon ·
1/4 teaspoon each, cardamom,
chili, black pepper,
all ground ·
6 onions,
about 2 pounds, sliced ·
2 tablespoons each,
water and dry vermouth ·
2 tablespoons golden raisins
for garnish (optional) ·
Cookware spray ·

The Rice:
1 pound Patna,
or long grain rice ·
12 whole cloves ·
7 sticks cinnamon,
each 1 inch long ·
7 bay leaves ·
12 whole cardamoms ·
12 whole black peppercorns,
or 6 black and 6 green ·
1/2 tablespoon saffron ·
1 tablespoon coarse salt ·
2 teaspoons
skimmed milk, hot ·

This regal dish is vastly popular throughout India and Pakistan, where it is served on special festive occasions. It is ideal as a party dish. Its preparation seems complicated—it does take four hours to complete—but believe me, it is certainly worth the effort. I find it easier to prepare the ingredients the morning before, keep them refrigerated, then proceed with final cooking two hours before serving time.
YIELD: Six servings

1. Soak the rice in water to cover while preparing the BIRYANI, or meat portion of the recipe. Apply cookware spray to a 5-quart casserole with cover, and arrange the meat along the base of the casserole. In a bowl, combine the yoghurt, lemon juice, all the ground spices listed under ingredients for the BIRYANI, and the garlic, ginger, and salt; mix thoroughly.

2. If chicken is used, remove the skin and pierce each piece of chicken with the prongs of a fork. Spoon the yoghurt and spice mixture into the casserole, carefully covering all the chicken; set aside.

3. Apply cookware spray to a heavy skillet with cover; add the sliced onions and 2 tablespoons of water. Sauté over medium heat, covered, for approximately 10 minutes, shuffling the skillet occasionally to avoid burning. If extra moisture is necessary, add the dry vermouth. When cooked, mash one-half to two-thirds of the onions and stir into the meat mixture in the casserole, reserving the balance of the onions for garnishing; reserve 1 tablespoon or more of the onion liquor for sautéing the optional raisins, which will also be used as garnish.

4. Drain the rice. Add 3 quarts of water, the spices (except for the saffron) listed under the ingredients for the rice, and salt to a 4-quart pot and bring to a boil. Add the rice and continue cooking until partially done, approximately 10 minutes. Drain the rice through a sieve, reserving the spices. Blend the reserved spices with the rice mixture and place onto a platter to cool, approximately 15 minutes.

5. Mix the saffron with the hot skimmed milk; set aside. Spoon the cooled rice over the meat and yoghurt mixture in the casserole; add the oil and the saffron mixture, and place the reserved onions on top as a garnish. At this point, you may refrigerate the covered casserole until 2 hours before serving time.

6. Two hours before serving, place a sheet of wet paper toweling or aluminum foil between the casserole and the cover for a more thorough sealing, turning the ends of the paper over the top of the cover. Bring the contents to a boil, lower the heat, and simmer for 1-1/2 hours.

7. Meanwhile, prepare additional garnishing as you desire. To serve, remove the onions and rice from the casserole into separate dishes until the meat has been placed on a large serving platter. Now cover the meat with the rice and surround the periphery of the platter with the cooked onion garnish and sprigs of parsley or fresh coriander. For additional garnish, add 2 tablespoons of golden raisins, sautéed in the reserved onion liquor and dry vermouth, 2 tablespoons of blanched almonds or cashews or a combination of both; and the whites of 3 hard-boiled eggs, cut in strips lengthwise.

BONUS IDEAS: When buying a leg of lamb, have your butcher cut 3 pounds of the meat from the shank end. This can be reserved in the freezer, for this dish or for kabobs of lamb.

For a party dish, you may wish to use only skinned chicken legs and breasts. Disjoint the leg and thigh sections to facilitate serving, and be sure to puncture the meat.

Using aluminum foil for more thorough sealing, the casserole may be baked for 1 hour at 300°F. instead of being cooked on top of the range. If you have a large enough microwave oven to accept a 5-quart glass casserole, cook uncovered 7 minutes; cover the casserole tightly and rotate half way; cook an additional 20 minutes and let stand 10 minutes before serving.

Additional accoutrements include a refreshing plain yoghurt or RAITA (page 107), and simple vegetable dishes such as SPINACH AND PEAR PURÉE (Page 19) and ONION or CUCUMBER RELISH (page 115).

DOONG GWAAH JOONG Whole

Winter Melon Soup

CHINESE

**1 whole winter melon,
about 4 or 5 pounds ·
6 cups chicken broth
(page 117)
or canned consommé ·
1 cup chicken breast,
diced ·
1 cup roast duck or
raw lean pork, diced ·
1/2 cup Canadian bacon
or lean prosciutto,
diced ·
4 black mushrooms,
soaked and diced ·
1/2 cup mushrooms,
sliced lengthwise ·
1/2 cup bamboo shoots,
diced or tree-shaped ·
1/2 cup water chestnuts ·
3 teaspoons
light soy sauce ·
1/4 cup parboiled peas
or snow peas (optional) ·
Salt to taste ·
4 teaspoons each,
chopped scallions and
chopped parsley ·**

A flavorsome and hearty soup strikingly presented in its own shell. I wholeheartedly recommend your trying this traditional Chinese dish for entertaining. When selecting a Chinese winter melon, allow about 1/2 pound per serving, and be sure that you have a stock pot large enough for steaming the melon you purchase. There are far more ingredient variations than there are regions in China, and I have yet to taste one version that wasn't superb.

YIELD: Eight to ten servings

1. Scrub the winter melon thoroughly, and slice off the lid, including the stem, about 3 to 5 inches from the top. Reserve the melon lid; remove and discard the seeds and sponge-like pulp from the melon until you have a clean inner layer of melon pulp. Prepare a large stock pot to steam the melon by placing a metal trivet, a raised rack, or a heatproof bowl into the steamer; the rack or bowl should support the melon above the level of water required for steaming. Using strong twine, make a harness that will support the weight of the filled melon; this should have a handle or loop so that it can be safely removed from the pot later.

2. Place sufficient water to last for several hours of steaming—but not rising above the level of the trivet or raised rack, or not above 3/4 of the height of the bowl supporting the melon in the pot—into the pot or steamer. Fill the cavity of the melon with the chicken broth to 3/4 of its volume. Add all of the other ingredients except the optional peas or snow peas, the salt, and the chopped scallions and parsley. Partly cover with the melon lid. Steam, tightly covered, over medium heat for about 3-1/2 hours, or until the melon has become translucent and tender. Do not overcook since the melon must be sufficiently firm to maintain its shape. Continue to add additional stock as necessary to fill 3/4 of the volume of the melon. During the last 15 minutes of cooking, add the optional peas or snow peas.

3. When cooked, carefully lift the melon from the pot using the twine harness and, to support the melon, place it in a large bowl. Transfer to the table with the sliced melon lid fully in place. When serving, ladle out the soup and cooked ingredients, as well as some of the scooped out cooked melon. Each diner can add salt to taste, and garnish with the chopped scallions and parsley which are separately served at the table.

BONUS IDEAS: Shrimp, abalone, lobster, or other seafoods can be added to or substituted for the meats. Other possibilities include diced smoked ham, button mushrooms, and sherry.

Since winter melons vary in shape and size, be sure to select one that will stand upright and secure when placed at the table after it is cooked. Once you have cleaned the inside of the melon, you can determine how much chicken broth you will require by filling the melon with a quart or more of water. Prepare 1/4 more chicken broth than the amount of water that fills the cavity of the melon to 3/4 of its capacity; the extra broth will be used for adding additional broth during the last 15 minutes of cooking.

For certain festivals in China, the thick outer skin of the winter melon is scored with intricate designs. I have never found it necessary to do this, but you might have fun doing it. Also, when removing the lid you may wish to make V-shaped cuts to achieve a sawtooth effect (page 49).

FARINA PIE CASSEROLE

BERMUDIAN

YIELD: Eight to ten servings

1 3-1/2-pound chicken, cut into serving pieces •
2 pounds lean pork, cut into 3/4-inch cubes •
1 tablespoon salt or to taste •
4 egg whites •
1/4 cup melted polyunsaturated margarine •
1/2 cup honey •
1/2 teaspoon each, ground nutmeg and cinnamon •
5 cups farina •
1 tablespoon potato flour, rice flour, or cornstarch •
1 teaspoon baking powder •
Cookware spray •

1. In a large saucepan in barely enough water to cover, cook the chicken and pork with 3/4 tablespoon of the salt for about 1 hour over medium heat. Remove the meat, drain and discard the chicken bones; set aside and reserve the cooking liquid, about 2 cups.

2. Whisk the egg whites for about 1 minute until foamy, blend with the melted margarine, the remaining salt, and the balance of the ingredients except the farina, potato starch, and the baking powder. Gradually add the farina and mix well to a consistency of a light pastry dough. Add the potato starch and baking powder and blend into the dough thoroughly.

3. Preheat your oven to 350°F. Apply cookware spray to an ovenproof casserole and make a 1-inch shell of the farina mixture around the sides and base of the pan. Fill the shell with the cooked meat and add all but 1/2 cup of the reserved cooking liquid. Top the meat with the balance of the farina mixture, making indentations in the top layer with the back of a wooden spoon. Bake, uncovered, for about 1-1/2 hours, occasionally basting the pie with the reserved cooking liquid. Serve hot or cold.

* COTOLETTE CON MANICO ALLA MILANESE Milanese Veal Chops with Handle

ITALIAN

**4 rib veal chops, with the bone attached and unbroken ·
Salt and pepper to taste ·
2 egg whites ·
1/2 cup unsweetened wheat germ or toasted gluten bread crumbs ·
1 tablespoon grated Parmesan cheese ·
1 tablespoon polyunsaturated margarine (optional) ·
1 tablespoon water or dry vermouth ·
1 lemon, cut in quarters ·
Cookware spray ·**

This dish is the pride of virtually every Milanese chef, as well as being one of my very own specialties. It is easy to prepare, and a "must" for busy homemakers, since the prepared chops can be frozen, thawed, and cooked in short order. Whenever I make this dish, I generally prepare enough to reserve some in the freezer. The "handle" refers to the attached bone which, after the chop is cooked, is garnished with a paper frill. Sophia Loren, an outstanding cook in her own right, considers this an elegant dish, and she agrees with the Milanese chefs who insist that the German WIENER SCHNITZEL is an adaptation of it, rather than vice versa—as many Germans insist.

YIELD: Four servings

1. Have the butcher trim off all fat and skin from the chops and pound the meat-end of each chop until it is at least twice its original size, as he would do for Italian style veal cutlets; be sure the bone isn't removed or cracked. If you are doing this at home, cover each chop with a piece of waxed paper, and pound the meat-end of the chop with the side of a cleaver or cutlet mallet. Add salt and pepper to either side of the chop, press the seasonings into the meat with the side of the cleaver or a broad bladed knife, and set aside until all of the chops have been prepared in the same manner.

2. Whisk the egg whites for about 1 minute until foamy, and place in a bowl or soup plate wide enough to hold the chops. In a separate bowl or soup plate, mix the wheat germ or bread crumbs with the Parmesan cheese. Dip each chop into the egg whites, drain and place in the dish of wheat germ. With the edge of a knife, pat the crumbs into each side of the chop. If you are planning to freeze the chops for future use, wrap them in freezing packages at this point. Before using, be sure they are thoroughly defrosted.

3. Apply cookware spray to a large skillet, and sauté the chops on each side for about 3 minutes, with the water or dry vermouth, or the optional margarine. Apply paper frills to the end of the rib bone, and serve hot, with the lemon wedges.

BONUS IDEAS: You can prepare VEAL CORDON BLEU in the same manner, except that you will use Italian style veal cutlets, or breast of turkey or chicken. After the meat has been pounded and seasoned, place a slice of FROMAGE BLANC or Swiss cheese covered with a thin slice of lean boiled ham between two equal sized slices of the pounded veal. Pound the edges, or brush on some of the whisked egg whites to seal the edges of the meat and let them set for 10 minutes. Then dip the stuffed escallops into the egg white and wheat germ, as above, and cook as indicated for the Milanese veal chops.

As with most dishes calling for escallops of veal, you can substitute either chicken or turkey breasts and proceed with the same instructions for preparation and cooking.

Garnish with parsley or watercress, and serve the chops with a paper frill on the tip of the rib bone. The lemon sections are generally squeezed over the meat for added flavor.

* CONIGLIO IN CASSERUOLA Rabbit Casserole

ITALIAN

1 large rabbit, cut into serving pieces, or 1-1/2 pounds fresh or frozen pieces ∙ 3/4 pint red or white wine ∙ 1 large sprig each, fresh parsley and thyme, or 1/4 teaspoon of each, dried ∙ 1 large onion, chopped ∙ 2 shallots or scallions, chopped ∙ 1/2 pound sliced mushrooms ∙ 1 tablespoon minced fresh parsley ∙ Salt and pepper to taste ∙ Cookware spray ∙

Rabbit is a delicate meat—not unlike chicken and veal—and is very popular in Europe. And now it is becoming increasingly available in the United States, both fresh and frozen. This recipe can be made either with red wine, as is done in Italy, or with white wine. As in the case of CoQ AU VIN, the red wine, while producing a particularly delicious dish, colors the delicate meat to a mahogany shade. You may wish to consider this fact when deciding which wine to use.

YIELD: Four servings

1. Place the serving pieces of rabbit into an earthenware or glass bowl, and add the wine, thyme, and parsley. Cover and marinate in a cool place, or in the refrigerator, for 3 hours. When marinated, begin preparing the casserole by sautéing the onion and shallots with a tablespoon of the marinade, in a large heavy pan to which cookware spray has been applied. When the onions and shallots are translucent, remove with a slotted spoon, and set aside.

2. Drain the pieces of rabbit, but do not pat dry, and reserve the marinade and the liver of the rabbit if it is available. In the skillet over high heat, brown all sides of the rabbit pieces. When brown add the reserved marinade with the sprigs of thyme and parsley; season to taste, and simmer over low heat for 1 hour.

3. Dice the reserved liver, mix it with the parsley and mushrooms, add to the pan, and stirring continuously, simmer for 7 minutes more. Serve.

BONUS IDEAS: Serve with ITALIAN POTATO GNOCCHI (page 26-27) dressed with the casserole sauce, or with boiled or mashed potatoes, and a green or fruit salad.

* BOUDIN BLANC White Forcemeat Sausage

FRENCH

3 cups
thinly sliced onions ·
1 tablespoon white wine
or dry vermouth ·
1-1/3 cups veal or
chicken broth,
or canned consommé ·
2 tablespoons
polyunsaturated margarine ·
1/2 cup uncooked rice ·
1 cup each,
lean veal and boned
raw chicken breast,
with its skin removed ·
1 slice of gluten bread,
crust removed ·
3 egg whites ·
1-1/2 teaspoons salt ·
1/4 teaspoon each,
dried rosemary, thyme,
sage, and ground nutmeg ·
1/8 teaspoon
ground white pepper ·
1/2 cup evaporated
skimmed milk ·
6 feet of
sausage casing, or
cheesecloth and string ·
Cookware spray ·

Optional:
2 ounces mushrooms,
finely chopped ·
1 ounce turnip, minced ·

A traditional supper dish during the French Christmas holidays, these delicate white sausages are also ideal for luncheon meals throughout the year. They require a little effort to prepare, but since they freeze well, you can make large quantities, as I do, and reserve them in conveniently sized packages for future use. They add great flavor to stuffings in such dishes as POULET VIVANDIÈRE (page 78–79) and CROWN ROAST OF LAMB (page 65) and can be enjoyed in their own right, served either as sausages or patties.

YIELD: Twelve servings

1. Apply the cookware spray to a large heavy saucepan and sauté the onions and the optional turnips with the white wine. When the onions turn translucent, add the optional mushrooms and sauté for about 1 minute, stirring constantly; set aside. Cook the rice in the broth and margarine, covered, over low heat for about 25 minutes, or until the liquid has been absorbed; set aside to cool.

2. Grind the meat with the cooled onion mixture as finely as possible, then combine with the cooked rice and grind the mixture once more. Add the slice of gluten bread as a visual guide to indicate that the sausage mixture has gone through the grinder. Stop grinding when the bread passes through the blades. Whisk the egg whites for 1 minute until foamy and add the herbs, seasonings, salt, and pepper. Beat this mixture well, gradually adding the skimmed milk. Combine the egg and milk mixture with the ground meat and rice mixture and beat together thoroughly until uniformly blended.

3. If the sausage casings are salted, soak for 20 minutes in warm water, and rinse thoroughly before using. If you do not have a sausage-making attachment to your grinder see Bonus Ideas; otherwise apply the sausage-making funnel to the blade-end of your grinder, gather the casing over the funnel, beginning with one end and sliding as much of the casing as possible toward the base end of the funnel attachment. Tie the end of the casing and force the sausage mixture through. As the mixture fills the casing, twist the filled casing to form whatever size links you prefer. Tie the twisted casing to securely separate each link and repeat the process until you have a string of 4 or 5 links. Continue until all of the mixture and casing has been utilized.

4. You can form your sausages by using double layers of cheesecloth, but here you must chill the mixture first. Cut the cloth into approximately 5- by 10-inch pieces, place over

96

wax paper or foil, and brush with corn oil. Roll about 1/2 cup of the chilled (20 minutes in the freezer will suffice) mixture into the shape of a sausage; place in the center of the cloth and roll tightly, tying both ends to form the link. For sausage patties, double the dimensions of each piece of double-layered cheesecloth, and form a large sausage with at least 1 cup of the mixture. Refrigerate, and slice into patties when ready to use. Whether you use the sausage casing or the cheesecloth, the BOUDIN BLANC must be refrigerated, in order to set, for at least two days before using; and you must simmer them, covered, for 20 to 30 minutes in enough water to cover before freezing them for future use.

BONUS IDEAS: I have made BOUDIN BLANC successfully by adapting an 8-inch long pastry decorator into a sausage-maker. I remove the decorating blades from the 2-inch funnel-like end, place one end of the casing over the funnel spout and slowly gather as much of the length of the casing that will fit onto it, generally about 24 inches at a time. Then I fill the long 2-inch diameter tube with the CHILLED mixture, and press it through with the wooden pestle that is part of the set. As each sausage comes through in the casing, I twist the sausage twice to form the size link I want, and tie the twisted area with kitchen string to secure each link. This process is repeated until I have a string of 3 or 4 sausages. You can also use a fabric or plastic lined pastry bag with a metal tube attached to its end, preferably the long Bismark tube designed for jelly doughnuts. Fill the bag 3/4 full with the sausage meat, apply the casing to the metal tube; squeeze the bag and proceed with the preparation of the sausages by twisting and tying them into links.

✻ FINKER Scandinavian Hunter's Casserole

SCANDINAVIAN

1-1/2 pounds top round or lean chuck of beef, cut into 1-inch cubes •
2 large onions, thinly sliced •
1 tablespoon water •
1 tablespoon dry vermouth, beef broth or consommé •
2 large carrots, thinly sliced •
4 russet potatoes, thinly sliced •
1 teaspoon coarse salt •
8 twists of pepper mill •
1/4 teaspoon ground nutmeg •
3/4 cup beef broth, or consommé •
4 cups mashed potatoes, or potato flakes prepared with skim milk, and up to 2 tablespoons polyunsaturated margarine •
1 cup thinly sliced apples •
1 cup thinly sliced, mature pear •
2 tablespoons unsweetened wheat germ •
Cookware spray •

This dish is not only very easy to prepare, but also very versatile; its combination of lightness and body makes it suitable any day or season of the year. In my own family, everyone has tried creating his own variation. We prefer to cook this meal in a glass casserole, so that the various layers are attractively visible when the dish is served.
YIELD: Four to six servings

1. Apply cookware spray to a large skillet and sauté the onions with the water and dry vermouth for 3 minutes. Add the sliced potatoes and carrots; cover, and continue sautéing for 7 minutes longer, shuffling the pan occasionally. Remove the contents and set aside.

2. Dip the meat cubes in cold water, drain, but do not pat dry. Place the meat in the skillet and brown over high heat, stirring until all sides of the meat are browned. Add the salt, pepper, and nutmeg and the broth and cook over a low heat for 5 minutes.

3. Apply cookware spray to a 2-quart, preferably clear glass, casserole. Arrange the cooked sliced of carrots vertically around the perimeter of the dish. Use mashed potatoes, as necessary, to hold the carrot trim in place. Add alternate layers of meat, onions, carrots, sliced potatoes and sliced fruit, finishing with a top layer of mashed potatoes. Pour the broth and meat juices into the casserole. Sprinkle with the wheat germ and make a ring or geometric design of sliced carrots for garnish. At this point, the dish may be refrigerated or frozen for future use.

4. When ready to serve, bake in an oven at 375°F. for approximately 25 minutes. If dish has been frozen but not completely thawed, increase the baking time to 40 minutes. Complete the garnishing with sprigs of green parsley and serve hot.

BONUS IDEAS: This dish can also be made easily and attractively in a microwave oven, utilizing a heatproof, clear glass, covered casserole. Cook covered for 6 minutes, let stand 5 minutes, turn the casserole half round and cook for 5 minutes longer. Let the dish stand 10 minutes before serving.

Instead of combinations, potatoes can be entirely sliced or entirely mashed, as you prefer. Pearl onions, fresh peas, string beans, button mushrooms, rutabaga, or other vegetables—are all fine accoutrements to this versatile dish.

Additional garnishing ideas include using some of the vegetable ingredients, in addition to the carrots, as a garnish; you can make rings of pearl onions, button mushrooms, fresh peas, or asparagus tips. Geometric patterns of mushrooms in the shape of anvils also can be used, and the red touch of cherry tomatoes, pimiento, or other edibles can complement the dish.

This is a one-dish meal that you can just as easily prepare in two casseroles at the same time, reserving one in the freezer for future use.

PETTI DI POLLO CON ZUCCHINI
Breasts of Chicken with Zucchini

ITALIAN

3 chicken breasts, each cut into 6 filets ·
2 tablespoons oil, half of which is olive oil ·
Juice of 1/2 lemon ·
1/4 teaspoon coarse salt ·
4 twists of pepper mill ·
1-3/4 cups zucchini, unpeeled and sliced 1/4 inch thick ·
1 onion, diced ·
1 cup tomato sauce, or 1 cup canned Spanish style tomato sauce plus 1 tablespoon canned tomato paste ·
4 sprigs parsley, chopped ·
3 tablespoons Parmesan cheese ·
2 egg whites ·
Cookware spray ·

This is an attractive and tasty blend of chicken and zucchini that serves admirably either as a main-course dish or as part of a party buffet. It can be made in advance and freezes well, so you may wish to consider making more than one recipe at a time to reserve for future use.
YIELD: Six servings

1. Mix the oil, lemon juice, salt, and pepper in a bowl. Add the chicken breasts and marinate for several hours, or overnight.

2. Drain the chicken and reserve the marinade. Apply cookware spray into a large skillet and sauté the drained chicken breasts a few minutes on both sides until they turn white. Apply cookware spray to a large quiche dish or glass pie plate and lay the cooked chicken along the bottom of the dish.

3. Place the sliced zucchini into the bowl of marinade and stir until all slices are covered. Discard the cooking liquor from the skillet and sauté the diced onion with up to 1 tablespoon of water until the pieces are translucent. Add the zucchini and marinade to the skillet and cook for about 6 minutes over medium heat until they are translucent. Stir often but avoid breaking the slices. Add the tomato sauce and parsley, cover, and cook over lowered heat for 20 minutes, shuffling the skillet occasionally.

4. Adjust the seasonings to taste. Add 1 tablespoon of the Parmesan cheese and let the cooked mixture settle away from the heat for 5 minutes. With a slotted spoon, remove enough uniform zucchini slices to ring the inside edge of the quiche dish, standing vertically. Spoon the balance of the zucchini-tomato mixture over the chicken breasts, arranging the cooked zucchini slices in decorative patterns over the chicken.

5. When cooled, the dish may be frozen for future use. When ready to use it, thaw and continue with the recipe, allowing 15 extra minutes of cooking time.

6. Preheat the oven to 350°F. Whisk the egg whites until they foam and add them so they cover the surface of the zucchini slices. Sprinkle the balance of the Parmesan cheese over the egg whites and cook in the oven for approximately 10 minutes.

BONUS IDEAS: This attractive dish lends itself particularly to creative garnishing, but be sure that the garnishes are compatible with the delicate blending of the chicken, zucchini, and cheese.

Try garnishing with mushrooms, cut lengthwise into anvil shapes. Make a border along the outside edge of the dish with the stems facing toward the center. As a centerpiece decoration, you can create a geometric flower shaped with 6 mushroom slices with the stems coming to a point in the center. Parsley, fresh basil, or mint leaves can provide an added touch.

As is frequently the case with recipes calling for chicken breasts, filets of veal cutlet can be substituted for the chicken.

6.
Accoutrements

The side dishes you select to accompany your MINCEUR main dishes will play an important and complementary role. Whether your selection of an accoutrement is influenced by its particular flavor, color combination, texture, or suitability in terms of the main dish, you are encouraged—particularly in the MINCEUR concept—to make your selection in terms of enhancing rather than overpowering the PIÈCE DE RÉSISTANCE of the meal: the main dish itself.

MINCEUR SAUCES, GRAVIES, AND DRESSINGS

Most ethnic cuisines, and especially LA GRANDE CUISINE, feature a variety of sauces and gravies. As I have repeatedly stressed, these dressings when properly used bring out the natural taste of a particular dish; they must not be used to mask bad cooking. Too often these sauces are prepared with large quantities of butter, egg yolk, heavy cream, and refined wheat flour. The following MINCEUR recipes have successfully avoided these VERBOTEN ingredients which are, of course, incompatible with our new concept. At the same time they will titillate your palate and contribute significantly to your repertoire of MINCEUR dishes. By judiciously using these sauces or gravies with meats, poultry, and fish, and by using other dressings with vegetables and fruits, you will add a large number of interesting side dishes, or accoutrements to your menus. As we will see in this and in a later chapter, some of these sauces and aspics are equally applicable to appetizers and desserts.

First, let's begin with the basic categories of sauces— white, brown, and red sauces. In LA GRANDE CUISINE, white sauces are made with milk, cream, or a white stock, such as chicken, veal, or lamb stock, or fish broth or bouillon.

Brown sauces are made with the bones of meat—such as beef, veal, or poultry—that have been browned first. And, of course, the red sauces are made from a tomato base. From these basic sauces a great variety of special sauces can be made or compounded. Escoffier, in MA CUISINE, refers to them as the "mother sauces," and points out that in professional kitchens the basic sauces are prepared every morning and kept on hand throughout the day; they permit the rapid preparation of any required variation and thus are fundamental in providing rapid service. Of course, you don't have to prepare these basic sauces every morning, since both the basic brown, white, and tomato sauces can be prepared ahead and taken as needed from refrigerator or freezer. In order to facilitate making the basic brown sauce and many of its variations and gravies, you will want to prepare ahead basic fish, chicken, and meat stocks (pages 253–54); they can be frozen in practical quantities and are, therefore, readily available when you need them.

MOYIN MOYIN Bean and Shrimp Pudding

NIGERIAN YIELD: Four to six servings

1 cup dried black-eyed beans, soaked for 3 hours •
1 onion, peeled and quartered •
2 scallions, white part only, shredded and minced •
1 small green pepper, diced •
1/2 teaspoon coarse salt •
3 tablespoons of polyunsaturated oil, preferably sesame oil •
4 ounces fresh, frozen, or canned shrimp, diced •

1. After the beans have soaked for 3 hours, remove the skins and drain thoroughly. Using a mortar and pestle, grind the beans into a paste and gradually add water, stirring until you have a smooth but thick mixture the consistency of a batter for griddle cakes or fritters. Add the onion, scallions, diced pepper, salt, and oil to an electric blender and purée at medium speed for about 1 minute. Thoroughly blend the bean batter into the purée, then stir in the diced drained shrimp and mix thoroughly.

2. Pour the mixture into aluminum freezer foil containers with tight lids, or into covered ovenproof casseroles; and, with water not higher than 1/4 of the height of the container, steam for about 30 minutes until thoroughly cooked. You can test for doneness by inserting a toothpick into the mixture. If done, the toothpick should come out dry. Serve warm in place of bread or rolls.

BONUS IDEAS: After the bean and shrimp mixture has steamed for about 20 minutes, carefully remove the container covers and arrange fresh, frozen or freeze-dried cocktail shrimp or prawns on top of each pudding. Cover and continue to steam for about 10 minutes until thoroughly cooked.

DEMI-GLACE SAUCE VITE Quick
Demi-Glace Sauce

FRENCH/
INTERNATIONAL

YIELD: One cup

1 cup Enriched
Canned Bouillon
(page 114)·
1 teaspoon cornstarch
or arrowroot·
1/2 teaspoon
beef flavor
(Valentine's, B-V,
or Bovril)·
1 teaspoon canned
meat jelly
(available in
gourmet shops)·
Cookware spray·

Apply cookware spray to a saucepan, add the enriched bouillon, and gradually stir in the cornstarch. When smooth, add the beef flavor base and the meat jelly; continue stirring until the mixture is smooth. Simmer, stirring constantly, for about 10 minutes or until the sauce is thickened and completely blended.

BONUS IDEAS: You can prepare this quick DEMI-GLACE in the same saucepan in which you have prepared the ENRICHED CANNED BOUILLON, simply by adding the balance of the ingredients and simmering, stirring continuously, until the sauce is completely blended and thickened.

Transfer the sauce to the upper half of a double boiler to keep warm before serving. Add 4 tablespoons of dry sherry to enrich the flavor, if desired. Use this sauce with beef or in the preparation of other sauces.

* ENRICHED SAUCE ESPAGNOLE

FRENCH

4 cups Sauce
Espagnole (page 112–13)·
1 cup beef stock
or consommé·
2 tablespoons each,
minced tomatoes
and mushrooms·
1 teaspoon coarse salt
(optional)·
1/2 teaspoon
chopped parsley, or
1/4 teaspoon dried·
1/8 teaspoon
dried tarragon·
1 tablespoon arrowroot
or cornstarch·
1/2 cup Madeira
or sherry wine·
Cookware spray·

For those who prefer not to take the time to prepare the classic DEMI-GLACE SAUCE (page 105), this simplified version will prove suitable, and can be used both as a meat glaze and a base for other French sauces.
YIELD: Two-and-one-half cups

1. Apply cookware spray to a heavy saucepan, and add all of the ingredients except the arrowroot and the wine. (Use the salt only if you do not intend to use this sauce as a base for other sauces.) Cook uncovered over low heat for about 1 hour, or until reduced by half. Remove from the heat, strain, and transfer the strained sauce into a second saucepan. Mix the arrowroot with the Madeira wine, stir the mixture into the warm, strained sauce and blend until smooth.

2. Simmer the sauce, partially covered, for 1/2 hour or until it thickens. Cool and use. If storing in the freezer, brush melted margarine over the top to avoid crusting.

BONUS IDEAS: This sauce can be further enriched by adding 4 tablespoons of Madeira, port, champagne, or brandy, and simmering the sauce about 5 minutes, until the alcohol content has evaporated.

MILK AND MUSTARD SALAD

AUSTRALIAN

YIELD: Four servings

1 large
head of lettuce,
washed, drained, and
shredded •
3 tablespoons
evaporated skimmed milk •
1/4 teaspoon
dry mustard •
3 tablespoons vinegar •
2 hard-boiled
egg whites, or
1 hard-boiled egg •
1/4 teaspoon salt
or to taste •

Place the shredded lettuce in a salad bowl. In a separate serving bowl mix the balance of the ingredients thoroughly. Chill the lettuce and the dressing separately, and in traditional Australian fashion, serve the dressing separately so that it can be added to the shredded lettuce by each diner.

BONUS IDEAS: Try varying this pleasant salad by using a smaller head of lettuce and combining it with 1/2 pound of fresh spinach leaves. Remove the stems from the spinach and shred the leaves in the same manner as the lettuce. I like to garnish this salad with 1/2-inch crouton cubes and T-shaped slices of fresh mushrooms. Several red radish flowers add a welcome accent of color.

Other garnishing suggestions include scallion brushes, either green or black olives, or strips of pimiento.

SALSIFY PARISIEN Oyster Root, Parisian Style

FRENCH

1 pound oyster root
or rutabaga,
peeled and cut into
1-1/2-inch pieces •
1/4 teaspoon
coarse salt •
1 tablespoon
polyunsaturated margarine •
3 tablespoons oil,
preferably olive •
1 large clove garlic,
minced •
2 tablespoons parsley,
minced •
Cookware spray •

A taste I developed during my stay in Paris was for the haunting flavor of salsify, which I first experienced in an unpretentious restaurant in the Avenue George V. I frequented this establishment after working hours a great deal because they served dinner at a later hour, and eventually got to know the chef. When he showed me how to prepare salsify, I found myself buying the root in Parisian markets and preparing it in any available kitchen I could find. Salsify, or oyster root, was immensely popular in the United States around the turn of the century, but now is relatively difficult to find; you may even have to import the seeds to grow your own; I assure you it is well worth the effort. The nearest substitute I have found is rutabaga—a large yellow turnip sometimes referred to as Swedish turnip.

YIELD: Four servings

Parboil the oyster root or rutabaga, covered, in salted water for about 15 minutes; drain and pat dry. Apply cookware spray to a skillet, add the margarine, and melt over medium heat; then add the oil, garlic, and parsley and sauté for 5 minutes. Add the drained salsify and sauté, turning often, for 15 minutes until golden and beginning to brown. Remove from the heat, cover, and let set for 5 minutes. Serve hot with grilled meat.

SAUCE DEMI-GLACE Demi-Glace Sauce

FRENCH

1 scant cup
(about 7 ounces)
Sauce Espagnole
(page 112–13)·
1 teaspoon
meat jelly,
chopped (page 110–11)·
Cookware spray·

YIELD: One serving, about a quarter cup

Apply cookware spray to a small saucepan and heat the
SAUCE ESPAGNOLE briefly; then add the meat jelly. Simmer
over low heat for about 15 minutes, until the sauce is thickened and blended.

BONUS IDEAS: This classic sauce is used as the base to
expediently prepare many famous and popular French
sauces: SAUCE CHASSEUR (Hunter's Sauce), page 121; SAUCE
ITALIENNE (Italian Sauce with Tomatoes), page 113; and
SAUCE PIQUANTE (Piquant Sauce), page 123.

YAM Thai Salad

THAI

3 small heads
of Iceberg lettuce,
halved, or 6 heads of
Boston lettuce·
2 large cucumbers,
peeled and sliced·
1 medium onion,
thinly sliced·
3 large tomatoes, sliced·
5 ounces dried beef
or prosciutto cut into strips·
2 hard-boiled
egg whites, or 1
hard-boiled egg, sliced·

Thai Dressing:
1 teaspoon
dry red bell pepper
or red chilies, crushed·
5 cloves garlic·
3/4 cup
roasted peanuts, ground·
1/4 teaspoon salt·
1/3 cup honey·
1/4 cup vinegar·

This unusual and tangy salad is simple to prepare, and has
the advantage that the dressing can be made well in advance. You will probably want to prepare extra quantities of
the dressing to reserve for future use.
YIELD: Six servings

1. Wash, drain, and dry the lettuce and place in a large
salad bowl or in small individual ones. Arrange the other
vegetables, the egg, and the beef decoratively over and
around the lettuce.

2. To prepare the dressing, place the red pepper and the
garlic in a mortar and grind with a pestle, then blend into a
smooth dressing with the ground peanuts and the balance of
the ingredients. Pour over the salad and serve chilled.

BONUS IDEAS: You can score the unpeeled cucumber (see
page 49) to achieve decorative cucumber slices and add
scallion brushes and chopped scallions or parsley.

An effective variation is to serve this salad on individual
plates rather than in bowls. Place 2 or 3 leaves of Boston
lettuce on each plate to form a natural bowl for the other
ingredients. Overlap 5 or 6 slices of cucumber with slices of
hard-boiled egg whites and onion slices in a circular pattern
and top with a slice of tomato. Cut 5 strips of the dried beef
and tuck the cut ends under the overlapping slices so that
the curved part of each strip extends onto the bed of lettuce
leaves.

The chilled dressing may be served separately.

105

MIA'S INSALATA DI PESCE Mia's
Mediterranean Fish Salad

MEDITERRANEAN

2 cups cooked fresh, frozen, or canned fish and shellfish ·
6 or more fresh lettuce leaves ·
1 tablespoon small capers, or to taste ·
1 tablespoon fresh lemon juice ·
1 garlic clove, minced ·
2 pimientos, cut in thin strips ·
2 tablespoons chopped fresh parsley or mint ·
1 tablespoon olive oil, or to taste ·
Salt and pepper to taste ·

This is a quickly and easily made appetizer, side dish, or "Emergency" meal—especially if you have on hand cooked fish and shellfish reserved from other meals. If not, you can use frozen fish and canned shellfish with excellent results. YIELD: Six servings

1. Place the reserved (or freshly cooked) pieces of fish and shellfish, with the skin and shells removed, on a bed of lettuce leaves on each serving plate. Add the capers, lemon juice, and seasonings to each plate in equal proportions and garnish with the strips of pimiento and chopped parsley or mint.

2. Sprinkle each plate with a few drops of the oil, and serve at room temperature, or slightly chilled.

BONUS IDEAS: You can add any precooked fresh, frozen, or canned fish or seafood you like. Clams, mussels, squid, and lobster are excellent options you may wish to consider.

If you serve this fish salad in individual salad plates, you are assured of a more even distribution of the ingredients for each serving. Also, less attention is required to the possibility of disturbing your garnishing pattern.

* SAUCE VITE ESPAGNOLE Quick Brown
Sauce Espagnole

FRENCH/ INTERNATIONAL

1-1/2 cups beef stock, or Enriched Canned Bouillon (page 114) ·
6 tablespoons polyunsaturated margarine ·
5 tablespoons cornstarch ·
Salt and pepper to taste ·
Cookware spray ·

YIELD: Approximately one-and-one-half cups

1. Heat the stock in a saucepan. Apply cookware spray to a second saucepan and cook the margarine over medium heat for about 3 minutes until it browns. Gradually add the cornstarch and stir until the mixture is smooth. Add the hot stock, or enriched canned bouillon, and stir with a wooden spoon until the mixture is completely blended.

2. Season to taste, and simmer for about 20 minutes. If the sauce is too thick, add additional hot stock, and adjust the seasonings.

BONUS IDEAS: Add 3 tablespoons of wine or brandy as recommended for ENRICHED SAUCE ESPAGNOLE (page 112–13) and simmer for 5 minutes.

106

RAITA Yoghurt Cucumber Salad

6 ounces plain yoghurt·
1 tomato, cut in bits·
1/2 teaspoon each
minced fresh orange
and lemon peel, or
half the quantity dried·
1 medium cucumber·
1/4 teaspoon
Tabasco sauce·
4 twists of pepper mill·
1/8 teaspoon
toasted cumin seeds,
ground·
1 teaspoon
minced fresh parsley,
or 1/2 teaspoon dried·
1 teaspoon coriander,
ground (optional)·
1/8 teaspoon paprika·

This refreshing salad is the GAZPACHO of Indian cuisine. The traditional accompaniment to Mogul dishes in India, it works equally well with any main course meat dish. The same vegetables that are blended into the yoghurt can be used as a garnish. It couldn't be simpler or faster to make.
YIELD: Four to six servings

1. Parboil the minced orange and lemon peel for a few minutes; drain and add to the yoghurt and mix well. Cut 5 slices of unpeeled cucumber and reserve for garnishing. Peel the balance of the cucumber and dice. Add the balance of the ingredients to the yoghurt and mix well to blend.

2. Garnish with reserved cucumber slices, additional bits or slices of tomatoes, thin slivers of orange peel that have been parboiled to remove acidity, sprigs of parsley, paprika, and fresh coriander leaves to taste. Chill before serving.

BONUS IDEAS: This simple salad lends itself to a variety of garnishes. Try adding caviar for an added taste sensation.

Since I find that, for many, the taste for fresh coriander is an acquired one, I generally serve the fresh coriander leaves separately, letting each guest experiment with what is often a new experience. A refreshing alternate is fresh mint.

There isn't a homemaker too busy to whip together this delightful and satisfying salad dish in a few minutes while preparing the rest of the meal.

SAUCE AU RAIFORT Horseradish Sauce

1 cup sour cream
or plain yoghurt·
1 shallot or
scallion, minced·
1/2 teaspoon each,
horseradish and
mustard, either
Dijon or Homemade
Mustard·
Salt and ground
white pepper to taste·

YIELD: One cup

Combine all of the ingredients in a bowl and mix thoroughly. Serve with smoked fish, boiled beef, or boiled fish.

BONUS IDEAS: Whenever possible use freshly grated horseradish, which is especially plentiful in the spring. With braised beef, consider HOT HORSERADISH SAUCE. Boil 2 tablespoons of horseradish with 1/4 cup of consommé for 15 minutes. Add 1/4 cup each of margarine, plain yoghurt and wheat germ or bread crumbs. Reduce the mixture over high heat, strain, and thicken with 1 teaspoon of cornstarch dissolved in 2 tablespoons of consommé. Dilute 1/2 teaspoon of mustard in 1/4 teaspoon of vinegar and add to the hot sauce before serving.

CACIK Turkish Cucumber Salad

TURKISH

YIELD: Four servings

4 cups plain yoghurt •
1 large cucumber •
1 clove garlic,
minced •
Salt to taste •
3 sprigs of fresh
mint leaves, minced,
or 1 teaspoon dried •
1 tablespoon oil,
preferably olive •

Peel the cucumber, cut it into 1/4-inch cubes and set aside. Whisk the yoghurt in a bowl until it is smooth; blend in all of the other ingredients except the oil. Mix thoroughly, then gradually add the oil until thoroughly blended. Chill and serve with meat, poultry, or fish.

BONUS IDEAS: Try garnishing with cucumber petals (page 49) topped with a small mound of plain yoghurt and accented with a fresh mint leaf or a floret of fresh parsley.

DAL Curried Lentils

CEYLONESE

YIELD: Six servings

1 cup red lentils
or yellow peas •
3 cups water •
1/4 teaspoon
red bell pepper or
1/8 teaspoon Tabasco •
1/2 teaspoon
coarse salt •
1 teaspoon
minced fresh ginger •
1/2 teaspoon tumeric •
2 medium onions •
1 garlic clove, chopped •
2 tablespoons
double-strength chicken
or beef broth •
Cookware spray •

Place the lentils and water in a saucepan; add the pepper, salt, ginger, and tumeric; cook over low heat, stirring occasionally, until the lentils are soft, or about 1 hour. Apply cookware spray to a skillet and sauté the onions and garlic in the concentrated broth until the onions turn translucent. Before serving, pour the cooked onion mixture over the lentils and garnish with minced coriander leaves or parsley.

BONUS IDEAS: A slow-cooking crockery pot can be used by placing the lentils, water, pepper, salt and tumeric in the pot, covering, and cooking on low heat for about 9 hours or until the lentils are soft. Pour the cooked onion mixture over the lentils and garnish before serving.

A pressure cooker is NOT recommended unless the lentils have been reconstituted before cooking. Dried beans have a tendency to clog the valve during the cooking process, which can be dangerous. First reconstitute the lentils as recommended for the preparation of CANADIAN PEA SOUP (page 162). Cook at 15-pound pressure for 15 minutes; then add the onion mixture, garnish, and serve.

If using a microwave oven, combine the lentils, water and seasonings in a non-metal casserole and cook for 25 minutes, stirring occasionally. Let the lentils stand at least 5 minutes before adding the cooked onion mixture. Garnish and serve.

MAJANI YA MABOGA Squash Leaves with Rice

TANZANIAN

YIELD: Four to six servings

2 pounds tender squash
or pumpkin leaves •
2 tablespoons
chicken broth
or dry vermouth •
1 medium onion,
peeled and sliced •
1 green tomato,
chopped •
2 chilies or
1/2 teaspoon Tabasco •
1 cup skimmed milk •
Salt to taste •
Cookware spray •

Use young squash or pumpkin leaves; remove ribs and fibers and mince fine. Wash and drain, but do not pat dry. Apply cookware spray to a skillet and cook the leaves AU SEC for 3 minutes, covered tightly; remove and set aside. Place the chicken broth or dry vermouth in the skillet, and sauté the onion until it turns translucent. Add the chopped green tomato and sauté, stirring occasionally, for 5 minutes. Add the cooked squash leaves and the balance of the ingredients, simmer for 5 minutes, and serve hot over rice (page 249).

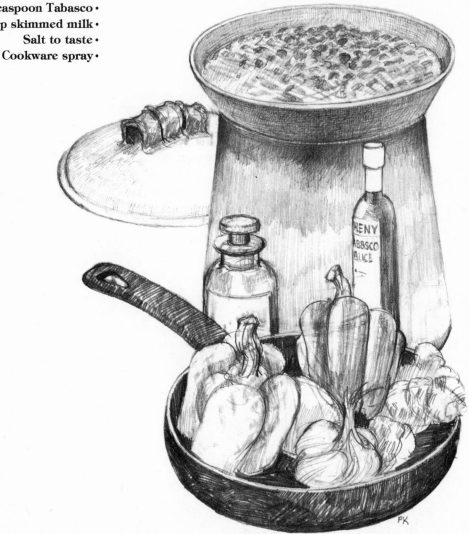

109

STEWED GREEN TOMATOES

AMERICAN YIELD: Six servings

2 tablespoons
diced onion ·
2 tablespoons ·
shredded scallion,
white part only ·
2 tablespoons
chicken broth or
dry vermouth ·
3 cups
thinly sliced
green tomatoes ·
1 teaspoon
coarse salt ·
1/2 teaspoon cayenne
or paprika ·
Cookware spray ·

Apply cookware spray to a skillet and sauté the onion and scallion over medium heat in half of the broth until the onions are translucent. Add the balance of the broth, the sliced tomatoes and all of the seasonings; cook for about 15 minutes, stirring occasionally, until the tomatoes are tender. Serve with meat or poultry, garnished with minced parsley or paprika.

BONUS IDEAS: If you like the special flavor of green tomatoes, as I do, try preparing your own GREEN TOMATO RELISH: In a quart jar blend 2 cups of sliced green tomatoes, 2 shredded scallions, 1-1/2 cups of Chinese lettuce or cabbage, shredded, 1/2 cup of diced celery, 1/4 cup diced green pepper, and 1 tablespoon of salt; fill the jar with water to cover the ingredients. Put aside for a half hour, then rinse and drain the vegetables.

Transfer the ingredients to a saucepan; add 1/4 cup of white wine, 1 cup of diced red and green peppers, 1/3 cup of honey, 1 cup of malt vinegar, 1 teaspoon of dry mustard, 8 cloves, 6 each of black and green peppercorns, 4 each of juniper and allspice berries, 1 teaspoon of ground cinnamon, and 1/8 teaspoon of dried dillweed. Bring to a boil, and simmer covered over low heat for 20 minutes, stirring occasionally. Transfer the cooked relish to a pint jar with a cover. Serve at room temperature with meat or poultry.

✳ GLACE DE VIANDE Meat Glaze or Jelly

FRENCH YIELD: Two cups

Veal bones,
reserved from
Sauce Espagnole ·
Beef stock,
or water to cover ·
3 layers of
cheesecloth ·
Cookware spray (optional) ·
Sauce Espagnole ·

1. Apply the optional cookware spray to a heavy saucepan; place the veal bones into the pan and barely cover with the beef stock or water. Partially cover the saucepan, and cook slowly, simmering for 4 or 5 hours, until all the gelatinous matter has been released from the bones. Discard the bones, sieve the stock mixture through the triple layer of cheesecloth, and reserve the stock.

2. Mix the reserved stock with equal parts of SAUCE ESPAGNOLE (page 112–13), and cook the mixture about 20 to 30 minutes over medium heat until it is reduced to a thick, brown sauce—so that it evenly coats a spoon inserted into it.

110

BONUS IDEAS: Use as a glaze to coat meats attractively, but use judiciously since this is strong, concentrated stock, and should not mask or overpower other sauces or gravies you may be using, nor the basic ingredients.

The glaze hardens upon cooling. To facilitate its melting, always chop the meat jelly before using as a glaze.

PATATAS ASADAS A LA CABAÑA
Roast Potatoes a la Cabaña

ARGENTINIAN

6 medium
Idaho potatoes,
peeled and
cut into quarters,
lengthwise ·
3/4 cup cooking water ·
3/4 cup
chicken stock,
or consommé ·
2 celery stalks,
scraped and cut into
3-inch lengths ·
1 carrot,
scraped and cut into
3-inch lengths ·
4 sprigs
fresh parsley ·
1 tablespoon oil ·
1 bay leaf ·
Salt to taste,
about 1/2 teaspoon ·
Strips of pimiento ·
Cookware spray ·

A decorative and savory accompaniment to roast meat dishes, this is extremely simple to make. You will find that the potatoes become moist and deliciously flavored by the chicken stock and the aromatic vegetables. An added advantage is that you can cook this dish in the oven along with your main roast.

YIELD: Six to eight servings

1. Preheat the oven to 350°F. Place the cut potatoes in 2 quarts of salted water and cook for approximately 5 minutes after the water has reached the boiling point. Apply cookware spray to a roasting pan or casserole large enough to hold the potatoes on one level.

2. Drain the partially cooked potatoes and reserve 3/4 cup of the cooking water. Lay the potatoes along the base of the roasting pan, then add the cooking water and chicken stock, the celery, carrot, and parsley. Spoon a drop of oil onto each piece of potato. Add the bay leaf.

3. Cook in the oven approximately 1/2 hour or until almost fork-tender. Increase the oven heat to 400°F. for 10 minutes. Remove and serve hot, garnishing each piece of potato with parsley flakes and slivers of pimiento.

BONUS IDEAS: As indicated, use the reserved water from cooking the potatoes for added flavor and richness. Reserved cooking liquors from other vegetable dishes can also be used.

Once the potatoes are peeled and quartered, place them in a bowl of cold water until ready for use, to avoid discoloration.

This is an excellent accompaniment to lamb and other meat roasts and can be used as a main-platter garnish along with tasteful and colorful edibles such as carrot purée and/or baked fruit.

111

* SAUCE BRUNE OU SAUCE ESPAGNOLE Basic Brown Sauce, or Sauce Espagnole

FRENCH

2 or more
cracked veal bones,
about 2 pounds·
6 cups hot beef stock
(55 ounces) canned·
1 onion,
thinly sliced·
2 carrots, chopped·
1 celery stalk, chopped·
1/4 cup diced
Canadian bacon (optional)·
6 sliced mushrooms
(optional)·
4 tablespoons
cornstarch·
1/2 cup red wine,
preferably Burgundy·
1/2 cup
dry white wine,
sherry, or
dry vermouth·
3 tablespoons
tomato paste·
1/2 teaspoon
coarse salt·
5 twists of pepper mill·

Bouquet Garni,
tied in cheesecloth,
consisting of:
4 sprigs parsley,
or 3/4 teaspoon dried·
1/4 teaspoon thyme,
dried·
1 bay leaf·
1 small clove garlic,
mashed·
Cheesecloth for straining·
Cookware spray·

This is the most fundamental of the "mother sauces," as Escoffier called them, and the basis of many variations, including DEMI-GLACE SAUCE, from which many of the outstanding sauces are derived. In adapting this sauce, you will have a number of options, all of which are interesting. Whatever short cuts you elect, however, please try the classic concept in the MINCEUR style at least once. In the long run, it does not take that much more time to prepare although long periods of simmering are initially required. And, once frozen, this basic sauce is available for many weeks, and even months, for use in the compounding of other sauces. Remember—these are rich sauces that must be used judiciously; although the recipe is MINCEUR, if you use the sauces to mask, rather than bring out, the basic ingredients of the dishes you are preparing, you are defeating your purpose.

YIELD: One quart

1. Place the veal bones in a heavy saucepan with enough water to barely cover them. Bring to a boil; after 5 minutes, remove the bones and drain them, discarding the cooking water. Place the bones in a pan in an oven at 500 °F. for 15 minutes to brown. In a separate pan, heat the beef stock over medium heat.

2. Apply cookware spray to a heavy saucepan and sauté the onions, carrots, celery, and the optional Canadian bacon and mushrooms, with 2 tablespoons of the beef stock, until the onions turn translucent, stirring often. Sprinkle the cornstarch into the pan, and stir with a wooden spoon until it is thoroughly blended with the vegetable mixture, adding additional stock as necessary and continuing to cook for 3 minutes.

3. Remove the pan from the heat, and gradually add the wine and the hot beef stock, blending the mixture with a wire whisk until completely smooth. Return the pan to the heat; add the tomato paste, the BOUQUET GARNI, the salt and pepper, and simmer briefly over low heat. Add the browned veal bones, cover the pan, and continue to simmer for 1 hour. Uncover the pan, increase the heat and cook for another 1/2 hour to reduce the sauce and augment its flavor.

4. When cooked, strain the sauce, pressing the vegetables against a sieve and utilizing all juices. Reserve the veal

bones for GLACE DE VIANDE (see Bonus Ideas). Wet and squeeze dry 3 layers of cheesecloth and line the sieve with it, then strain the sauce again through the triple layers. Depending on the thickness of the sauce, you may have to squeeze the last quantities through the cheesecloth with your hands before the cloth is discarded. Just before using, place the cooled sauce in the refrigerator or freezer; and when thoroughly chilled, skim off any of the remaining fat.

BONUS IDEAS: An alternate but more lengthy method for cooking this sauce is to prepare SAUCE ESPAGNOLE the day before. If you do, let it simmer slowly, partially covered, for 3 to 5 hours, skimming off any fat or foam that rises to the top. If the liquid of the sauce appears to be evaporating too quickly, periodically add a little extra water.

If you reserve the bones from this sauce, you can use Escoffier's trick of the trade and prepare GLACE DE VIANDE— meat jelly—which can be used as a glaze to coat meats attractively, and is an essential ingredient of the classic DEMI-GLACE SAUCE (page 105), which in turn is used as the basis for quickly compounding other popular sauces such as SAUCE CHASSEUR, or HUNTER'S SAUCE.

Once the fat has been skimmed off the chilled sauce, brush the top with melted polyunsaturated margarine, to prevent crusting, before you store it in the refrigerator or freezer.

✴ SAUCE ITALIENNE Italian Sauce

FRENCH YIELD: Three-and-one-half cups

2 cups
Demi-Glace Sauce
(page 105)·
1-1/2 cups
Tomato Sauce Minceur
(page 16–17)·
1/3 cup finely
shredded mushrooms·
4 ounces
shredded Canadian bacon·
2 sprigs of parsley,
chopped·
Cookware spray·

1. Apply cookware spray to a saucepan and add all of the ingredients except the parsley. Stir with a wooden spoon, bring the mixture to a boil, and cook over high heat for 5 minutes, stirring occasionally.

2. Remove from heat, and add the parsley. Serve.

BONUS IDEAS: If you use the Bolognese version of TOMATO SAUCE MINCEUR (page 16–17), eliminate the Canadian bacon from the above ingredients.

To use fresh tomatoes instead of the tomato sauce, halve and seed 6 pounds of tomatoes and place them in a pan with 3 tablespoons each of oil and margarine, 1/8 teaspoon of salt and pepper, 1 small clove of mashed garlic and 1 basil leaf. Cover, simmer for 30 minutes; strain before use.

ENRICHED CANNED BOUILLON

2 cups
canned beef bouillon ·
1 tablespoon
tomato paste ·
3-1/2 tablespoons each,
minced onions
and carrots ·
1-1/2 tablespoons
minced celery ·
2 tablespoons
fresh parsley, or
1 tablespoon dried ·
1/8 teaspoon thyme,
dried ·
1/2 bay leaf ·

YIELD: Approximately two-and-one-half cups

Combine all the ingredients in a saucepan, bring to a boil, and simmer for 20 minutes. Strain through a fine sieve.

BONUS IDEAS: This enriched bouillon can be used satisfactorily whenever a recipe calls for beef, or brown, stock. To prepare an aspic, however, it is necessary to add unflavored gelatin powder in the proportion of 1 tablespoon dissolved for every 3 cups of bouillon. This aspic can be used for a favorite dish of mine: BOEUF FROID EN GELÉE, or BRAISED BEEF IN ASPIC. This dish can be made with any marinated beef that has been braised until tender and cut into slices. It lends itself particularly to leftover slices of SAUERBRATEN MINCEUR (page 213–14).

Prepare the aspic and pour a thin layer, about 1/8 inch, into a chilled serving platter; chill until it begins to set. Arrange the beef slices and braised vegetables—such as pearl onions, carrot slices, and peas—on the platter with several gherkins that have been cut into fan-like shapes. Chill 2 additional cups of aspic in the freezer or in a mixing bowl over ice cubes. Spoon the chilled aspic over the garnished meat and place in the freezer for 15 minutes, until the aspic is firm. Chill the balance of the aspic and cut it into 1/4-inch cubes; arrange the cubes around the platter of meat. Refrigerate and serve cold.

SAUCE AUX CHAMPIGNONS
Mushroom Sauce

1/2 pound
sliced fresh mushrooms ·
1 tablespoon
dry vermouth ·
1 tablespoon
Armagnac or brandy ·
1 cup
Sauce Espagnole
(page 112–13) ·
Cookware spray ·

YIELD: One cup

1. Apply cookware spray to a heavy skillet and sauté the mushrooms with the dry vermouth for 3 minutes. Meanwhile heat the Armagnac in a separate saucepan; ignite and add to the mushrooms. When the flames are spent, remove the mushrooms to a warm place.

2. Add the SAUCE ESPAGNOLE, or any of our alternate MINCEUR versions of this sauce, and cook over medium heat for several minutes. Add the reserved mushrooms. Serve with poultry, roasted meats, or as a garnish for casseroles.

KOCHUMBER Onion or Cucumber Relish

**INDIAN/
PAKISTANI**

1 large onion,
sliced paper-thin,
and soaked
in iced water
for half an hour;
or 1 cucumber
peeled and diced ·
1/2 pound tomatoes,
cut into bits ·
1 minced green chili
or 1/8 teaspoon
chili powder ·
1/2 teaspoon
coarse salt ·
1 tablespoon
fresh lemon juice,
or to taste ·

These are traditional Indian relishes served on festive occasions but suitable as accompaniments to many dishes. They are easy to make and you can prepare both kinds (see Bonus Ideas) while your main course is cooking.
YIELD: Four servings

For the onion relish, drain the sliced onions thoroughly. Mix all the other ingredients in a bowl, except the lemon juice, and stir in the drained onions. Chill before serving, adding the lemon juice and stirring the mixture once more. For the cucumber relish, substitute the diced cucumber for the onions and proceed as above.

BONUS IDEAS: For a festive occasion, especially when you're serving Indian food such as BIRYANI (page 90–91), you can save time by preparing both the onion and the cucumber relishes simultaneously. Simply double the quantity of all ingredients except the onion and cucumber, and place half in separate mixing bowls; then add the drained onion to one bowl, and the diced cucumber to the other. You can also save time by preparing these simple relishes in the serving bowls you plan to use. Chill about 30 minutes before serving.

I like to add 4 grinds of a pepper mill, and 1 teaspoon of toasted and ground cumin seeds to these relishes in step 1.

WITLOF Braised Endive

BELGIAN

6 heads Belgian endive ·
2 tablespoons
polyunsaturated margarine ·
1 cup chicken broth
or consommé ·
1 teaspoon lemon juice ·
White pepper to taste ·
Cookware spray ·

Belgian endive and its relatives, fennel and celery, are, when braised, marvelous accoutrements to most meat dishes. They can also be featured in the French style, with assorted hors d'oeuvres, as well as varied by the addition of ham and other ingredients (see Bonus Ideas below).
YIELD: Four to six servings

Soak the endives in cold water for about 20 minutes, drain and cut each in half lengthwise. Allow 2 or 3 halves per serving. Apply cookware spray to a skillet and over low heat braise the endive sections with the margarine, covered, for 3 minutes. Add the broth and cook, covered, for about 10 minutes longer or until tender but AL DENTE. Sprinkle with lemon juice and white pepper, and serve.

115

BONUS IDEAS: For Finocchio al Formaggio, or Sautéed Fennel with Cheese, use 3 large fennel bulbs, trimmed of leaves and wilted outer parts. Slice 1/2-inch thick and soak in cold water, drain and dry; sauté the slices in margarine for 1 minute. Add water barely to cover, salt to taste, and simmer for 8 minutes; turn the slices, cover and cook 3 minutes longer. Uncover, add 1/4 cup of additional water and cook over medium heat for about 1/2 hour, or until all of the liquid is absorbed and the tender fennel is lightly golden in color. Season to taste, add 2 or 3 tablespoons of Parmesan cheese, and serve hot with roasted meats.

For Braised Celery, serving 6, slice 6 stalks of celery into 1-inch sections. Sauté with 3 slices of onion in 2 tablespoons of margarine for 3 minutes until the onions are golden, then add 1/4 cup of chicken stock or tomato juice and cook for 10 minutes over low heat until the celery is tender but al dente.

* FONDS DE VEAU BLANC Basic Veal Stock

2 veal knuckles,
cracked, about 2 pounds ·
2 pounds
shoulder of veal ·
Bones of 1 chicken,
including the neck
and gizzard ·
1 onion, cut in two,
each half pierced
with a whole clove ·
2 well-trimmed leeks ·
2 celery stalks ·

Bouquet Garni,
tied in cheesecloth,
consisting of:
4 sprigs fresh parsley,
or 1/2 teaspoon dried ·
1 bay leaf ·
1/4 teaspoon thyme,
dried · ·

10 whole
white peppercorns ·
Salt to taste ·
3 quarts of cold water ·

YIELD: 2 quarts

Place the veal knuckles in a large heavy stock pot, barely cover with water and boil for 5 minutes. Drain the bones, discarding the cooking water. Replace the bones and add all the other ingredients with 3 quarts of cold water. Bring to a boil, and simmer slowly for about 4 hours, reducing the volume of the mixture by a third. Cool, skim off the fat, then strain through a fine sieve. Freeze in 1-cup or 1-quart quantities to facilitate future use.

BONUS IDEAS: For a more richly colored stock, place the bones in a roasting pan and place them in an oven, preheated to 500 °F., for about 10 minutes. Some experts roast the onion, leeks and celery in this manner, with the bones, for about 7 minutes to avoid their becoming scorched. I find browning the vegetables unnecessary, but I do recommend adding 1 pound of lean brisket or shin of beef in preparing the basic stock. Roast the meat with the veal bones for added richness of flavor.

After preparing the stock, reserve the cooked veal bones and meat to prepare VEAL ASPIC. Add them to a stock pot with 1 small onion and 1 carrot, chopped; 1/2 cup of diced celery, 1 teaspoon of coarse salt and 2 twists of a pepper mill. Add boiling water to cover and simmer for 2 hours, or until the liquid has been reduced by half. Cool, remove any remaining fat, and strain through a fine sieve or several layers of cheesecloth. Clarify the stock (page 249). Pour the aspic in a cooled mold and, when it begins to set, add 1 teaspoon of fresh thyme or tarragon and diced bits of the cooked veal. When firm, unmold, slice and serve.

To prepare FONDS DE VOLAILLE, or BASIC CHICKEN STOCK, substitute 1 fowl for 2 pounds of veal in the ingredients. Wrap the fowl in aluminum foil and place in an oven at 500°F. Remove the fowl; discard the skin and the excess fat under the skin and in the cavity, and proceed with the recipe.

TOMATO ASPIC

INTERNATIONAL

YIELD: About 2 cups

1 cup
chicken broth or
canned consommé ·
3 cups
chopped tomatoes or
1 cup canned tomato juice ·
2 tablespoons
powdered gelatin ·
1/2 teaspoon salt
or to taste ·
1/4 teaspoon each,
ground pepper and honey ·
2 tablespoons each,
chopped onion and
lemon juice ·
3 sprigs parsley
or 1/4 teaspoon dried ·
1 bay leaf ·
1/4 teaspoon each,
dried basil and tarragon ·
2 egg whites ·
2 eggshells, crushed ·
Dash to taste of sherry,
Madeira, or cognac ·
Triple layers of
cheesecloth ·

1. Combine all of the ingredients, except the sherry, in a large saucepan and stir occasionally over medium heat until the mixture comes to a boil. Remove from the heat and let stand for about 10 minutes. Strain through several layers of cheesecloth, correct seasonings, and add the sherry or Madeira wine to taste.

2. Chill the aspic about half an hour and when it is about to set, add the various ingredients you plan to present within the aspic, see below.

BONUS IDEAS: When the chilled aspic begins to set, I often add about 1 cup of diced carrots, celery or green peppers. Well-drained clams, oysters, mussels, shrimp or crabmeat can also be added before the aspic is thoroughly set.

You may also use the aspic from TONGUE IN ASPIC (page 142–143), PÂTÉ MULCAHY (page 142–143) or any other dish in this genre. Wherever possible, use a stock made out of the principal ingredient you will be embedding in the aspic, such as chicken, beef, or fish.

This versatile dish can be varied by serving on a bed of lettuce with a mound of ricotta or a favorite dressing. (A bed of watercress or the center leaves of escarole can be substituted for the lettuce.) The aspic lends itself as well to being served as a luncheon salad or a colorful tasty beginning to a special meal.

The aspic may be chilled in individual molds or in a large ring mold. To serve, unmold the aspic, fill the center area with meat or seafood, and cover with EGGLESS (page 124) or BONUS MAYONNAISE (page 124).

BRINGAL Eggplant Curry

YIELD: Six servings

1 medium eggplant,
unpeeled,
about 2 pounds •
1 teaspoon salt •
1/2 teaspoon tumeric •
2 tablespoons
double-strength
chicken broth, or
dry vermouth •
1 onion,
finely chopped •
1/4 teaspoon
fenugreek, ground •
1 teaspoon
cumin seeds,
toasted and ground •
1 teaspoon each,
ground coriander
and cayenne •
2 cloves garlic,
finely chopped •
2 slices fresh ginger,
shredded and minced •
2 tablespoons vinegar •
2 cups water •
1/3 cup evaporated
skimmed milk •
Cookware spray •

1. Wash the eggplant and cut it into 1/4-inch cubes. Sprinkle the cubes with the salt and tumeric. Apply cookware spray to a saucepan and sauté the cubes in 1 tablespoon of the concentrated broth over medium heat, until they are lightly browned. Remove from the heat, and set aside.

2. Apply cookware spray to a second pan, and sauté the onion seasoned with the fenugreek in the balance of the broth until translucent. Toast and grind the cumin seed and add to the onion with the ground coriander and cayenne; sauté 1 minute longer, stirring well. Add the balance of the ingredients except the milk; bring to a boil and add the reserved eggplant cubes; simmer over low heat, stirring occasionally, for about 10 minutes, or until the sauce is thickened. Add the milk and simmer about 5 minutes longer. Serve hot with mashed potatoes, rice, or pita bread.

BONUS IDEAS: Few people seem to be aware that white eggplants, when in season, can be found in Oriental markets. Whenever possible, I prefer using the white eggplant in cooking, since I find it is less bitter than the purple variety. Also, the pearl-colored skin contrasted with the green stem offers a striking color combination. Occasionally, I combine both white and purple eggplants in preparing those dishes calling for unpeeled eggplant.

I have found that the shape of an eggplant, as well as its color, seems to have a relationship to its flavor. Therefore, I generally choose the smaller, elongated eggplants rather than the overly large ones, which have passed their peak of flavor.

* SAUCE PÉRIGUEUX Demi-Glace Sauce
with Truffles

FRENCH YIELD: Two cups

2-1/2 cups
Demi-Glace Sauce
(page 105)·
2 tablespoons
chopped truffles·
2 tablespoons
truffle liquid·
2 tablespoons
Madeira wine·
Cookware spray·

1. Apply cookware spray to a saucepan, add the DEMI-GLACE SAUCE and reduce over high heat, for about 5 minutes. Add the truffles, their liquid, and the Madeira. Stir briefly to combine and remove from the heat.

2. Serve. Especially good with grilled or broiled meats or roasts.

BONUS IDEAS: If you eliminate the truffles and their liquid, you have prepared MADEIRA SAUCE, which also complements broiled and grilled roasts of meat.

* SAUCE POIVRADE VERTE Sauce with
Green Peppercorns

FRENCH YIELD: Three-and-one-half cups

1 medium onion,
thinly sliced·
1 carrot, scraped
and thinly sliced·
2 sprigs parsley·
1 bay leaf·
1/2 teaspoon thyme,
dried·
12 green peppercorns·
3/4 cup each,
wine vinegar and
red wine·
2-1/2 cups
Demi-Glace Sauce
(page 105)·
1 teaspoon cornstarch·
2 tablespoons brandy·
Cookware spray·

1. Apply cookware spray to a saucepan, and sauté the onion, carrot, and parsley until the onions are translucent. Add the bay leaf, thyme, the peppercorns, and the vinegar, and boil over high heat until the liquid is reduced by half. Add the DEMI-GLACE SAUCE; cook over high heat 7 minutes longer. Stir in the cornstarch, and blend it into the mixture with a wooden spoon, cooking 3 minutes more. Add the wine; cover and simmer for 30 minutes.

2. Strain the sauce through a fine sieve or cheesecloth, add the brandy, and serve. Highly recommended for game, rabbit and venison.

BONUS IDEAS: Of course, this same recipe can be prepared substituting 8 black peppercorns for the green ones, to make SAUCE POIVRADE ORDINAIRE, or simply, PEPPER SAUCE.

To enrich the sauce, add 4 tablespoons of red currant jelly or 2 tablespoons of margarine. QUICK PEPPER SAUCE can be made by using any of the brown sauces as in QUICK PIQUANT SAUCE (page 123), then adding the cornstarch, wine, peppercorns and brandy as per the above recipe.

* SAUCE CHASSEUR Hunter's Sauce

FRENCH YIELD: One-and-one-half cups

6 ounces
chopped mushrooms·
1 teaspoon
chopped shallots·
6 tablespoons
white wine, or
dry vermouth·
3 tablespoons brandy·
1-1/4 cups
Demi-Glace Sauce
(page 105)·
3 tablespoons
tomato sauce, or
1 cup of
chopped tomatoes·
1 tablespoon
meat jelly
(Glace de Viande)
(page 110-11)·
1 tablespoon
chopped fresh parsley,
or fresh oregano·
Cookware spray·

1. Apply cookware spray to a saucepan and sauté the mushrooms and shallots with 1 tablespoon of the white wine for 2 minutes. Add the brandy and cook 2 minutes longer, then add the balance of the white wine. Increase the heat and reduce the liquid to half its volume, cooking about 10 minutes longer. (Some chefs prefer to reduce the wine in a separate saucepan, then add it to the sauce mixture.)

2. Add the DEMI-GLACE SAUCE, the tomato sauce, and the meat jelly. Bring to a boil for 3 minutes, add the chopped parsley and serve.

BONUS IDEAS: In emergencies, some chefs have been known to use commercially prepared meat extracts—such as Bovril, B-V, and Valentine's Beef Flavor Base—instead of the more preferable, rich meat jelly. If a more strongly flavored sauce is desired, add a small clove of garlic in addition to the shallots.

SAUCE CHASSEUR is served with filet of beef (TOURNEDOS), filet of chicken, and lamb stews.

Before serving, place the cooked meat in a skillet, spread a thin layer of the sauce over it, and simmer over medium heat, covered, for about 5 minutes, turning the slices at least once. Serve hot and add additional fresh parsley or oregano to taste.

SAUCE RUSSE Russian Dressing

FRENCH YIELD: Two scant cups

1-1/4 cups Minceur
Mayonnaise (page 124)·
1 tablespoon horseradish,
preferably freshly grated·
1 teaspoon onion,
finely minced or grated·
1 tablespoon
tomato paste or
1/4 cup chili sauce·
1 gherkin, finely diced·

Combine all of the ingredients, blend well, and thoroughly chill before using. Serve with seafood, your favorite salads, and, instead of mayonnaise, with many other foods.

BONUS IDEAS: In place of the gherkin, try using 1/4 cup of domestic or imported caviar; accent with a dash of Worcestershire sauce.

You can prepare UKRAINIAN DRESSING by mixing 1/2 cup of finely chopped, boiled beets with 1-1/2 cups of mayonnaise and thoroughly blending 1 tablespoon of caviar into the mixture. Add a dash of horseradish or salt to taste, and serve chilled.

121

PEAS AND RICE CASSEROLE

JAMAICAN **YIELD:** Four to six servings

1 cup freshly grated
coconut or shredded,
unsweetened coconut·
2 pounds unshelled peas
or 1 10-ounce package
frozen peas·
1 cup canned red
or white kidney beans·
1 cup Carolina rice·
2 scant cups water·
1 teaspoon coarse salt,
or to taste·

If using fresh coconut, crack the shell, remove and grate the meat; shell the fresh peas. Place all of the ingredients except the rice and peas in a large saucepan, and bring to a boil, covered. Add the peas, and continue boiling, covered, for 5 minutes. Lower the heat; add the rice gradually, stirring the mixture well, and simmer, covered, for about 20 minutes, or until the liquid has been absorbed and the rice is cooked and fluffy. Transfer to a covered serving dish to accompany meat or poultry.

BONUS IDEAS: Garnish with bits or strips of pimiento and small florets of fresh parsley, or with julienned strips of carrot that have been parboiled for several minutes.

* SAUCE PIQUANTE Piquant Sauce

FRENCH   YIELD: Two cups

1/2 cup white wine,
or dry vermouth ·
1/4 cup
wine vinegar ·
2 tablespoons
chopped shallots ·
2 cups
Demi-Glace Sauce
(page 105) ·
2 tablespoons
chopped gherkins ·
1 teaspoon
chopped parsley ·
1 teaspoon tarragon,
dried ·
Salt and pepper to taste ·
Cookware spray ·

Apply cookware spray to a saucepan and boil the wine, vinegar, and shallots over high heat, until the mixture is reduced by one-half. Add the sauce and simmer for 10 minutes. Remove from heat and add the gherkins, parsley, and tarragon. Season to taste and serve especially with boiled beef and roasted, grilled, or broiled pork.

BONUS IDEAS: Try adding 3 tablespoons of brandy, Calvados or applejack during the last 3 minutes of simmering. For extra flavor, consider adding 1/2 teaspoon of cayenne pepper and 2 tablespoons of capers when adding the chopped gherkins.

QUICK PIQUANT SAUCE can be made effectively by using 1 cup of SAUCE ESPAGNOLE (page 112–13), ENRICHED SAUCE ESPAGNOLE (page 103) or QUICK BROWN SAUCE (page 106). Simmer for 7 minutes, add 2 tablespoons of brandy and continue simmering for 3 minutes. Remove the sauce from the heat and add 1/4 teaspoon of cayenne pepper, and 1 tablespoon each of chopped gherkins and capers. Season with salt and pepper to taste and add 1/2 teaspoon of chopped, fresh parsley. Serve the sauce hot.

* SAUCE DIABLE Devil Sauce

FRENCH   YIELD: 1 cup

1/2 cup each,
white wine and
wine vinegar ·
2 finely chopped
shallots ·
1 cup
Demi-Glace Sauce
(page 105) ·
1 tablespoon tomato paste ·
1/4 teaspoon
cayenne pepper ·
Cookware spray ·

1. Apply cookware spray to a saucepan. Add the wine, vinegar, and the shallots and cook over high heat for 20 minutes, reducing the mixture by two-thirds. Add the DEMI-GLACE SAUCE and the tomato paste, and boil 3 minutes longer. Remove from the heat.

2. Stir in the cayenne pepper, and serve.

BONUS IDEAS: Especially recommended for chicken, cornish hens, and grilled fish. If 1 tablespoon of mustard, Worcestershire sauce, or minced anchovies is added you will have an enticing variation.

QUICK DEVIL SAUCE can be made by using 1 cup of SAUCE ESPAGNOLE (page 112–13) or QUICK BROWN SAUCE (page 106). Simmer for 7 minutes, add 2 tablespoons of brandy and simmer 3 minutes longer. Remove from the heat and stir in 1/4 teaspoon of cayenne and salt to taste. Serve hot.

EGGLESS MAYONNAISE

AMERICAN   YIELD: One scant cup

2 teaspoons Dijon mustard·
1-1/2 tablespoons
olive oil·
1/2 cup plain yoghurt·
2 teaspoons
fresh lemon juice·
1 teaspoon
diced scallions·
1 tablespoon tomato paste·
1 tablespoon
fresh parsley or
1/2 tablespoon dried·
1/2 teaspoon fresh basil
or 1/4 teaspoon dried·
Salt and pepper,
to taste·
Dash of Tabasco to taste·

Place the mustard in a mixing bowl and gradually add the oil, whisking constantly. Add the yoghurt and blend thoroughly; then add the balance of the ingredients, except the Tabasco, and whisk for 5 minutes or longer, until you have a smooth mixture. If using an electric blender, start with the yoghurt and mustard; blend for 5 seconds, adding the oil gradually. Then add all of the other ingredients, except the Tabasco and blend for 15 seconds until smooth. In either case, add the Tabasco last. Refrigerate.

BONUS IDEAS: Try using this dressing with what the French refer to as "mayonnaise dishes." Uniform pieces or slices of precooked seafood or poultry are placed on a bed of lettuce, covered with mayonnaise and garnished with anchovy filets, capers, olives, hard-boiled egg whites, and either shredded lettuce or hearts of lettuce. These mayonnaise dishes are served thoroughly chilled, and sprinkled with paprika or curry.

BONUS MAYONNAISE

INTERNATIONAL   YIELD: One-and-one-third cup

1 egg, hard-boiled·
2 egg yolks·
1 cup part-skim
ricotta, or yoghurt·
1 teaspoon mustard
powder·
1 teaspoon lemon juice·
1 teaspoon diced scallions·
1/8 teaspoon
minced basil, dried·
1 tablespoon
fresh parsley, minced
or 1/2 tablespoon dried·
Salt and white pepper
to taste (optional)·
4 drops Tabasco·

1. Mash the cooked egg, press through a sieve, and blend with the egg yolks. Place the egg mixture in a blender, add the ricotta cheese, and beat for 45 seconds. Add the balance of the ingredients except the Tabasco, and blend for an additional 30 seconds.

2. Adjust the seasonings to taste, add the Tabasco, and as many additional drops of lemon juice as you consider necessary. Refrigerate until chilled, or place in the freezer for 15 minutes before serving.

BONUS IDEAS: This is one of the few recipes in the book where egg yolks are provided as a bonus option. The 3 egg yolks are well within the parameters prescribed by most doctors. Since only 1 tablespoon of mayonnaise is generally used per serving, the quantity of egg yolk consumed is minimal. EGGLESS MAYONNAISE (page 124) may be used instead.

* SAUCE BÉCHAMEL, Basic White Sauce

FRENCH/ INTERNATIONAL

YIELD: 1 cup

1-1/2 tablespoons polyunsaturated margarine·
1-1/2 tablespoons potato or rice flour, or cornstarch or arrowroot·
4 tablespoons powdered non-fat milk·
1 cup water·
1 teaspoon sherry (optional)·
1/2 teaspoon salt·
1/4 teaspoon ground white pepper·
Cookware spray·

Apply cookware spray to a saucepan and melt the margarine. Stir in the potato flour and cook slowly for 3 minutes to make a ROUX. Add the milk and water, and continue to cook over low heat for about 10 minutes, stirring constantly until the sauce is thick and smooth. Season with the optional sherry, the salt and the ground pepper.

BONUS IDEAS: The above recipe is for a medium-thick sauce, suitable for general use. For thicker sauce, use 2 tablespoons of potato starch, and for a soufflé base, use 3 tablespoons per cup of liquid.

To prepare SAUCE VELOUTÉ, or velvet-smooth sauce, replace the water with an equal quantity of veal, chicken, or fish stock, depending on the main ingredient of the dish this sauce is to enhance.

SAUCE MOELLE, Marrow Sauce

FRENCH

YIELD: One-half cup

1-1/2 cups Demi-Glace Sauce (page 105)·
1 tablespoon polyunsaturated margarine·
4 ounces fresh beef marrow, diced and poached for 3 minutes·
1 sprig parsley, minced·
Cookware spray·

Apply cookware spray to a saucepan, and add the DEMI-GLACE SAUCE. Cook over high heat for 20 minutes, until the sauce is reduced to a thick concentrate, like meat jelly. Remove from the heat and stir in the margarine, the diced marrow, and the parsley. Serve.

BONUS IDEAS: An excellent variation utilizing beef marrow is SAUCE BORDELAISE, Bordelaise Sauce, served on broiled and grilled meats. First sauté 3 chopped shallots or scallions with 1/2 garlic clove in 3/4 cup Bordeaux or other good red wine, with pinch of cayenne and 6 crushed peppercorns. Simmer gently until reduced by half. Add the DEMI-GLACE SAUCE, bring to a boil and add 1 tablespoon of brandy. Remove from heat and stir in the margarine, the diced marrow and the parsley. You may wish to add salt to taste.

Some chefs strain the sauce through triple layers of cheesecloth before adding the margarine, diced marrow, and the parsley.

* PESTO ALLA GENOVESE Genoese
Basil Sauce

YIELD: One scant cup

2 cups fresh or
frozen basil leaves ·
2 tablespoons pine nuts
or walnut meats, chopped ·
2 cloves garlic,
mashed ·
Pinch of coarse salt ·
1/2 cup grated
Parmesan cheese,
preferably combined
with 2 tablespoons
Romano-style
pecorino cheese ·
1/2 cup oil,
preferably olive ·
1 tablespoon
polyunsaturated margarine ·

1. Use a large mortar to obtain greater flavor. Combine the basil, nuts, garlic, and salt; grind with a pestle, crushing the ingredients to form a paste. Add the grated cheese, and grind again until the mixture is blended. (If freezing, do not add the grated cheese, but proceed with adding the oil, as in step 2.)

2. Add the oil and blend it into the mixture. Use a wooden spoon to blend in the margarine until the mixture has the consistency of a smooth paste similar to mayonnaise. Serve with pasta, and especially white or green GNOCCHI, in soups, and over broiled or baked potatoes. (If freezing, do not add the margarine.)

BONUS IDEAS: If using an electric blender, combine all of the ingredients except the grated cheese and margarine, and blend at high speed until finely minced. (If freezing, place the mixture in tightly sealed jars.) If the mixture is not being frozen, transfer it to a bowl and blend in the grated cheese and then the margarine, until the paste has a smooth consistency. Serve.

When refrigerating or freezing PESTO, brushing the top of the paste with oil will prevent discoloration. Avoid adding the grated cheese and margarine before freezing.

Frozen PESTO should be thawed in the refrigerator overnight before it is used. When thoroughly thawed, blend in the grated cheese and then the margarine as in step 2.

Many variations of this dish combine parsley with the basil, and call for as little as several sprigs of parsley to as much as 1/4 or 1/2 cup of chopped parsley, combined with the chopped basil leaves to produce a total of 2 cups. If fresh basil leaves are not available, you can use 2 cups of chopped parsley and 1/2 teaspoon dried basil.

Sardinian sheep's milk cheese, called Sardo PECORINO, is preferred to the Romano-style PECORINO cheese, but unfortunately, the former is not as commonly available. If the Sardo is used, allow only 1 tablespoon, since it is a stronger cheese and can overpower the delicate blend of flavors of the PESTO.

Some experts do not include the grated cheese and margarine in the recipe, but serve them at the table to be added to each dish of PESTO separately. Others blend the PESTO with 1 or more tablespoons of hot cooking water, from the pasta that is being served, before using.

Generally, 2 or 3 tablespoons of PESTO are sufficient for one serving of pasta, and only 1 tablespoon in soups or on potatoes. When serving PESTO with the grated cheese already incorporated into it, do not serve additional cheese or you will be disturbing the balance of flavors.

My favorite use of PESTO is on GNOCCHI VERDI (page 76–77) and with MINESTRONE FREDDO ALLA MILANESE (page 155).

* FUMET BLANC DE POISSON Basic
Fish Stock

FRENCH/ INTERNATIONAL

1 pound fish bones, preferably heads from flounder, whiting, or halibut •
1 onion, sliced and blanched •
6 parsley stems or 1 tablespoon parsley roots •
Juice of 1/2 lemon •
1 cup white wine, or dry vermouth •
2 quarts cold water •
2 each, carrots and celery stalks, chopped •
2 bay leaves •
1/4 teaspoon coarse salt •
6 whole white peppercorns •
1/8 teaspoon thyme, dried •
Cookware spray •

YIELD: Two quarts

1. Apply cookware spray to a heavy saucepan and line the bottom with the blanched onions and parsley stems. Cover these ingredients with fish parts; add the lemon juice and 1 tablespoon of the white wine. Tightly cover, and cook AU SEC over medium heat for about 5 minutes, shuffling the pan occasionally. Remove the cover, and continue to cook about 10 minutes longer, or until the liquid is reduced by half.

2. Add the water and the balance of the ingredients, and bring to a boil, skim and continue to simmer over moderate heat for about 20 minutes. Strain through a fine sieve, and adjust the seasonings as necessary. Refrigerate or freeze in convenient 1-cup or 1-quart quantities.

BONUS IDEAS: As we have noted in other MINCEUR recipes, wherever fish stock is called for, the same quantity of clam juice can be substituted. Whenever possible, first enrich the clam juice by adding to it half its volume of a mixture of water and white wine. Then add the sliced and blanched onion and the parsley stems and simmer for half an hour. Do not use salt with clam juice, but dilute it with water, if necessary, before using.

After preparing the stock, reserve the fish bones and trimmings to prepare FISH ASPIC. Place the reserved bones and an additional fish head in a stock pot and cover with fish stock and simmer for 2 hours or until the stock is reduced by half. Clarify (page 249) and pour into a chilled mold. When almost set, add flakes of cooked fish or seafood; and when firm, unmold, slice and serve over a bed of lettuce or other salad greens.

GAZPACHO SEVILLANO Sevillian Style Gazpacho

SPANISH

1 large ripe tomato, finely chopped •
2 cups tomato juice or ice water •
1/2 cup each, diced celery, cucumber, and green pepper •
1/4 cup minced onion •
1 small garlic clove, minced •
3 tablespoons olive oil •
2 tablespoons wine vinegar, preferably tarragon •
1 teaspoon each, parsley and chives, minced (optional) •
Salt and freshly ground pepper to taste •

There are as many variations of this delightful "salad soup" as there are regions in Spain and strong personal preferences among the cooks preparing it. GAZPACHO probably challenges our own CHILI CON CARNE as the most controversial dish, not only in terms of its ingredients but in the manner of its preparation. Some enthusiasts insist that the ingredients must be blended into a smooth purée, while others are equally vehement in insisting the ingredients be diced and that their distinctive textures be maintained. There isn't even full agreement that this dish should be served chilled, which it generally is—and most deliciously so.

YIELD: Six servings

Combine all of the ingredients in a ceramic, glass, or earthenware bowl, mix thoroughly, and refrigerate covered for at least 4 hours to chill completely.

If you prefer GAZPACHO with a smooth texture, use a blender: blend 1/2 or 3/4 of the ingredients for 10 to 15 seconds at medium speed. Combine with the balance of the ingredients and refrigerate for 4 hours. Serve topped with croutons and diced bits of the basic vegetable ingredients.

BONUS IDEAS: Some versions of this recipe call for croutons or cubes of stale bread marinated in the mixture. Other variations include 18 ground almonds and seasoning with cayenne, lemon juice, or Worcestershire sauce. Whatever choice you make, a great deal of the charm and satisfaction of GAZPACHO is topping the cold soup with diced vegetables of varied colors and textures.

DODO Banana Fritters

NIGERIAN

4 very ripe bananas •
1 teaspoon fresh lemon juice •
1 tablespoon cornstarch or water-chestnut flour •
3 egg whites •
1/2 teaspoon vanilla •
1 tablespoon honey •
1/2 cup corn oil •

YIELD: Four servings

Mash the bananas with a fork; add the lemon juice and cornstarch, mixing well until smooth. Beat the egg whites until they are stiff, and adding the vanilla and honey, fold into the banana mixture. Heat the oil in a small skillet over medium heat; spoon in the banana mixture 1 tablespoon at a time. When the fritters are browned on both sides, remove with a slotted spoon and drain on a double thickness of paper towels. Serve hot, sprinkled with lemon juice and additional honey to taste.

BONUS IDEAS: Some garnishing suggestions include cubes of pineapple, sliced kumquats or minced mint leaves sprinkled over the fritters.

✱ ROUILLE Pimiento and Garlic Sauce

FRENCH

1/4 cup
canned pimiento pieces·
1/4 teaspoon
Tabasco sauce·
4 cloves garlic,
mashed·
4 green peppercorns·
4 twists of pepper mill·
1 teaspoon thyme,
or basil·
1 tablespoon oil,
preferably olive·
1/4 teaspoon
coarse salt·
4 tablespoons
hot fish stock, or
clam juice·
1 medium potato,
peeled, quartered,
and cooked in
fish soup or clam juice·

Most of us wouldn't consider eating a BOUILLABAISSE or a delicately strained fish soup without the complementing flavors of a good ROUILLE. Try this pimiento and garlic sauce spooned directly into the soup or as a topping to toasted rounds floating on the surface of the soup. Be sure always to serve additional ROUILLE in a sauceboat or in small individual bowls for each guest, along with a dish of extra toast rounds.

YIELD: One cup

1. Place all ingredients into a large mortar or bowl, and grind with pestle or similar instrument to form a thick but smooth paste, blending with a few drops of the oil until proper consistency is reached.

2. Serve on rounds of toast floating in accompanying fish soup, in individual small bowls for each guest, and/or in a sauceboat.

BONUS IDEAS: When preparing fish soup, either BOUILLABAISSE (page 87) or MEDITERRANEAN FISH SOUP (pages 180–81), you'll save time and effort if you cook two peeled, quartered potatoes, reserving one of them for this recipe.

The ROUILLE may be frozen in a glass jar and reserved for later use. Be sure to leave some space for expansion.

SAUCE TARTARE Tartar Sauce

FRENCH

YIELD: One-and-one-fourth cups

1 cup Minceur Mayonnaise
(page 124)·
1 tablespoon each,
gherkin, capers,
parsley, and
onion—all minced·
1/8 teaspoon each,
paprika, salt, and
white ground pepper·

Combine all the ingredients in a bowl and beat until completely blended. Thoroughly chill before using and serve principally with fish.

BONUS IDEAS: This sauce can be enhanced by adding the white part of a hard-boiled egg, chopped; 1 teaspoon of minced tarragon leaves; and 1/2 garlic clove, minced. The minced onion may be replaced with 1 tablespoon of minced shallots, scallions, or fresh chives. If the sauce is too thick, it can be thinned with 1/2 teaspoon of fresh lemon juice or tarragon vinegar.

SAUCE AUX FINES HERBES French
Herb Sauce

FRENCH

YIELD: Two scant cups

1 cup plain yoghurt •
1/2 teaspoon each,
fresh tarragon, thyme,
chervil, chives,
and parsley—
all finely chopped;
or 1/4 teaspoon of each,
dried •
2 teaspoons Dijon
or Homemade Mustard
(page 246) •
1/4 teaspoon fresh
lemon juice (optional) •
1/8 teaspoon ground
white pepper (optional) •

Mix the combined herbs with all of the other ingredients, except the mustard, and blend. Add the mustard and beat well until completely blended. Thoroughly chill before using. Adjust lemon juice and seasonings before serving with fish and other dishes.

BONUS IDEAS: You may wish to consider a cooked version of this sauce, which is served hot with meat dishes. To prepare FRENCH HOT HERB SAUCE, bring to a boil 1/2 cup of white wine or dry vermouth with 1/2 cup of finely chopped, fresh parsley, tarragon and chervil and cook over high heat until reduced by half. Add 1 cup of DEMI-GLACE SAUCE (page 105) or QUICK DEMI-GLACE SAUCE (page 103). Just before serving, add an additional tablespoon of finely chopped tarragon. Garnish the meat being served with the hot sauce and with fresh tarragon leaves that have been dipped into boiling, salted water, cooled in cold water, and drained thoroughly.

SAUCE VERTE AUX ANCHOIS Piquant
Green Anchovy Sauce

FRENCH

YIELD: Four servings

6 anchovy filets,
mashed, or 2 teaspoons
anchovy paste •
3 teaspoons minced
capers •
1/2 garlic clove, minced •
1/2 teaspoon Dijon
or Homemade Mustard
(page 246) •
1 tablespoon
fresh lemon juice •
1/2 cup oil,
preferably a
polyunsaturated oil
combined with olive oil •
Salt to taste •

Combine all the ingredients except the oil and the lemon juice in a bowl, and mix thoroughly. Stir in the lemon juice and blend. Add the olive oil and beat vigorously until completely blended. Serve with boiled meat or poached or steamed fish.

BONUS IDEAS: For some meats you may want an even more piquant flavor, in which case substitute 1/2 teaspoon or more of red wine vinegar for the lemon juice.

This sauce is similar to an Italian version, SALSA VERDE, which can be prepared by adding 1/4 cup of a combination of chopped parsley and spinach or watercress; 1 finely chopped onion; and 1 small, boiled potato, diced. Serve thoroughly chilled with salads, boiled meats or chilled seafood.

SAUCE BÉARNAISE MINCEUR Bonus

Minceur Béarnaise Sauce

FRENCH

YIELD: One cup

1 teaspoon
polyunsaturated
margarine
or oil·
2 teaspoons
cornstarch or arrowroot·
1/2 cup chicken
consommé or broth·
1 egg yolk,
at room temperature·
1/8 teaspoon salt·
1/8 teaspoon
white pepper·

Bouquet de Vinaigrette,
consisting of:
1/4 cup wine vinegar,
preferably tarragon,
or sherry vinegar·
1/4 cup white wine
or dry vermouth·
1 tablespoon
minced shallots or
scallions·
2 tablespoons
fresh minced tarragon,
or 1 tablespoon dried·
1/2 teaspoon
minced fresh parsley,
or 1/4 teaspoon dried·

1. Prepare the BOUQUET DE VINAIGRETTE by placing all its ingredients in a saucepan and bringing them to a boil. Reduce the heat to medium and cook about 15 minutes, until the mixture is reduced to about 2 tablespoons of concentrated BOUQUET.

2. Blend together the cornstarch and margarine in a double boiler or BAIN-MARIE, and add the consommé. Cook over medium heat for about 5 minutes, stirring constantly until thickened.

3. Beat the egg yolk about 1 minute and blend with 2 tablespoons of the thickened sauce before adding it gradually to the remaining sauce. Continue to cook over low heat for 2 minutes, stirring constantly. Remove from heat, and blend in the BOUQUET DE VINAIGRETTE. Add salt and pepper to taste.

BONUS IDEAS: You can prepare BONUS HOLLANDAISE SAUCE in virtually the same way, but instead of preparing and blending in the BOUQUET DE VINAIGRETTE, substitute 1 teaspoon of fresh lemon juice; blend it into the sauce after removing it from the heat.

The BÉARNAISE SAUCE can be enriched in a number of ways. Try adding 1/4 teaspoon of nutmeg to the BOUQUET DE VINAIGRETTE; or, after blending, add 1 teaspoon of meat glaze (page 110–11) and whisk the sauce lightly for 5 seconds. Especially for use with grilled meats, consider adding 2-1/2 tablespoons of tomato paste to 1 cup of the BÉARNAISE, to prepare CHORON SAUCE, or BÉARNAISE AND TOMATO SAUCE.

Because of the egg yolk, this is a Bonus recipe; however, 2 egg whites whisked for 1 minute until foamy may be substituted for the egg yolk.

BARBECUE SAUCE

AMERICAN   YIELD: Two cups

1/4 cup chopped onions ·
1 tablespoon dry vermouth ·
1/2 cup water ·
2 tablespoons vinegar ·
3 tablespoons oil ·
2 tablespoons
Worcestershire sauce ·
1 cup chili sauce ·
2 tablespoons honey ·
1 tablespoon dry mustard ·
1/2 teaspoon each,
salt and ground pepper ·
1/4 teaspoon paprika ·
Cookware spray ·

Apply cookware spray to a heavy saucepan, and sauté the onions with the dry vermouth AU SEC until they turn translucent. Add the balance of the ingredients and simmer for 20 minutes, stirring occasionally. Remove from heat and let the sauce set. Serve with barbecued meats, especially pork, beef, and chicken.

BONUS IDEAS: This is essentially a basting sauce and should be applied to meat or poultry only during the final 10 or 15 minutes of cooking outdoors. The sauce can be varied to taste by adding: 1/4 cup of diced Canadian bacon; 1/2 teaspoon of toasted cumin, ground; 1/4 teaspoon of ground ginger; and 1/4 teaspoon of Tabasco sauce or 1 small clove of garlic, mashed. Remove the garlic after several hours, before storing, lest it overpower the other ingredients.

SALSA GORGONZOLA Gorgonzola Sauce

ITALIAN   YIELD: Six servings

1/2 cup Gorgonzola
cheese ·
1/3 cup combination of
skimmed milk and
skimmed evaporated milk ·
3 tablespoons
polyunsaturated
margarine ·
1 teaspoon salt,
or to taste ·

Mash the Gorgonzola cheese with a fork and blend it into a paste with 1 tablespoon or more of the milk mixture. Combine the cheese paste with the other ingredients in an enameled or glass double-boiler or BAIN-MARIE. Cook for several minutes over medium heat, stirring constantly with a wooden spoon until the mixture is blended and creamy. Cover, and remove from the heat. Serve with any pasta of your choice, particularly GNOCCHI VERDI (page 76–77) or POTATO GNOCCHI (page 26–27).

BONUS IDEAS: You can substitute other blue cheeses, such as Roquefort, which, when it is freshly cut, I have found to be subtly sharper than Gorgonzola.

LO SUY Chinese Master Sauce

CHINESE This is one of the most fascinating sauces, and a tradition in many Chinese families—a "perpetual" sauce, maintained and passed down from generation to generation even for hundreds of years. You can begin your own master sauce simply by preparing any Chinese recipe calling for "red-simmering," the slow cooking or braising of meats or poultry in the reddish sauce produced by the addition of soy sauce. RED-SIMMERED PORK (page 71) is one such recipe. To maintain this sauce for re-use in other dishes of this kind, you will either have to use it repeatedly, or bring it to a boil once a week and replenish it with additional ingredients. It takes only one red-simmered meat dish to begin a master sauce, but perseverence and almost Oriental patience to maintain it. Try it for as long as you find it worthwhile.

YIELD: Depends on starter recipe

1. To begin: Prepare any Chinese recipe for red-simmered meat or poultry. Reserve the meat, strain the sauce through a layer of cheesecloth, and refrigerate or freeze until the top layer of fat has congealed. Skim off and discard the fat and keep the sauce refrigerated in a covered jar until ready for future use.

2. To use: In a large pan, bring the sauce to a boil and add large cuts or cubes of pork, beef, lamb, or poultry. Simmer, covered, slowly for 2 or more hours until the meat is tender and thoroughly penetrated by the sauce. It is preferable to preboil the meat for 5 minutes in water, and rinse, before adding to the boiling sauce. Parboiling seals in the juices of the meat, achieving greater flavor. Once the meat has been completely cooked, serve it either hot or cold, with appropriate CHINESE DIPPING SAUCES but without its own sauce, which is reserved for future use after straining and skimming. The sauce becomes richer each time it is used.

3. To replenish: After the sauce is used 3 or more times, add 1/4 cup each of soy sauce and sherry, a sliced scallion stalk, 2 thin slices of ginger, 1/2 teaspoon honey, and a pinch of salt. After using the sauce 8 times, add a pinch each of seasonings such as: star anise, cinnamon, five spice powder, or several Szechwan peppercorns.

Of course, you can freeze the sauce. Otherwise if the sauce is NOT used for a period of one week, you must bring it to a boil, cool, and refrigerate again—or it will turn sour.

NOTE: Other Chinese red-simmered recipes you may consider to start a master sauce include: RED-SIMMERED CHICKEN (page 82–83), CAPON (page 83), BEEF (page 83) and RABBIT (page 83).

VINAIGRETTE MINCEUR

FRENCH

1 cup water ·
1 tablespoon
cornstarch or arrowroot ·
2 tablespoons
rice wine vinegar or
other wine vinegar ·
2 tablespoons
lemon juice ·
1 tablespoon each,
olive and safflower oil,
combined ·
1 teaspoon honey ·
1 teaspoon salt ·
1 teaspoon
dry horseradish ·
1 teaspoon dry mustard ·
2 tablespoons
chopped gherkins ·
1 teaspoon
Worcestershire sauce ·
1/4 teaspoon paprika ·
1 tablespoon
minced parsley ·
1 hard-boiled egg,
white part only, chopped ·

A versatile MINCEUR sauce that adds zest to many vegetable dishes, including MORNING DEW VEGETABLES (page 27) and steamed artichokes. VINAIGRETTE can also be used as a coating for salad greens, as a sauce for grilled, poached, or baked fish, or as a marinade for grilled barbecued meats. In the latter case you will want to add only two tablespoons of water for a more concentrated mixture. This VINAIGRETTE dressing keeps well in the refrigerator, but should be beaten or shaken before using.

YIELD: One cup

1. Mix the cornstarch and water; bring to a boil over low heat, stirring constantly, until the mixture clears and begins to thicken.

2. Remove from the heat and let cool; then add the balance of the ingredients. Beat the mixture well for 30 seconds with a whisk, an eggbeater, or in an electric blender. Place in a covered glass jar, and refrigerate; shake well before serving.

BONUS IDEAS: You can vary this recipe in many ways, depending on your own preferences. Try adding 4 twists of a pepper mill, and 1 teaspoon each of chives, shallots and/or capers.

Other ingredients you may wish to add include: 1 tablespoon of chopped onion or scallions, 1 tablespoon chili sauce, or 1 clove of garlic mashed. Remove the garlic after several hours, before storing, to avoid its overpowering the other ingredients.

This dressing is sometimes called RAVIGOTE SAUCE or FRENCH DRESSING and is excellent with salads and cold fish or meat. It is also delicious served lukewarm with hot, boiled meat dishes.

PURÉE DE CHOU-FLEUR Cauliflower Purée

FRENCH

1 medium cauliflower ·
1/4 teaspoon
coarse salt,
or to taste ·
1 tablespoon
sherry or dry vermouth ·
1/2 cup
reserved cooking liquor,
or chicken or
beef consommé ·
Cookware spray ·

I have always been intrigued by the fact that a particular familiar food can take on an entirely new taste and quality—merely by being prepared in a different manner. Like most of us, I have often used whole cauliflower florets as part of certain dishes and as a garnish for others. When puréed, however, cauliflower is transformed into an entirely different food that is both pleasant and interesting—and a wonderful variation from the standard mashed potatoes so frequently served with meat dishes.

YIELD: Two scant cups

1. Remove the green leaves from the cauliflower, wash and drain, but do not pat dry. Cut away the tough stalks and reserve the florets, which should be cut into approximately 2-inch sections. Apply cookware spray to a saucepan and cook the florets AU SEC over medium heat with the sherry and salt, covered, for about 20 minutes, or until tender but crisply AL DENTE.

2. Transfer the cooked florets and their cooking liquid, together with the reserved liquor or consommé, to an electric blender; blend at medium speed for about 2 minutes, or until you have a textured but smooth purée.

BONUS IDEAS: This purée can be endlessly varied in flavor, depending on the reserved cooking liquor you use. The reserved cooking liquor from BLANQUETTE DE VEAU (page 20) is particularly effective. Try adding 1 chopped leek and 1 chopped carrot, cooked AU SEC with the florets, and then puréed with the mixture of vegetables and cooking liquid. A tablespoon of grated FROMAGE BLANC can be added to the blender while puréeing the cauliflower mixture for still another variation in flavor.

SAUCE AU CURRIE Curry Sauce

FRENCH

YIELD: One cup

1 cup plain yoghurt ·
4 tablespoons
Minceur Mayonnaise
(page 124) ·
1 teaspoon Dijon
or Homemade Mustard
(page 246) ·
1 tablespoon
fresh lemon juice ·
2 teaspoons
curry powder or
to taste ·

Combine all of the ingredients except the lemon juice and curry powder in a bowl. Beat vigorously with a fork, add the lemon juice and then the curry powder. Blend until smooth, and thoroughly chill before using. Serve as a dip for CRU-DITÉS, or crisp raw vegetables.

BONUS IDEAS: A variation is SAUCE INDIENNE, or INDIAN SAUCE, which is served hot. Sauté AU SEC in 3 tablespoons of consommé: 1 onion and 1 clove of garlic, chopped; 2 sprigs of parsley; 1 chopped celery stalk; 1 small bay leaf; and 1/2 teaspoon of mace. Sauté until the onions are translucent. Blend 2 tablespoons of cornstarch and 1 teaspoon of curry powder into the mixture and cook 5 minutes longer. Add 2 cups of consommé and 1/2 cup of coconut milk, simmer for 50 minutes, then drain by pressing the solids through a sieve. Add 1 teaspoon of lemon juice to the heated sauce before serving.

SEUN MEI CHEUN Plum Sauce

CHINESE

1 cup unsweetened
plum jam ·
1/2 cup chopped
mango chutney ·
1 tablespoon honey ·
1 teaspoon vinegar ·
Salt and pepper to taste ·

This is an often-used dipping sauce for Chinese meals. Of course you can purchase it already prepared in Oriental shops, but if you prepare it yourself, you can make a number of pleasant variations.

YIELD: About one-and-one-half cups

1. Sieve the plum jam and mince the chutney fine; then combine all of the ingredients in a saucepan and blend thoroughly. Heat the mixture over low heat for 15 minutes, stirring periodically.

2. If the mixture is too thick, thin it with a little water. Transfer to a jar with a tightly closing cap, and store in a cool place. Serve in condiment dishes as a dip.

BONUS IDEAS: Unsweetened peach or apricot preserves can be used instead of the plum jam, or you can vary the dip with combinations of one or more of these ingredients. Lemon juice can be used instead of the vinegar.

SAUCE À L'AIL Garlic Sauce

PROVENÇAL

YIELD: One half cup

1 slice gluten bread,
white part only,
soaked in skimmed milk •
2 cloves garlic,
minced •
2 egg whites •
1 teaspoon
polyunsaturated margarine •
1/8 teaspoon salt •
1/2 cup
polyunsaturated oil
combined with olive oil •
1 teaspoon
fresh lemon juice •
2 tablespoons skimmed milk •

Wring out the uncrusted bread, reserving 2 tablespoons of the skimmed milk. Mash the bread with a fork in a bowl and combine with the minced garlic and the egg whites which have been beaten for 1 minute until foamy. Add the margarine and the salt. Beat the mixture constantly, gradually adding the oil, until it begins to thicken. Then add in the lemon juice and reserved tablespoons of skimmed milk, and continue to beat until thickened. Serve over fish, boiled meats, or boiled vegetables.

BONUS IDEAS: Either EGGLESS MAYONNAISE (page 124) or BONUS MAYONNAISE may be used in preparing QUICK GARLIC SAUCE. Grind the garlic and the mashed bread in a mortar and add the mixture to 1/2 cup of the mayonnaise.

TIM SEUN CHEUN Sweet and Sour Sauce

CHINESE

YIELD: One cup

2 tablespoons cornstarch •
1/2 cup water or
unsweetened pineapple
juice •
1 teaspoon soy sauce
or salt •
1/2 teaspoon
ground pepper •
1/4 cup malt vinegar •
1 tablespoon molasses •
3 tablespoons
tomato catsup or
tomato sauce •
2 tablespoons sherry •
2 tablespoons
Chinese pickles or
sweet mixed pickles,
shredded •

Blend the cornstarch with 1 tablespoon of the water; set aside. Place all of the other ingredients except the pickles in an enameled or glass saucepan and bring to a boil. Add the cornstarch mixture and boil for 2 minutes longer, stirring constantly. Add the pickles and let them heat through. Remove the pan from the heat and set aside, covered, for 5 minutes before using. Serve with meats or fish.

BONUS IDEAS: This sauce is used so extensively in Chinese cuisine that there are necessarily a number of variations. Additional ingredients that can be added, or substituted for some of those in the basic recipe include: several drops to taste of Tabasco sauce, Worcestershire sauce, or sesame oil; 2 minced garlic cloves; juice of 1/2 lemon; and chicken broth, instead of the water or pineapple juice.

To enhance the flavor, and for accents of color, I generally add 1/2 cup of pineapple chunks and 1/2 cup each of diced green and red peppers.

* SALSA DI NOCI Guido's Walnut Sauce

ITALIAN

6 tablespoons grated walnut meats •
1/4 pound soft polyunsaturated margarine •
Salt to taste •

This is a memorable variation for saucing pasta. Generally unknown even in Italy, the recipe has, however, been passed down for generations in some remote regions of the country. I find it best with small-sized pasta varieties, but it can be used as well with any of your favorites.
YIELD: Six servings

1. Grate the walnut meats with a Mouli or other grinder, and press firmly into the measuring spoon so that you have 6 level tablespoons. The margarine must be softened at room temperature for proper blending.

2. Blend the ground walnuts with the softened margarine thoroughly, and refrigerate or freeze until ready to use. When ready to serve, drain the pasta, and mix with the creamed walnut mixture until the pasta is well coated. Serve immediately.

140

7.
Tasty Beginnings

It is especially important in the MINCEUR concept that the first course establish the tone of the meal as a whole and provide an anticipation of the courses to follow. Once you have selected your main dish and its accoutrements, the judicious selection of the first course can be made from a wide variety of possibilities. It must be both delicious and satisfying in its own right as well as serve as a bridge to the heart of the meal, your main course. I am certain you will find that the principles and techniques used in preparing these appetizers and hors d'oeuvres will stimulate you to adapt other of your own favorites to MINCEUR CUISINE as well.

SEEKH KABOB Hot Beef Hors d'Oeuvres

PAKISTANI

YIELD: Six to eight servings

1 pound lean beef, cut into cubes or ground •
3 scallions, chopped •
1/4 teaspoon each, ground cinnamon, cloves, and cayenne •
2 teaspoons cumin, toasted and ground •
2 teaspoons coriander, ground •
1 teaspoon each, paprika and coarse salt •
3 tablespoons beef broth or dry vermouth (optional) •
Cookware spray (optional) •

Place the cubed or ground beef in a mixing bowl and stir in the balance of the ingredients, except the broth or vermouth. Allow the mixture to stand for about 1 hour in order for it to absorb the spices and seasonings. If using cubes of beef, skewer them on wet bamboo strips or metal skewers and broil or barbecue for about 10 minutes until tender. If using ground or chopped beef, mold the meat mixture into balls about 1 inch in diameter, dip them in water for a moment, drain, and pat dry. Apply cookware spray to a skillet and over high heat brown the meat balls on all sides in 1 tablespoon of the broth. Lower the heat, add the balance of the broth and simmer, covered, for about 10 minutes until the meat balls are tender. Serve hot as hors d'oeuvres.

BONUS IDEAS: In preparing the skewers, try alternating pieces of cubed meat with chunks of pineapple, green pepper, fresh tomato, and mushrooms for a hearty luncheon dish.

141

✳ PÂTÉ MULCAHY

AUSTRALIAN

3/4 pound chicken
or pork liver ·
1 pound chicken meat,
both dark and light ·
1-1/4 pounds
lean ground veal ·
1/2 cup Madeira,
port, or sherry ·
2 teaspoons each,
salt and freshly ground
white pepper ·
1 teaspoon
ground allspice ·
1 teaspoon fresh
tarragon or
1/2 teaspoon dried ·
1 large onion,
chopped ·
1 tablespoon each,
water and
dry vermouth ·
1/2 cup evaporated
skimmed milk ·
3 egg whites ·
2 tablespoons
potato flour, rice flour,
or cornstarch ·
1/2 cup softened
polyunsaturated margarine ·
2 slices gluten
or white bread ·
1 teaspoon each,
grated orange and
lemon zest, or
1/2 teaspoon each, dried ·
2 tablespoon each,
orange and lemon juice ·
2 garlic cloves,
minced ·
4 bay leaves ·
1 or 2 truffles or
black olives, sliced ·
1 cup aspic ·
Cookware spray ·

One of my favorites for entertaining. Since it freezes well, you can make convenient serving quantities in a number of variously sized molds for any occasion. This, in fact, keeps me prepared for months of entertaining. As for the aspic, which I insist on using as an accoutrement, there are a number of time-saving hints in the Bonus Ideas, below. Although the liver is not entirely acceptable from the point of view of cholesterol, very little is used, and other saturated fats are avoided without minimizing the pâté's overall satisfying blend of flavors.

YIELD: Three quarts

1. Trim the excess fat and the membranes from all of the meats, cut the liver and chicken into 1/2-inch cubes and place with the veal in a ceramic or glass bowl with the Madeira wine, salt, pepper, allspice and tarragon; marinate for at least 3 hours or, preferably, overnight. Apply cookware spray to a skillet and sauté the onions in the water and vermouth until they turn translucent.

2. Using an electric blender—and because of the volume of ingredients you may have to fill the blender 2/3 full several times—blend the meat, livers, wine marinade, evaporated milk, and egg whites beaten 1 minute until foamy. Occasionally add a portion of the cooked onions, flour, softened margarine, and slices of bread.

3. Place the puréed mixture into a large mixing bowl, add all of the other ingredients except the bay leaves, truffles, olives, and aspic and mix thoroughly. Apply cookware spray to a large 3-quart mold or a number of smaller ones, rub the inside surfaces with margarine or corn oil, and pour in the blended mixture. Place the bay leaves on top of the pâté mixture in one large mold. Cover the top of the mold with a double thickness of aluminum foil.

4. Preheat your oven to 325°F. Place the mold in a roasting pan with water added to a level no higher than 1/2 the mold's height and bake for 1-1/2 hours. Remove the pâté and let it cool for at least 15 minutes, then set it in the refrigerator for several hours or preferably overnight before serving. This permits the flavors to mature. Remove and discard the bay leaves and decorate the top of the pâté with slices of truffles or black olives and a clear aspic, either poured over it or chopped to top and surround it.

BONUS IDEAS: If you are planning to freeze the pâté, let it cool thoroughly, then place in the refrigerator for about 3 hours before packaging it for the freezer. Thaw thoroughly before serving and avoid reheating.

Prepare aspic as you would for TONGUE IN ASPIC (page 59), but for the 1 tablespoon of Madeira substitute 1 tablespoon of either sherry or cognac as you prefer. I find using canned consommé with gelatin simple and most satisfactory. Open a can of chicken or beef consommé and add 1 teaspoon of Madeira, other wine, or cognac. Be sure the consommé is the type that has gelatin and will form into an aspic when cold. I prefer a turtle consommé which has marvelous flavor and, with the addition of Madeira, a tawny color that is most appealing.

LOBSTER CANAPÉS

BRITISH   YIELD: About two dozen

1 tablespoon minced onion •
1 tablespoon broth or dry vermouth •
1 tablespoon chopped watercress or parsley •
1/8 teaspoon curry powder •
1/3 cup evaporated skimmed milk •
Salt and freshly ground pepper to taste •
3/4 cup fresh or canned lobster meat, chopped •
1/8 teaspoon paprika •
24 croutons •
24 lemon wedges •
3 tablespoons chopped fresh parsley •
Cookware spray •

Preheat your oven to 400°F. Apply cookware spray to a skillet and sauté the onion in the broth until it turns translucent. Add all of the other ingredients except the lobster, paprika, croutons, lemon wedges, and parsley, and simmer for 5 minutes, stirring occasionally, until the mixture is smooth. Add the lobster meat and heat for 3 minutes. Place the croutons in a casserole; spoon the mixture over the croutons and sprinkle with the paprika. Bake covered for several minutes until brown. Serve garnished with the chopped parsley and lemon wedges.

BONUS IDEAS: You can vary this recipe by substituting 3/4 cup of chopped clams, oysters, mussels, shrimp or crabmeat for the lobster meat.

Another variation is LOBSTER ROLLS. Sauté the onions in the broth until translucent, then add all of the other ingredients except the lobster and paprika, and simmer for 5 minutes, stirring the mixture into a smooth paste. Add the seafood meat and heat for 3 minutes. Trim the crusts from 8 slices of bread, place the bread on a damp cloth, and flatten each slice with a rolling pin. Then spread the seafood mixture on each slice of bread and roll as you would a jelly roll. Dip into melted margarine and roll in chopped parsley or chives. Place the rolls in the freezer for 20 minutes, or freeze for future use. When ready to serve, preheat your oven to 350°F. Cut each roll into thirds, bake for 5 minutes, and serve hot, sprinkled with paprika.

143

BISQUE DE HOMARD Lobster Bisque

FRENCH

1 lobster,
about 2 pounds ·
1/2 cup fish stock,
clam juice, or consommé ·
1 each, onion,
celery stalk, and
carrot, diced ·
3 tablespoons cognac
or brandy ·
1/2 cup of champagne
or dry white wine ·

1 Bouquet Garni
wrapped in cheesecloth,
consisting of:
1 stalk celery ·
1 bay leaf ·
3 sprigs
fresh parsley or
1/2 teaspoon dried ·
1/2 teaspoon
fresh thyme or
1/4 teaspoon dried ·

3 tablespoons
polyunsaturated margarine ·
3 tablespoons
potato starch or
cornstarch ·
3 cups
boiling skimmed milk ·
1/3 cup
evaporated skimmed milk ·
1 tablespoon sherry
or Madeira wine ·
Dash of
cayenne or nutmeg ·
Cookware spray ·

One of the marvelous specialties of French cuisine. It does take a bit of doing, but you must try it and enjoy the rewards of a superbly blended combination of tastes that will royally introduce any meal you are contemplating.

YIELD: Four to six servings

1. Remove and reserve the coral from the lobster, cut the lobster in its shell into about 5 pieces, and crack the claws. Apply cookware spray to a large saucepan and cook the diced onion, celery, and carrot in 2 tablespoons of the fish stock, AU SEC, for about 5 minutes, or until the onions are translucent. Add the lobster pieces, the claws, and the coral to the saucepan and cook with the balance of the fish stock over medium heat for about 10 minutes, or until the lobster shells turn red.

2. Meanwhile, heat the cognac, ignite, and pour over the lobster pieces. Add the champagne and the BOUQUET GARNI, cover, and simmer for about 20 minutes. Remove the lobster to cool; then remove the lobster meat from the shells, reserving the shells, and cut it into diced pieces. Discard the BOUQUET GARNI, strain the sauce, and grind or crush the lobster shells and set aside.

3. Apply cookware spray to a saucepan, melt the margarine and with a wire whisk, blend in the potato starch to make a ROUX. Add the skimmed milk and bring to a boil; continue to whisk the hot milk into the ROUX, blending constantly. Add the ground lobster shells and about 1/2 cup of the reserved lobster sauce; simmer, covered, over low heat about 1 hour.

4. Strain the sauce, return it to the saucepan and bring to a boil. Reduce the heat, then stir in the evaporated milk; add the reserved diced lobster, and serve hot with a dash of cayenne and sherry to taste.

BONUS IDEAS: If you use frozen lobster tails, I have found that many varieties do not lend themselves to the grinding of the shells. Instead, cut the shells into pieces and cook with the sauce. If preparing CLAM BISQUE, BISQUE DE CLAMS, substitute 2 dozen clams and do not break the shells, but simply add them to the sauce while cooking. SHRIMP BISQUE, BISQUE DE CREVETTES, is made in the same manner, with 1-1/2 dozen large shrimp substituted for the lobster. OYSTER BISQUE, BISQUE DE HUÎTRES, can be made by using 1 pint of shelled oysters in their own liquor instead of the lobster.

BAKED CUCUMBERS

YIELD: Six or more servings

6 cucumbers,
about 8 inches long ·
2 tablespoons wine
or rice vinegar ·
1/2 teaspoon honey ·
3 tablespoons melted
polyunsaturated margarine ·
1/2 teaspoon
dried dill or basil ·
1/8 teaspoon
ground pepper or
to taste ·
2 scallions, minced ·
Cookware spray ·

Preheat your oven to 375°F. Peel the cucumbers and cut lengthwise into strips slightly less than 1/2 inch wide; then cut the strips into 2-inch lengths. Apply cookware spray to a casserole and add all of the ingredients except the minced scallions. Bake uncovered for 1 hour or until tender, tossing the mixture occasionally. Add the minced scallions and serve. This dish can be prepared in advance and reheated before serving hot with the minced scallions.

BONUS IDEAS: You can vary this recipe by sprinkling 1/4 cup Parmesan cheese over the mixture and browning it in the oven. It can also be blended with 1/4 pound sliced mushrooms and served with a BÉCHAMEL sauce (page 125) to which 1/4 cup FROMAGE BLANC has been added.

STUFFED MUSHROOMS

AMERICAN

YIELD: Six to twelve servings

12 mushrooms ·
1 tablespoon
broth or dry vermouth ·
1 tablespoon
chopped onion ·
3 tablespoons
Canadian bacon, chopped ·
1/8 teaspoon
Worcestershire sauce ·
Salt and fresh
ground pepper to taste ·
3 tablespoons
unsweetened wheat germ ·
1 tablespoon
polyunsaturated
margarine ·
2 tablespoons
chopped parsley ·
Cookware spray ·

Preheat your oven to 350°F. Gently clean the mushrooms with a damp cloth and remove the stems. Using a round cutter, trim the mushroom caps to a uniform size, reserving the trimmings to add to the stuffing. Apply cookware spray to a skillet and add the broth or vermouth; add the mushroom trimmings with all of the other ingredients except the wheat germ, margarine, and parsley; sauté AU SEC for 2 minutes until the onions are translucent. Spoon the mixture into the center of each mushroom cap, sprinkle with wheat germ, place a dot of margarine on top of each, and bake for about 10 minutes. Serve garnished with the chopped parsley on croutons, crackers, or separately.

BONUS IDEAS: You can prepare the mushrooms by replacing the Canadian bacon with 12 clams, oysters, shrimp, or snails or 3/4 cup of crabmeat. Top the seafood with 1 teaspoon of horseradish, or MINCEUR MAYONNAISE (page 85) and a dash of either Tabasco or Worcestershire sauce, before sprinkling with wheat germ and dotting with margarine. Bake for 10 minutes in an oven set at 350°F. and garnish with 2 tablespoons of finely chopped parsley or fresh chives. Serve hot on croutons or crackers.

ARTICHAUTS MONTRÉAL Montreal
Artichokes

CANADIAN

4 medium artichokes •
Water to suit the
cooking process you elect •
3 tablespoons vinegar
or lemon juice •
2 onions,
thinly sliced •
1/4 cup white wine
or dry vermouth •
1 tablespoon oil •
1 tablespoon
polyunsaturated
margarine •
1 bay leaf •
3 tablespoons
cider vinegar •
Salt and pepper to taste •
Cookware spray •

This elegant dish is so versatile it can be served hot or at room temperature, as an appetizer or as the PIÈCE DE RÉSISTANCE of a luncheon meal. The natural juices blend with the other ingredients to become a pleasantly different sauce.
YIELD: Four servings

1. Prepare the artichokes (see page 237) by slicing off the upper third of each, and trimming the tough tops of the individual leaves and the stems. Place in cold water with the 3 tablespoons of vinegar or lemon juice, and let stand for about a half hour. Drain well before cooking.

2. Apply cookware spray to a skillet and sauté the onions with 1 tablespoon of the wine or water, until translucent, then add the oil and the margarine and cook until the margarine is melted. Transfer the mixture to a baking dish deep enough to contain the artichokes; stir in the balance of the ingredients, except the drained artichokes, the salt, and the pepper and blend thoroughly. Add the artichokes and place in the upper tier of a steamer, or over a legged trivet with about 2 inches of boiling water beneath it. Cover the steamer and cook for 35 to 45 minutes, depending on the size of the artichokes, or until tender, occasionally turning them in the sauce. Remove the artichokes from the heat, season the sauce to taste, and serve.

BONUS IDEAS: Montreal style artichokes can be cooked in a pressure cooker at 15 pounds pressure for 10 to 15 minutes, depending on their size. For cooking in a microwave oven, sauté the onions as in step 1 in the baking dish covered with wax paper for 3 minutes; stir well, then sauté 3 minutes longer. Add the artichokes, leaving the center area of the dish free, and cook covered with wax paper for 7 minutes, turning the artichokes in the sauce occasionally; then repeat the process for 2 more 7-minute cooking intervals. Remove from the oven and let stand covered for 10 minutes, before seasoning to taste and serving. Of course, you can also cook the artichokes in a heavy-based casserole on top of the range. Add all of the ingredients except the salt and pepper, and enough cold water to cover a third of the height of the artichokes. Cover tightly, using wet paper towels for improving the seal (see Chapter 11, page 237).

ESCARGOTS AU VIN Snails in Wine

FRENCH

6 dozen canned
snails with shells ·
3 cups
dry white wine or
dry vermouth ·
1 tablespoon shallots
or scallions, chopped ·
1 garlic clove,
mashed or minced ·
3 teaspoons
fine gluten bread crumbs
(optional) ·
3 tablespoons fresh
parsley, finely chopped ·
Salt and freshly ground
pepper to taste ·

A delicate light sauce that refreshingly accents the distinctive flavor of the snails.
YIELD: Six servings

Combine the wine, shallots, and garlic in a saucepan and boil until the wine is reduced by half. Place a little of this mixture in each snail shell; insert a snail in each; then press the optional bread crumbs into each shell, adding a little more wine mixture. If you don't use the bread crumbs, just add extra wine mixture on top of each snail. Bake in a snail dish or muffin tin in a preheated oven set at 375°F. for about 8 minutes. Season to taste and sprinkle with the parsley. Serve hot.

BONUS IDEAS: If you wish, the snails can be served without their shells; cook them for only 5 minutes in a snail dish. If the shells are used, another trick for holding them in place during baking is to crumple a sheet of aluminum foil, place it in a pie dish, and lodge the shells in the depressions of the foil.

* TERRIN'S CAVIAR PIE

AMERICAN

1 2-ounce jar (56 grams)
of red or black
caviar or fish roe ·
1 8-ounce bar of
low-fat cream cheese ·
8 ounces whipped
skimmed cottage cheese
or ricotta ·
2 tablespoons
sour cream or
plain yoghurt ·
1 teaspoon lemon juice ·
4 tablespoons
minced fresh onions
or 2 tablespoons dried ·
1 9-inch pie plate ·
Cookware spray ·

This is a simple but strikingly attractive dish for entertaining that I have enjoyed many times at the home of Terrin Levitt, an excellent cook and the most creative potter I know. The intriguing part of this dish is that although it always tastes exciting, the garnishing can be varied to suit your personal fancy.
YIELD: Twelve servings

Apply cookware spray to the pie plate, and mix all of the ingredients, except the caviar, thoroughly. Spread the mixture in the pie plate, smooth the top with a knife or the back of a wooden spoon to suggest a filled cream pie. Spoon the caviar into a circular border about 2-1/2 inches from the rim. Depending on the color of the caviar used, make a border immediately inside the rim of the pie with edible vegetable garnishes of contrasting colors, such as chopped scallions, parsley, radish slices, or olives. The original recipe used a sieved hard-boiled egg yolk in the center of the pie, but you can use grated carrot, sliced kumquats, or sprinkled paprika. Chill and serve.

BONUS IDEAS: You can prepare the caviar pie ahead, cover it with plastic, and store in the refrigerator to chill. Occasionally there will be enough of the blended cheese filling left over so that you can roll it into a small ball or a sausage shape and then roll in minced parsley or grated nuts to cover and freeze for future use.

* MOULES FARCIES Stuffed Mussels

FRENCH

2 quarts mussels,
as prepared for
Mussels à la Marinière ·
4 tablespoons each,
finely chopped onion,
celery and parsley ·
1 tablespoon green pepper,
finely diced ·
1 tablespoon water
or 1 tablespoon consommé
or dry vermouth ·
1 cup toasted
gluten bread crumbs,
or unsweetened
wheat germ ·
1 teaspoon each,
dry mustard and
coarse salt ·
1/2 teaspoon
cayenne pepper ·
Cookware spray ·

Until only recently the French and other Europeans have generally held mussels in higher regard than Americans. Now, however, they are popular in the United States, and there are dozens of marvelous recipes for mussels. Many of these recipes call for preparing MUSSELS À LA MARINIÈRE (page 72) as an important first step; I generally at least double the MARINIÈRE recipe and use the extra portion for MOULES FARCIES. Since this dish freezes so well, I often make large quantities and freeze on freezer-proof trays ready to serve as needed.

YIELD: Four to six servings

1. Remove the mussels from the shells, reserving the shells. Dice the cooked mussels. Apply cookware spray to a skillet and sauté the onion, celery, and pepper with 1 tablespoon of water, consommé or dry vermouth until translucent.

2. Add to the skillet the chopped mussels, the bread crumbs or wheat germ, and all other ingredients using sufficient reserved MARINIÈRE broth, or clam juice, to achieve a moist mixture, blend well. Spoon this mixture into the reserved half shells, patting into smooth mounds. Add additional broth or clam juice as necessary.

3. Apply cookware spray to an ovenproof serving tray or casserole. The stuffed mussels can be frozen at this point, preferably in packages of 12 to 18 mussels to facilitate serving. When ready to serve, preheat oven to 450°F. Brown the frozen mussels on an ovenproof dish for several minutes and serve hot.

BONUS IDEAS: You may wish to enrich the stuffed mussels before browning by topping each mussel with a dot of polyunsaturated margarine; or possibly a touch of sherry wine.

This is an excellent dish for entertaining or for quick treats. Other FARCI variations, based on the above recipe, are MOULES FARCIES AU CURRIE (add 1 teaspoon of curry powder); and MOULES CRÉOLES (add 1 minced clove garlic, 2/3 cup tomato purée, and 1/8 teaspoon thyme or basil).

If clam juice is used instead of MARINIÈRE broth in these recipes, eliminate the salt, or, depending on taste, use it sparingly.

* QUICHE NIÇOISE Tomato Quiche with Olives

PROVENCAL

1 small onion
thinly sliced,
about 1/2 cup •
1 tablespoon
white wine or
dry vermouth •
2 pounds fresh tomatoes,
peeled and seeded,
or canned
Italian style
plum tomatoes •
1 large clove garlic,
mashed •
1/2 teaspoon each,
dried basil, thyme,
and salt •
1/8 teaspoon
ground pepper •
4 egg whites •
3 chopped flat anchovies •
4 tablespoons oil,
preferably olive,
or a combination of
olive and corn oils •
3 tablespoons canned
Italian tomato paste •
2-1/2 tablespoons
chopped parsley •
1 teaspoon paprika •
1/8 teaspoon cayenne •
16 pitted black olives •
1/4 cup grated
Parmesan cheese or
fromage blanc,
singly or combined •
1 9-inch Minceur Pie Crust
(page 170–71) or
frozen pie crust •
Cookware spray •

This is one of my favorite dishes and a welcome change from other kinds of quiche. It's a conversation piece when served as an hors d'oeuvre, and equally successful for luncheon or as part of a dinner buffet. It freezes well, and I've found it a welcome gift when visiting friends. Besides tasting marvelous, it lends itself to creative garnishing.

YIELD: 6 servings

1. Apply cookware spray to a skillet and sauté the onions with the white wine until they are translucent. Add the tomatoes, garlic, basil, thyme, salt, and pepper, and stir well. Cover, and cook for 7 minutes, shuffling the pan occasionally. Uncover and cook over high heat for 3 minutes to reduce. Set aside.

2. Set your oven at 375°F. Beat the egg whites for about 1 minute until foamy. In a bowl, combine all of the remaining ingredients except the pie crust, cheese, olives, and 1 tablespoon of the oil; mix until blended. Pour the mixture into the pie crust and let it settle for 5 minutes; sprinkle with the cheese, and garnish with whole or halved olives in a decorative pattern. Sprinkle the remaining oil over all, and bake for 25 minutes. Serve.

BONUS IDEAS: As garnish, I like to use miniature pear-shaped tomatoes, preferably the delicate tasting, orange-colored ones; I split them in half and make decorative patterns on the quiche, intermingling or alternating them with the black olives.

Many dishes that are frozen for future use are garnished after they are thoroughly thawed and ready to serve. This dish, however, is a convenient exception, since the tomato and olive garnishes freeze as well as the quiche itself. Once thawed and baked as directed, it is ready to serve.

* PIROZHKI Russian Meat Pastries

RUSSIAN

1 thin layer of
dough from Minceur
Pie Crust (page 170–71) ·
1 cup of fish,
beef, or cabbage filling
(see Bonus Ideas) ·
1 egg white ·

This is an authentic Russian delicacy, especially good when the filling is varied with meat, fish, and cabbage. These filled pastries are similar to Chinese WON TON, Italian RAVIOLI, Israeli KREPLACH, Mexican ENCHILADAS, and, of course, our own pot pies.

YIELD: Twenty servings

1. Roll out the MINCEUR pie dough, following instructions on page 170–71, into a thin 1/8-inch layer. Cut the rolled dough into 3- to 4-inch squares or rounds and fill the centers with the filling of your choice (from Bonus Ideas). Moisten the edges of the dough, fold in half, covering the filling, to form semicircles, rectangles, or triangles. Seal the edges with the prongs of a fork, and brush the surfaces and the edges with the egg white that has been whisked for 1 minute until foamy.

2. Preheat your oven to 450°F. and bake the pastries 20 minutes until brown. Serve hot.

BONUS IDEAS: Any reserved ground meat moistened with SAUCE ESPAGNOLE (page 112–13), or any other reserved sauce or gravy, can be used as filling. Add seasonings to taste, and accent with Worcestershire or other gourmet sauces.

The Russians traditionally serve one of 3 main fillings, as follows:

1. MEAT FILLING
YIELD: 1 cup
Combine 1 cup of cooked meat (chopped fine or ground) that you may have reserved from any roasted or stewed dish with 1 teaspoon of minced onion, 2 tablespoons of yoghurt or sour cream, 1 tablespoon tomato paste, and 1 tablespoon of sherry or Madeira. Season to taste.

2. FISH FILLING
YIELD: 3/4 cup
Combine 1/2 cup of cooked white-fleshed fish such as halibut or sole, the whites of 2 hard-boiled eggs, 1 tablespoon of yoghurt or sour cream, and 1/2 teaspoon of fresh lemon juice. Season to taste.

3. CABBAGE FILLING

YIELD: 3/4 cup

Combine 1 cup shredded cabbage (sautéed with dry vermouth AU SEC until soft), 1/2 teaspoon salt, 2 tablespoons of yoghurt or sour cream, 1/2 teaspoon fresh lemon juice, and 1 pinch of ground nutmeg, ginger, or cinnamon. To avoid leakage, brush the sealed edges of the PIROZHKI with egg white, and permit them to set for 5 minutes before baking.

CARCIOFI CON PARMIGIANA
Artichokes with Parmesan Cheese

ITALIAN

6 small artichokes •
1 tablespoon vinegar
or fresh lemon juice •
3 cups
chicken stock or
consommé •
3 tablespoons melted
polyunsaturated
margarine •
1/2 cup freshly grated
Parmesan cheese •
1/8 teaspoon each,
salt and pepper •
1/4 cup good white wine
or dry vermouth •
2 tablespoons fresh
chopped parsley or chives •
1 lemon, juiced •
Cookware spray •

One of my favorite ways of preparing artichokes and a successful appetizer or side dish to any meal.

YIELD: Six servings

1. Prepare the artichokes (page 237) by slicing off the upper thirds, and trimming off the tough leaf tops. Scrape the outer layers of the stems, but do not remove the stems. Cut the artichokes in half lengthwise and soak in 4 quarts of water to which the vinegar or lemon juice has been added to prevent discoloration. After 15 minutes, drain the artichokes and pat dry.

2. Preheat your oven to 400°F. Bring the chicken stock to a boil, add the artichokes, and cook over medium heat for 35 minutes, or until tender. Drain the artichokes and remove the choke and inner sharp leaves. Roll the artichokes first in half of the melted margarine and then in the Parmesan cheese. Place the artichokes in an ovenproof dish or casserole, sprinkle with salt and pepper, and pour the wine over them. Bake in the oven for 7 minutes or until hot, then add the balance of the melted margarine; sprinkle with the chopped parsley or chives and additional lemon juice. Serve hot.

BONUS IDEAS: You can substitute 2 tablespoons of chopped scallions for the parsley or chives. If reheating, add additional white wine and bake in the oven or in a microwave oven for several minutes until hot.

MINESTRONE FREDDO ALLA
MILANESE Milanese Cold Vegetable Soup

ITALIAN

2 cups fresh or
canned vegetable broth ·
2 cups water ·
1 tablespoon
dry vermouth ·
2 carrots, diced ·
2 stalks celery, diced ·
2 sprigs parsley,
chopped ·
3/4 cup rice ·
1 teaspoon coarse salt ·
8 twists of pepper mill ·
1/4 cup grated
Parmesan cheese ·
8 large fresh
basil leaves, julienned,
or 4 tablespoons
pesto (page 126–27) ·
Cookware spray ·

One of the most popular first-course summer dishes in the restaurants of Milan. The Milanese generally prepare MINE-STRONE in the morning, and set it out in individual plates, so that by serving time the soup has settled and cooled to the perfect temperature. Each cook likes to vary the traditional ingredients to include his favorites. My preference in this recipe is to limit the number of vegetables included, using just enough to flavor the cooked rice, and to accent the dish with basil. Try adding one tablespoon of PESTO (GENOESE BASIL SAUCE, page 126–27) to each plate before setting it out to cool.

YIELD: Four servings

1. In a large stock pot, bring the vegetable broth and water to a boil; turn down the heat and let it simmer. Apply cookware spray to a saucepan and sauté the carrots and celery AU SEC with the dry vermouth for 5 minutes. Add the sautéed mixture to the soup and bring it to a boil. Add the rice, parsley, salt, and pepper; stir with a wooden spoon. Cover, and cook over medium heat for 12 minutes, stirring occasionally. When the rice is cooked but still firm, adjust the seasonings to taste.

2. Ladle the soup into each plate, blend in the grated cheese and the strips of fresh basil, or PESTO. Set aside to cool, and serve at room temperature.

BONUS IDEAS: Some favorite ingredients others like to use in preparing MINESTRONE include: 1 small cabbage, shredded; 1 pound of whole peeled potatoes; 1 head of celery, diced; 1 pound of tomatoes, sieved; 2 large leeks, diced; 1 thinly sliced zucchini; 3/4 cup dried kidney or haricot beans, soaked overnight; 1 clove of garlic; and then there are those cooks who prefer to substitute their favorite pasta for the rice.

Whatever the variation, it is a most satisfying dish. MINESTRONE FREDDO ALLA MILANESE should be cooled but not refrigerated. However, if you eliminate the rice or pasta and include all of the above bonus options, you will have MINE-STRONE IN STAGIONE, or MINESTRONE IN SEASON, which will keep for over a week in the refrigerator and improves greatly with reheating.

✱ PHO Many-Flavored Beef Soup

VIETNAMESE

YIELD: Ten servings

8 cups beef stock
or canned broth ·
2 scallions, shredded ·
1 slice fresh ginger,
shredded ·
1 star anise
or to taste ·
2 pounds
vermicelli noodles ·
2 tablespoons
unsweetened
shredded coconut ·
1/2 cup water ·
1/2 pound lean
flank steak, uncooked
and shredded ·
8 scallions,
white part only,
finely chopped ·
5 sprigs fresh mint,
preferably apple mint ·
3 tablespoons
double-strength
fish stock or
1 tablespoon
Chinese Oyster Sauce
(page 58) ·
Lemon juice to taste ·

1. Combine the beef stock with the shredded scallions, ginger, and star anise and simmer covered, until required for serving. Cook the vermicelli in boiling water for 5 minutes, drain, and place in large individual soup bowls. Boil the shredded coconut in the 1/2 cup of water for 10 minutes. Cover the noodles with the uncooked shredded steak, chopped scallion, and mint leaves. In each bowl pour the coconut mixture over the meat and noodle combination.

2. When ready to serve, bring the simmering stock to a boil, and add the concentrated fish stock, which has been reduced to half its original volume, or use the oyster sauce. Remove the boiling stock from the heat and stir well. Pour the hot stock over the meat and noodle combination, add several drops of lemon juice to each bowl, and serve hot.

BONUS IDEAS: Traditionally, a special stock similar to a PE-TITE MARMITE (page 84) is prepared for this soup. Wrap 1 large knucklebone in aluminum foil and roast in an oven set at 500°F. for 15 minutes. Place the bone in a stock pot with 2 pounds of shank or shin of beef, with water to cover, and bring to a boil. Throw off the first water, rinse, and return the bone and meat to the pot with 2-1/2 quarts of cold water. Add the shredded scallion, star anise, slice of ginger, and 2 large onions cut into quarters. Bring to a boil and simmer for 3 hours or longer. Clarify the stock (page 249), dice the cooked meat, and reserve both the meat and the broth. Then proceed with the recipe as directed.

ENRICHED CLAM BROTH may be substituted for the fish stock. Bring 1/2 cup of clam juice to a boil, with 1 chopped stalk of celery and a pinch of cayenne, and cook over high heat until reduced by half. Add 1 tablespoon of minced clams and simmer for 10 minutes.

CALALOO Creole Soup

WEST INDIAN YIELD: Six servings

2 onions, minced ·
1 small pepper, diced ·
1/2 cup diced
Canadian bacon ·
2 tablespoons
broth or dry vermouth ·
2 pounds
fresh spinach or
2 10-ounce packages
frozen spinach, chopped ·
12 mussels or
clams in their shells,
or a combination
of both ·
12 pods okra,
fresh or frozen ·
2 quarts water ·
2 tablespoons
minced fresh chives
or 1 tablespoon dried ·
1 clove garlic, minced ·
1 teaspoon coarse salt ·
1/2 teaspoon each,
ground pepper, cayenne,
thyme, and basil ·
Cookware spray ·

Apply cookware spray to a large saucepan and sauté the onions, pepper, and Canadian bacon in the broth or dry vermouth until the onions are translucent. Add all of the remaining ingredients except the mussels or clams, cover, and bring to a boil. Simmer over low heat for 30 minutes, stirring regularly. Add the seafood and continue to simmer about 1 hour, stirring occasionally. Serve hot.

BONUS IDEAS: Adjust your cooking time according to which shellfish you use, since clams require longer cooking time than mussels before their shells open. Remove and discard any of the shellfish whose shells remain closed. You can enrich the flavor of the soup by combining 1 quart of water with 4 cups of chicken broth or consommé.

If using a slow-cooking crockery pot, combine all of the ingredients, except the shellfish, cover, and cook on low for 5 hours. Add the shellfish, cover, and cook on high for about 30 minutes, until the shells have opened.

The soup may be prepared in a microwave oven by combining all of the ingredients, except the shellfish, in a 5-quart non-metal casserole. Cook, covered, for 15 minutes. Let it stand for 10 minutes, stir well, then rotate the casserole 180°. Add the shellfish and cook, covered, for about 10 minutes, until the shells open. Let it stand 5 minutes before serving.

I find a microwave oven an excellent method for reheating cooked food, particularly soups. When reheating large quantities, cook, covered, for about 3 minutes. An individual bowl of soup may be reheated by cooking, covered, for about 1 minute.

* MIDWESTERN STEAK SOUP

AMERICAN

1 pound
lean ground beef ·
1 tablespoon
dry vermouth ·
4 ounces polyunsaturated
margarine ·
8 ounces potato
or rice flour ·
2 quarts water ·
1 cup each,
diced onions, carrots,
and celery, parboiled ·
2 cups fresh or
frozen vegetables ·
16-ounce can of
Italian style
plum tomatoes ·
2 tablespoons
beef base,
such as B-V or Bovril ·
1 teaspoon
ground black pepper ·
Cookware spray ·

This recipe was given to me by a friend who had obtained it from the chef of a popular restaurant somewhere in the Midwest. Although my friend raved about its flavor, the recipe, at first, seemed rather unappealing, which did not encourage my trying it. One day, however, I did—only to discover a most satisfying dish that was immediately adopted by my family. Although its name is a misnomer since it is not made with steak, it is a hearty soup that freezes well and, therefore, one you will want to consider making in large quantities.

YIELD: Eight servings or more

1. Apply cookware spray to a skillet and sauté the ground beef with the dry vermouth until the beef browns. Remove with a slotted spoon and reserve.

2. Combine all of the other ingredients in a large heavy pot; bring to a boil and add the reserved cooked meat. Lower the heat, and simmer for 45 minutes, or until the vegetables are cooked to taste. Generally it is not necessary to add salt, but you may do so to taste. Serve hot.

BONUS IDEAS: Serve either as an appetizer, for a family luncheon, or as a snack. This soup improves with longer simmering as well as with reheating (after being refrigerated or frozen).

158

TONG KWA JOONG Eight Precious
Melon Soup

CHINESE

1 pound winter melon
or the white part only
of watermelon,
pared and cut into
1-inch cubes ·
6 cups
chicken broth or
consommé ·
4 black mushrooms,
soaked and diced ·
1/2 cup bamboo shoots,
diced or tree-shaped ·
2 teaspoons
light soy sauce ·
1/8 teaspoon
white ground pepper ·
1/4 cup Canadian bacon
or lean prosciutto,
diced ·
2 teaspoons each,
chopped scallions
and chopped parsley ·

This is an easy-to-make relative of WHOLE WINTER MELON SOUP (page 192–93) and can be prepared with a one-pound slice either of winter melon or our own American watermelon.

YIELD: Four servings

Bring the chicken broth to a boil, add the melon, mushrooms, and bamboo shoots and cook over medium heat until the melon turns translucent, about 20 minutes. Add the balance of the ingredients except the scallions and parsley and cook for 5 more minutes. Serve hot, garnished with the chopped scallions and parsley.

BONUS IDEAS: You can add or substitute any of the ingredients called for in WHOLE WINTER MELON SOUP (page 192-93).

I like to add 1/2 cup of diced chicken, with the skin removed, or dried shrimp, which is available in Oriental markets. Soak the shrimp in sherry to cover for at least 20 minutes, or in very warm water for 30 minutes or longer, before adding them to the broth.

I also use 1/3 cup of button or T-shaped sliced mushrooms along with 2 dried, black mushrooms, which are also available in Oriental markets. Dried mushrooms should be soaked in very warm water for at least 20 minutes, and the hard stems should be discarded, before they are added to the broth.

CEVICHE ESTILO ACAPULCO
Marinated Fish Acapulco Style

MEXICAN

2 pounds swordfish,
flounder, or halibut filets ·
5 limes or small lemons,
juiced ·
1/2 cup chopped onion ·
4 chili serranos,
chopped, or
1 teaspoon Tabasco ·
1/2 cup oil ·
1 tablespoon vinegar ·
1/2 teaspoon thyme ·
1 tablespoon
chopped parsley ·
1/2 cup fresh red pepper
or pimiento, chopped ·
Salt and pepper to taste ·

An excellent appetizer that can also double as a first course for a special summer meal. An advantage is that you can blend any combination of firm white-flesh fish and seafood, such as scallops, as you wish.
YIELD: Eight servings

1. Cut the fish into 1/2-inch cubes, place with the lime or lemon juice in an earthenware or glass covered bowl, and refrigerate for 3 hours, occasionally turning the fish cubes with a wooden spoon.

2. Remove from the refrigerator and combine the balance of the ingredients with the marinated fish cubes; blend thoroughly using a wooden spoon. Refrigerate overnight before serving.

BONUS IDEAS: In Mexico, it is considered more authentic not to refrigerate the CEVICHE overnight. After the marinated fish is combined with the other ingredients, the CEVICHE is placed in sherbert glasses or on seashells, then chilled and served—with slices of onion and avocado for garnish.

MARINATED ASPARAGUS

INTERNATIONAL

1 pound fresh
green asparagus ·
1/4 cup oil,
preferably olive ·
1/8 teaspoon each,
salt and pepper ·
1 tablespoon
fresh lemon juice ·
2 tablespoons
tarragon vinegar ·
1/2 onion,
thinly sliced ·
8 to 10 slices
gluten bread ·
1/2 cup Bonus Mayonnaise
(page 124) ·

YIELD: Eight to ten servings

1. Scrape the asparagus with a vegetable peeler and cut off the tough bases of the stalks, so that the asparagus spears are uniform in length. Combine the oil, salt and pepper, lemon juice, and vinegar in a ceramic or glass dish. Layer the asparagus in the marinade. Spread the sliced onions on top, cover and refrigerate to marinate for at least 24 hours. Periodically toss the mixture gently.

2. After 24 hours, taste to see if additional tarragon vinegar is necessary. The asparagus improves in taste the longer it marinates, and can do so up to 3 days. However, after 24 hours, remove and discard 1/2 of the sliced onions.

3. To prepare as an hors d'oeuvre, trim the crusts from the bread and, using a rolling pin, flatten each slice slightly. Coat the slices with mayonnaise and cut each slice in half. Place one drained spear of asparagus lengthwise on each half slice of bread and roll. The mayonnaise and marinade will hold the rolled bread together.

4. Place the hors d'oeuvres on a platter, cover with plastic wrap, and refrigerate until chilled before serving.

BONUS IDEAS: The marinated asparagus can also be served as a salad, without the bread. Serve chilled with BONUS or EGGLESS MAYONNAISE (page 124) to taste.

* SOUPE AUX POIS Canadian Pea Soup

CANADIAN

YIELD: Eight to ten servings

2 cups dried
whole yellow or
split peas ·
2 quarts water ·
1 meaty ham bone
or prosciutto bone ·
1 onion, minced ·
1 carrot, minced ·
1 stalk celery, diced ·
1/2 teaspoon sage
or 1/4 teaspoon dried ·
1 teaspoon
chopped parsley ·

This soup is most easily made by combining all of the ingredients in a pressure cooker and cooking at 15-pound pressure for 40 minutes. If using a slow-cooking crockery pot, combine all the ingredients, cover, and cook on low for about 8 hours. If using the top of the range, you will first have to soak the peas in cold water overnight, then combine all the ingredients and simmer, covered, over low heat for about 3-1/2 hours. In all cases, remove and discard the bone, but remove any meat from the bone and return it to the soup before serving.

BONUS IDEAS: When using a pressure cooker, dried beans should be reconstituted before cooking, to avoid clogging the valve. A convenient substitute for soaking overnight is to cover each 1 cup of dried beans with 3 cups of cold water. Bring to a boil and cook for 4 minutes. Remove from the heat, cover, and let stand for 1 hour.

* ZUPA SZCZAWIOWA Polish Sorrel Soup

POLISH

1 pound each,
sorrel and spinach leaves,
chopped ·
8 cups chicken or
beef broth,
or canned consommé ·
3/4 cup diced onions ·
1 tablespoon white wine
or dry vermouth ·
1 pound peeled and
diced potatoes ·
1 teaspoon fresh chervil
or parsley or
1/2 teaspoon dried ·
1 teaspoon honey ·
Salt and freshly
ground pepper to taste ·
Cookware spray ·

A hearty blend of sorrel and spinach. This recipe has encouraged me to plant a sizable patch of the too-often-ignored sorrel plant in my garden. I find this soup far more memorable than the non-MINCEUR version—without the spinach but with the addition of egg yolks and butter.
YIELD: Eight to ten servings

Place the broth in a large saucepan and bring to a boil. Meanwhile, sauté the onions in the wine until they turn translucent. Combine all of the other ingredients with the onions and stir into the broth. When the broth again reaches the boiling point, reduce the heat, cover, and simmer for about 30 minutes. Serve hot.

BONUS IDEAS: Chervil, if at all available, is an important ingredient. The soup can be prepared ahead of time, and can be frozen; it improves with reheating.

Sorrel is available in jars in many gourmet shops. If necessary, however, the sorrel may be replaced with escarole or watercress, in which case an additional teaspoon of

162

chervil should be added. This soup is best cooked in an enameled pot because of the acid in the sorrel, which contributes to its distinctive taste.

Like most soups, POLISH SORREL SOUP lends itself easily to cooking in a microwave oven. However, because of the relatively short time required for cooking, there is little advantage to be gained by using a pressure cooker. A slow cooking crockery pot is a possibility, although this method cannot be particularly recommended here.

PAO YU TONG Abalone Soup

CHINESE

YIELD: Six servings

1/2 cup fresh, frozen, or canned abalone, diced •
1 tablespoon cornstarch •
4 Chinese mushrooms •
6 cups chicken broth or canned consommé •
2 slices Canadian bacon, diced •
1 tablespoon light soy sauce •
1/4 teaspoon honey •
1/4 teaspoon sesame oil or
1/2 teaspoon corn or peanut oil •
2 slices fresh ginger, chopped •
1/8 teaspoon freshly ground pepper, or to taste •
3 scallions, chopped •

Dissolve the cornstarch in 2 tablespoons of water; set aside. Soak the mushrooms for 30 minutes in warm water, discard the tough stems and cut into thin strips. Bring the broth to a boil, then add all of the remaining ingredients except the reserved cornstarch and the scallions. Reduce the heat and simmer covered for 3 minutes; stir in the dissolved cornstarch until the soup thickens. Adjust the seasonings, and serve hot, sprinkled with the chopped scallions.

BONUS IDEAS: This basic abalone soup can easily be converted into the much-cherished THREE FRESH FISH TREASURES SOUP, or SAAM SIN TONG: After the abalone soup has thickened, add 1 cup diced cooked shrimp and 3/4 cup diced cooked lobster meat; stir these ingredients into the soup; remove from the heat and serve hot with the chopped scallions. You can also substitute 1/2 cup diced chicken breast for the Canadian bacon, and add an optional tablespoon of sherry.

You can also add several water chestnuts, cubed bits of lean prosciutto, and 1/4 pound of mushrooms, sliced into T shapes. A word of caution, however, concerning the reheating of these delicate soups: Always remove the cooked ingredients and reheat the soup separately. When it is sufficiently hot, return the cooked ingredients and heat through for about 1 minute, thus avoiding overcooking.

ESCARGOTS AU CHAMPAGNE
Mushrooms Stuffed with Champagne-Marinated Snails

INTERNATIONAL

18 canned snails, drained •
2 cups champagne or good white wine •
1/2 cup polyunsaturated margarine •
1 teaspoon minced shallots or scallions •
1 garlic clove, minced •
1 tablespoon each, fresh chives, parsley, or thyme, or
1 teaspoon each dried •
Salt and freshly ground pepper to taste •
18 large mushroom caps •
6 10-inch squares of aluminum foil •
Cookware spray •

I was first introduced to this memorable dish in an imaginative restaurant in Columbus, Ohio, and was most pleased when the chef enthusiastically shared his recipe with me. I have converted it to the MINCEUR concept and used it on numerous occasions with notable success.

YIELD: Six servings

1. Place the drained snails in a ceramic, glass, or earthenware bowl; add the champagne, and marinate at least 3 hours, or preferably overnight. Prepare the herb and margarine mixture by thoroughly blending the balance of the ingredients except the mushroom caps and, of course, the aluminum foil squares, which will be used as PAPILLOTES for cooking. Brush the mushroom caps with a damp cloth and stuff with 1 drained snail and enough of the herb and margarine mixture to fill each cap. Reserve the marinade.

2. Preheat your oven to 350°F. Apply cookware spray to the dull side of the aluminum foil squares. Transfer 3 of the stuffed mushroom caps to each square and prepare a triangular pouch by folding over 1 corner of the square to meet its diametrically opposite corner. Fill the pouch with proportionate amounts of the reserved marinade, then seal the foil PAPILLOTE. Place the PAPILLOTES on a rack in the preheated oven and bake for about 15 minutes. Serve hot, placing the sealed PAPILLOTES on individual plates, to be opened by each diner.

BONUS IDEAS: You may prepare ahead and freeze the stuffed mushrooms for future use, but I suggest you store the marinade separately and fill the foil pouches with the thawed stuffed mushrooms and the marinade just before cooking. Any unused portions of the herb and margarine mixture can be frozen as well, and reserved for serving with fish or seafood.

SOUPE AU CHOU Saskatchewan Cabbage Soup

CANADIAN

YIELD: Six servings

2 cups
shredded cabbage ·
2 onions,
peeled and chopped ·
1 teaspoon
coarse salt ·
1/2 teaspoon honey ·
1-1/2 cups
skimmed milk ·
1/2 cup evaporated
skimmed milk ·
1 tablespoon
polyunsaturated margarine ·
1 tablespoon
cornstarch or arrowroot ·
Salt and freshly
ground pepper to taste ·
Cookware spray ·

Before shredding the cabbage, remove all the coarse ribs, then shred and dip in water; drain but do not pat dry. Apply cookware spray to a large saucepan, and cook the onions and the moist cabbage AU SEC for about 15 minutes until tender, shuffling the pot occasionally. Add the salt, honey, and both the skimmed and evaporated milk and cook over low heat for 2 minutes longer, stirring constantly. Blend the cornstarch with the margarine and stir this ROUX into the cabbage mixture and heat through. Season to taste and serve hot with croutons.

BONUS IDEAS: This soup can be prepared in a microwave oven by combining all of the ingredients, except the cornstarch and margarine, and cooking them, covered, for 10 minutes. Blend the cornstarch with the margarine, add this ROUX to the cabbage mixture, and cook 1 minute longer. Let it stand 5 minutes and serve hot.

If using a slow-cooking crockery pot, combine all of the ingredients, except the ROUX, and cook, covered, on high for 30 minutes, until the cabbage is tender. Add the ROUX and cook, covered, 5 minutes longer.

8.
Desserts and Beverages

Many of us consider a meal incomplete without a satisfying dessert, such as pastry, as its finale. Others, particularly Europeans, prefer fresh fruit and a variety of special cheeses at the meal's end, while the Chinese prefer savories to sweets. Many desserts in this chapter are strictly MINCEUR—utilizing no butter, cream, egg yolks, or saturated fat. Others are bonus recipes which, as we have previously indicated, use minimal amounts of egg yolks and, in some cases, sugar.

Since I do not intend to moralize in this book, especially in terms of the use of sugar—about which, however, a substantial number of doctors and food experts have expressed strong views (see Chapter 12)—you will find that where sweeteners are required I have avoided pure cane and beet sugars and artificial sweeteners and have used honey or blended, fruit (fructose) or date sugars, which can be found in health food shops. These natural sweeteners are equal to or have greater sweetening power than other sugars and, in my opinion and that of many experts, are substantially less harmful.

Just as you will learn in Chapter 9 to adapt your own main dish recipes to MINCEUR CUISINE, I am confident that you will be stimulated by the MINCEUR and "bonus" recipes in this chapter to adapt many of your favorite desserts—even breads and pastries—to the new French style of cooking.

167

* CRÈME FRAÎCHE MINCEUR

FRENCH/
INTERNATIONAL

3/4 cup (5.33-ounce can)
evaporated milk ·
1 teaspoon
powdered gelatin ·
2 tablespoons
cold water ·
1 teaspoon honey,
or to taste ·
1/4 teaspoon
flavoring to taste:
vanilla or
almond extract,
or liqueur ·

YIELD: One-and-one-half cups

1. Place the unopened can of milk in a saucepan, with water to cover, and boil over brisk heat for 15 minutes. Remove; use heat-resistant gloves to hold the hot can, and open carefully. Pour the heated milk into a mixing bowl. In a separate bowl, dissolve the gelatin powder in the cold water, and stir into the hot milk.

2. Place the mixture in the freezer for 1/2 hour, or in the refrigerator for several hours, or preferably overnight, so it becomes very cold. Just before serving, remove the milk mixture, immediately transfer to a large mixing bowl, and beat with a balloon whisk for about 5 minutes, until light and fluffy. Add the honey, and flavoring to taste—vanilla, almond, or liqueur.

BONUS IDEAS: This is a versatile CRÈME; it can be served over fruits or as part of many desserts. Although it freezes very well, allow it to thaw completely before serving. If necessary, add additional flavorings, and beat with a balloon whisk again before serving.

* CRÈME MINCEUR Minceur Cream

INTERNATIONAL

4 tablespoons
polyunsaturated margarine ·
2 tablespoons honey ·
2-1/2 tablespoons dry
non-fat milk powder ·
2-1/2 tablespoons
skimmed milk or water ·

A versatile cream that can be used as a dessert filling or topping. It is especially suitable for piping—as a garnish to many dessert dishes. CRÈME MINCEUR can be kept in the refrigerator for several days and may also be frozen for future use.

YIELD: Six to eight tablespoons

Bring the margarine to room temperature, and blend with the honey until thoroughly creamed. Add the milk powder to 1 tablespoon of the skimmed milk and stir until dissolved; then beat the milk mixture and add it gradually into the margarine and honey mixture with a fork or small whisk, slowly beating constantly until all of the milk has been added. Continue beating for a total of 3 minutes, until the combined mixture is light. Serve immediately, or store in the refrigerator or freezer.

BONUS IDEAS: Be sure the margarine is at room temperature before using, but under no circumstances should you heat the margarine, for this will change its flavor.

＊ GRANITA DI FRAGOLE Quick Strawberry Sherbert

ITALIAN **YIELD:** Four servings

2 pints fresh strawberries or 1 package frozen strawberries, thawed ·
1/4 cup maple syrup ·
2 tablespoons date sugar ·
1/2 cup water ·
Juice of 1/2 lemon ·

Purée the strawberries, and set aside. Combine the maple syrup, the date sugar, and the water in a saucepan and boil over medium heat for about 5 minutes, stirring occasionally. Allow to cool, then stir in the strawberry purée and add the lemon juice. Pour the well blended mixture into a freezer tray and freeze, stirring periodically.

BONUS IDEA: In season, raspberries can be used instead of strawberries.

169

* MINCEUR PIE CRUST

AMERICAN

1/2 cup each,
rice flour and
finely milled rye flour ·
1/2 cup dry non-fat
cottage cheese or
part-skim ricotta ·
1/2 cup
polyunsaturated margarine,
at room temperature ·
1/2 teaspoon fine salt ·
Cookware spray ·

A versatile pie crust that can be used as the basic crust for QUICHE NIÇOISE (page 151), for Russian PIROZHKI with a variety of fillings (page 152–153), and for a number of other recipes in this book. I like to double this recipe, reserving the extra dough for future use.
YIELD: One 9-inch crust

1. Sift the combined flour 4 or 5 times or place in an electric blender at medium speed for 2 minutes in order to aerate. Gently transfer the flour to a mixing bowl, gradually adding the balance of the ingredients while, at the same time, mixing constantly with a fork until smooth. Sprinkle in several drops of water if necessary. Continue mixing until the dough becomes a solid mixture, and you are able to gather it into a ball. Place in the refrigerator, covered with wax paper, for 2 hours or, preferably, overnight.

2. When ready to roll the dough, cover your work area with a pastry cloth or wax paper, taping two 1-1/2-foot strips together if necessary. Place the ball of dough on the wax paper and press it into a flattened circle, about 1/2 inch thick. (If you have doubled the recipe, cut the flattened circle in half, reshaping each half.)

3. Place a second layer of wax paper over the flattened circle of dough. (This avoids the necessity of flouring your rolling pin to avoid sticking.) Roll the dough from its center to its outward edges, lifting—not rolling—the roller back to the center each time. Continue until you have rolled the dough into a uniform 1/8-inch thickness, with a circumference about 2 inches larger than the inverted pie pan you are using. If the dough should break, patch it with extra pieces of dough and a little water, simply rolling the patch over the broken area.

4. Carefully peel off the top layer of wax paper. Spray the pie pan with cookware spray and invert the pie crust into the pan. Peel off the remaining layer of wax paper, or the pastry cloth, and ease the pie crust into the pan. For a one-crust pie, trim the overhanging pastry edge but leave at least 1 inch beyond the rim of the pan. Fold the outer edges under the lip of the pan. Flute, fork, or make other decorative edges on the border of the crust, but anchor at least a half dozen points of the edging to the underside of the rim of the pan to prevent shrinkage.

5. Prick the bottom of the pie shell with the prongs of a fork. Sprinkle 2 dozen uncooked beans along the bottom of the shell to prevent puffing during baking. Bake in a pre-heated oven set at 450°F. for about 10 minutes. Allow the pie crust to cool before filling.

BONUS IDEAS: Depending on your intended use for the pie shell, there are several tricks you can employ with the left-over pie dough. You can re-roll it into a thin layer and cut it into 1/2-inch strips with a pastry cutter or knife. Use these strips to crisscross or lattice the top of a filled pie. When joining any tears that might occur, always moisten the ends of the strips and press together.

ZABAGLIONE FREDDO Chilled Italian
Wine Pudding

ITALIAN

1 tablespoon powdered
unflavored gelatin ·
3 tablespoons water ·
2 egg yolks ·
3 tablespoons honey ·
6 tablespoons Marsala
or sherry wine ·
2 egg whites,
beaten until stiff ·
1-1/2 cups of
Crème Fraîche Minceur
(page 168) ·
2 maraschino cherries ·

This is a "bonus" recipe that will prove a delightful and refreshing finale to any meal. In its preparation, a BAIN-MARIE, or double boiler, is required or can be improvised (page 273). ZABAGLIONE is generally served in stemmed glasses or demitasse cups and for a color accent each portion can be topped with a slice of a maraschino cherry.

YIELD: Six servings

1. Sprinkle the gelatin over the water in a heatproof bowl; then place the bowl in a saucepan that has been filled with 2 inches of hot water, and heat slowly over low heat to dissolve the gelatin. Set aside.

2. Combine the egg yolks and honey in a mixing bowl and beat vigorously, preferably with an electric mixer at high speed, until the mixture is lemon-colored and thickened. Gradually add the Marsala wine and continue beating 3 minutes. Place the mixture in another heatproof bowl and place the bowl in the original saucepan with the hot water. Return to a boil and continue beating vigorously for about 10 minutes, until the ZABAGLIONE increases in volume and rises to the edges of the bowl. Fold in the liquefied gelatin with a wooden spoon.

3. Now transfer the mixture to a larger container and set it on a bed of ice. Mix slowly with a wooden spoon to cool. When cool, gently fold in the stiffly beaten egg whites; then fold in the CRÈME FRAÎCHE MINCEUR. Chill for 2 hours before serving and accent each portion with a slice of maraschino cherry or bits of mandarin oranges.

171

RAISIN PIE

SCOTTISH   YIELD: Eight servings

2 cups
seedless raisins·
2-1/2 cups water·
1/2 cup date sugar
or blended sugar·
3 tablespoons
arrowroot or cornstarch·
1/8 teaspoon salt·
1/2 teaspoon
ground cinnamon·
2 tablespoons
fresh lemon juice·
1/2 teaspoon
grated lemon zest,
or 1/4 teaspoon dried·
2 recipes for
Minceur Pie Crust
(page 170–71)·
Cookware spray·

Preheat your oven to 400°F. Wash the raisins and simmer them in 2 cups of the water over low heat for about 15 minutes. Blend the sugar, cinnamon, arrowroot, and salt with the balance of the water. Bring the raisins to a boil and add the sugar mixture, stirring constantly. After 3 minutes, remove the pan from the heat; add the juice and lemon zest. Prepare the pie dough for 2 9-inch round or, preferably, rectangular or square crusts. Roll out the pie crusts to about 1/8-inch thicknesses and apply cookware spray to a baking pan. Place one crust in the pan and pour in the raisin mixture; top with the second pie crust. Using the prongs of a fork, make steam vents in the top crust and bake for 30 minutes. Cut the raisin pie into serving sections and top with MINCEUR CRÈME FRAÎCHE (page 168). The raisin pie may be served either hot or at room temperature.

BONUS IDEAS: I like to sprinkle an additional teaspoon of grated lemon or orange zest over the CRÈME FRAÎCHE, or garnish the pie with slices of stewed pears, before serving.

* MINCEUR TORTONI

AMERICAN   YIELD: Six to eight servings

3/4 cup
Almond Macaroons
(page 178), crushed·
3/4 cup evaporated
skimmed milk·
1/4 cup ground fruit,
blended, or date sugar·
1 teaspoon
vanilla extract·
1 cup
Crème Fraîche Minceur
(page 168)·
Grand Marnier or
Cointreau·

1. Combine the crushed macaroons, the evaporated skimmed milk, and the date sugar; blend very well. Place in the refrigerator for 1 hour until chilled. Prepare the CRÈME FRAÎCHE MINCEUR (page 168), adding the teaspoon of vanilla, and fold into the chilled macaroon mixture.

2. Spoon the combined mixture into paper muffin cups, sprinkle with the Grand Marnier, and decorate with whole or crushed almonds, maraschino cherries or crystallized angelica. Place on a tray in the refrigerator and chill thoroughly before serving.

MACAROON JAM TARTS

AMERICAN

YIELD: Six to eight servings

2 9-inch baked
Minceur Pie Crusts
(page 170–71) ·
1 recipe for
Almond Macaroons
(page 178), uncooked ·
Unsweetened jam ·
Honey ·
Cookware spray ·

1. Preheat the oven to 325°F. With a cookie cutter or knife, cut the baked pie crusts into 3-inch rounds. Place the uncooked .macaroon paste in a pastry bag or tubular cookie decorator (or use a spatula or a spoon) and make a 3/4-inch border around the outer edge of the cookie round. As a variation you can add a diagonal strip of the paste to provide two semicircular pockets to receive the jam after baking.

2. Apply cookware spray to a cookie sheet and bake the unfilled tarts in the oven for about 20 minutes. Remove, and when thoroughly cooled, fill the spaces within the macaroon borders with your favorite unsweetened jam. Brush the raised borders with honey. Serve.

✳ MOUSSE MINCEUR

INTERNATIONAL/
FRENCH

YIELD: Two cups

3/4 cup (5.33-ounce can)
chilled evaporated milk ·
1 teaspoon
powdered gelatin ·
2 tablespoons
cool water ·
1 teaspoon honey ·
1/4 teaspoon
flavoring to taste:
vanilla or
almond extract, or
1/2 teaspoon liqueur,
such as Cointreau ·
Fruits and garnishes
to taste (optional) ·

1. Chill the can of milk in the refrigerator or in the freezer for 1/2 hour until very cold. At the same time, cool the mixing bowl with ice cubes or in the refrigerator. Beat the milk with an electric hand beater for 5 minutes, or with a whisk for 7 minutes, until it thickens. Meanwhile, dissolve the gelatin in cool water, and then heat slightly for 3 minutes until the mixture is clear. Set aside to cool.

2. Add the honey and the cooled gelatin to the thickened milk, and then the flavorings to taste. Refrigerate for about 15 minutes until firm and chilled, then add optional fruits and garnishes before serving.

BONUS IDEAS: Use bits of mandarin orange sections in the body of the mousse, and whole sections as garnishes on top, plus a maraschino cherry if you like.

Other fruits that can be used are bits or slices of banana, peaches, nectarines, and kumquats.

Powdered almonds, or a sprinkling of cinnamon or nutmeg can be added to the top.

Serve in clear sherbert glasses, stemmed glassware, or in individual soufflé or custard cups.

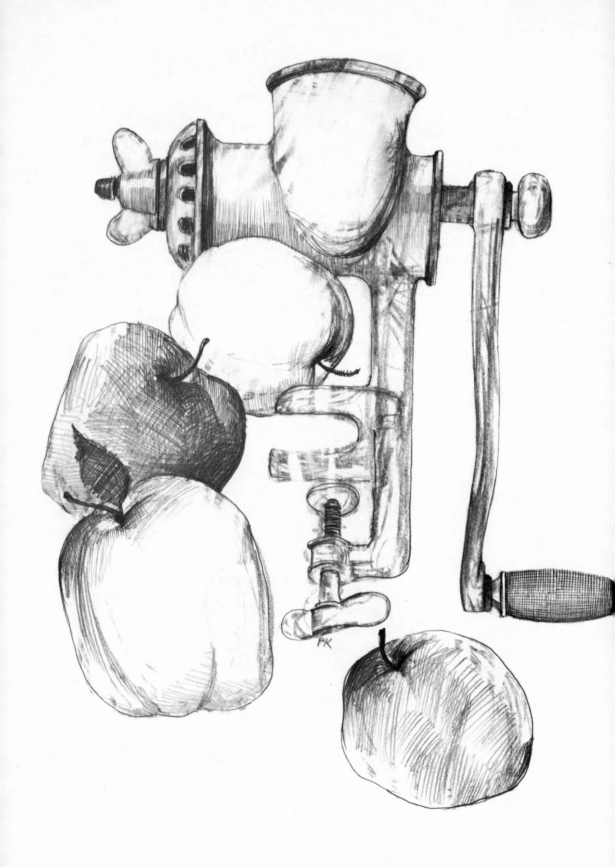

PASTILA Apple Rum Sweets

RUSSIAN

1-3/4 pounds whole apples ·
1 teaspoon fresh lemon juice ·
1 cup date sugar ·
2 egg whites ·
1/2 teaspoon rum or rum flavoring ·
14 to 16 small paper muffin cups ·
Cookware spray ·

For those who occasionally want to satisfy a sweet tooth, this delightful confection can be made and stored for long periods. In Russia, PASTILA is traditionally prepared whenever there is a surplus crop of apples, but make it whenever your favorite apples are available.

YIELD: About fourteen

1. Preheat the oven to 375°F. Place the apples in a covered ovenproof dish, to which cookware spray has been applied, without peeling or coring, and bake for about 1 hour, or until the apples are soft. When cooked, but while they are still warm, press the apples through a sieve. Put the strained pulp in a mixing bowl. Add the lemon juice and strenuously beat the pulp until it is very light, about 20 minutes.

2. Gradually beat in the date sugar, and continue beating for an additional 10 minutes. In a separate bowl, beat the egg whites—which should be at room temperature—until they are stiff; fold them into the apple mixture, adding the rum during the process. Fill the paper cups and bake on a cookie sheet for 15 minutes. Reduce the oven temperature to 275°F. and bake slowly for 6 or more hours until the PASTILA is thoroughly firm. Remove the confections from the paper cups and dip each PASTILA in additional date sugar. Serve or store for future use.

BONUS IDEAS: Once you have tried these delicious sweets, you will probably wish to increase the quantity to more efficiently utilize the 6-hour baking time. Since the PASTILA keep very well, there is little problem in doing this. You can vary the flavor by substituting 1/4 teaspoon of vanilla for the rum, or using your own favorite flavoring.

175

* MERINGUE TORTE Meringue Shells

UKRAINIAN

**6 egg whites,
about 3/4 cup •
1-1/2 teaspoons
fresh lemon juice or
1/2 teaspoon
cream of tartar •
2 cups blended
or date sugar •
1 tablespoon
polyunsaturated
margarine •
Cookware spray •**

A versatile torte, pie, or tart shell that can be filled with any of your favorite fruit fillings, topped with a layer of meringue and decorated with CRÈME FRAÎCHE MINCEUR (page 168) or garnished with any fresh fruit you choose.
YIELD: Two 9-inch shells

1. Preheat the oven to 275°F. Beat the egg whites with the lemon juice or the cream of tartar until they are frothy. Add the fruit sugar gradually, 1 tablespoon at a time, beating constantly for several minutes until the egg whites are very stiff and glossy.

2. Apply cookware spray to a 9-inch pie plate; line with a circle of paper cut from a brown paper bag and rubbed with the margarine. (You can sprinkle flour on the pie plate instead of using the greased paper.) Spoon in the meringue lightly, spreading just to the rim of the pan and leaving a slight mound in the center to minimize cracking. If using the brown paper, raise one edge slightly with a spatula, Bake in the oven for 1 hour, or until delicately browned. Turn off the heat and leave to cool slowly in the oven to prevent shrinkage. It is not unusual if the meringue cracks or falls in the center. If it is sticky, reheat in the oven for 10 minutes. If not used immediately, store in a dry, cool place. When ready to use, fill the shells with fruit and honey, or fruits prepared for fruit pies; decorate with a second layer of meringue, additional fruit, or the MINCEUR CRÈME FRAÎCHE (page 168) to which diced fruits or sliced strawberries have been added.

BONUS IDEAS: Instead of large shells, you can make MERINGUE TARTS, or individual shells. Heap several spoons of the meringue mixture in circles on a baking sheet lined with margarine-brushed brown paper; or sprinkle flour onto the sheet and shake off the excess. Hollow out the centers of each circle with the back of a spoon, and bake as directed above in an oven set at 275°F.

MERINGUE-CAPPED COOKIES can be made by cutting 3-inch circles out of a MINCEUR PIE CRUST (page 170–71), topping each cookie with the meringue. Bake in a preheated oven set at 350°F. for about 12 minutes, or until delicately browned. These are very elegant cookies.

SANGRÍA Spanish Wine Punch

SPANISH

2 bottles full-bodied red wine or dry white wine •
2 lemons juiced, plus 1 lemon thinly sliced •
1 quart sparkling water or club soda •

There are many versions of this refreshing and popular beverage, and you can certainly create one of your own. SANGRÍA can be made with either red or white wine, accented with a number of liqueurs, and garnished with fresh fruit; it can be served fresh and iced or refrigerated overnight before serving. The Spaniards like to serve SANGRÍA both before and during meals.
YIELD: Twenty servings

Combine all ingredients in one large or two small pitchers, and stir well. Chill, or serve with ice cubes. Garnish each glass with a lemon slice and some of the optional garnishes (see Bonus Ideas).

BONUS IDEAS: If using white wine, consider accenting with one of the orange-based liqueurs such as Grand Marnier or Cointreau. Fresh strawberries, grapes, sliced or cubed peaches, or other favorite fruits can be added as garnish.

Other options are blending both red and white wines together, using a rosé wine, champagne, or other sparkling wine; and instead of serving in pitchers you can present SANGRÍA elegantly as a punch with a block of ice, garnished with fruits and long strings of orange peel.

For FIESTA SANGRÍA, add 1 orange, sliced; 1/4 cup of brandy, or to taste; and 1 teaspoon Curaçao to the basic ingredients list. Refrigerate overnight and serve cold.

LASSI Yoghurt and Rose Water Highball

INDIAN

1/4 cup rose water •
2 tablespoons plain yoghurt •
Crushed ice or ice cubes •

An easy-to-prepare and pleasantly refreshing summer drink.
YIELD: Two servings

Half fill each of 2 12-ounce highball glasses with crushed ice or cubes. Into each glass, add half of the rose water and yoghurt and stir briskly until the yoghurt is liquefied. Serve chilled.

BONUS IDEAS: In the Philippines, a similar summer drink is made by substituting mashed avocado pulp for the yoghurt. Coconut milk or skimmed milk can also be substituted for the rose water.

COCONUT MACAROONS

AMERICAN

1 cup unsweetened shredded coconut ·
2-1/2 tablespoons honey ·
1 teaspoon vanilla ·
1/2 teaspoon almond extract ·
2 cups corn flakes or rice crisp cereal ·
1/4 cup evaporated skimmed milk ·
1/8 teaspoon fine salt ·
3 egg whites ·
1 tablespoon polyunsaturated margarine ·
Cookware spray ·

These popular accents to many of your dessert dishes can also be used to create other desserts such as PESCHE RIGALO (page 178–79), MACAROON JAM TARTS (page 173) and MINCEUR TORTONI (page 172).

YIELD: About thirty 1-inch macaroons

1. Preheat the oven to 350°F. Combine the coconut, honey, vanilla, almond extract, and corn flakes, and blend thoroughly. Add the evaporated skimmed milk and mix to form a thick paste.

2. Add the salt to the egg whites and beat until stiff but not dry. Fold the coconut paste into the egg whites. Apply cookware spray to a cookie sheet, rub with margarine, then drop the batter, 1 teaspoon at a time, about 1 inch apart onto the greased surface. Bake at 350°F. for 15 minutes. You should be able to remove the macaroon balls from the sheet with a spatula without breaking. If they are still sticky, cook a few minutes longer or place them on a wet cloth.

BONUS IDEAS: If the macaroons are not sweet enough, they can be rolled in 1/4 cup of date sugar. For ALMOND MACAROONS, you may substitute 1/2 pound of blanched and ground almonds for the shredded coconut, in which case do not include the corn flakes among the ingredients. I find it helpful to use a slotted spoon to fold the coconut or almond paste into the egg whites.

PESCHE RIGALO Macaroon Stuffed Peaches

ITALIAN

1 peach, unpeeled and halved, with the stone removed ·
3 teaspoons orange juice or unsweetened pineapple juice ·
2 macaroons (page 178) or imported from Italy ·
2 whole almonds, shells removed ·
Grand Marnier or Cointreau to taste ·

We all have had dishes that have become especially memorable; and when such a dish turns out to be simple to prepare, it's all the more appealing. I first tasted this dessert in Milan, at a restaurant called Rigalo, which is in the old quarter of the city—the section favored by the artist colony. I had no intention of having a dessert after a superb meal, but when I saw so many other diners savoring this dessert I was compelled to try it. I have been making it—in its MINCEUR version, of course—regularly ever since.

YIELD: One serving

Preheat your oven to 350°F. Place the peach halves on a cookie pan, and pour 1/2 of the orange or pineapple juice into the cavity of each half. Place 1 macaroon into each cavity and pour the balance of the juice over all. Top each

178

moistened macaroon with 1 whole almond and bake for 5 minutes until thoroughly heated. Remove, place on a serving dish and sprinkle to taste with Grand Marnier.

BONUS IDEAS: Stuffed peaches with macaroons is a traditional dish in the Piedmonte areas of Italy. PESCHE ALLA PIEMONTESE, or PIEDMONT STUFFED PEACHES, generally calls for 5 peaches to serve 4; the extra peach is mashed into a purée and blended with 2 egg whites, 4 crumbled macaroons, 1 tablespoon of honey, and 1 tablespoon of polyunsaturated margarine. The mixture is spooned into the cavity of each peach half, and the tops dotted with polyunsaturated margarine. The stuffed peaches are then baked in an oven set at 375°F. for about 1 hour and served either hot or cold.

TISANES Herb Teas

INTERNATIONAL

1 teaspoon of the
herb or herbs of your
choice, singly or
in combination
(see below)·
1 cup of boiling water·

A favorite beverage that can be served either hot or cold, herb teas are especially popular in many foreign countries and are becoming more so in the United States. Served hot, with the possible addition of honey and lemon, they are a pleasant variation from coffee and standard teas. Served cold, you can replace pre-dinner cocktails with your tisanes attractively presented in chilled glasses, as you would PLANTER'S PUNCH (page 183) or MINT JULEP (page 184).

If properly prepared and garnished, these tisanes can become satisfying beverages you will want to serve regularly, encouraged by the fact that they may be good for you as well: as you will note below, many of the herbs recommended for tisanes are diuretics.

YIELD: One cup

1. Use a ceramic, glass, or enameled pot and pour the boiling water over the herb or herbs of your choice. Let steep at least 5 minutes if fresh herbs are used, and at least 10 minutes if you're using dry herbs. However, for maximum enjoyment it is preferable that the herbs be steeped between 15 and 30 minutes. Strain, and serve hot with honey and lemon; or chill and serve cold in chilled glasses garnished with fruit.

2. The flavorsome diuretic herbs you may wish to consider using (singly, or in combinations of as many as five simultaneously) include: borage, bearberry, cherry stems, corn silk, dandelion, heather flowers, horsetail, pine needles and yerba maté.

BONUS IDEAS: Other pleasant tisanes include TISANE OF SPEARMINT, infused as suggested above, and served hot with honey and lemon. A particular favorite of mine is TISANE OF SPEARMINT AND LEMON BALM, which I infuse with 2-inch curls each of lemon and orange zest, steep for 30 minutes, strain and then serve either hot or cold.

KANDEEL Hot, Spiced Wine

BELGIAN **YIELD:** Six servings

1 bottle
dry white wine •
1 cinnamon stick
or 1/2 teaspoon
ground cinnamon •
10 cloves, crushed •
Zest of 1 lemon,
cut into thin strips •
1 cup water •
1/4 cup honey •
4 egg whites •
1 whole egg •

Place the cinnamon, cloves, and strips of lemon zest into a very heavy saucepan with the water; simmer very slowly for about 45 minutes. Strain the mixture and stir in the honey; set aside to cool. Beat the egg and egg whites together for 1 minute until foamy; add to the cooled liquid. Add the wine and stir the mixture thoroughly. Simmer the mixture over very low heat, stirring constantly, until it thickens, but do not let the mixture boil. Serve hot in individual mugs.

BONUS IDEAS: This is a Bonus recipe using 1 egg yolk. For those who prefer not to use the yolk, replace the whole egg with 2 additional egg whites, or with 1/2 teaspoon of arrowroot dissolved in lukewarm water.

HEET BIER Beer Toddy

DUTCH **YIELD:** Six servings

4 cups beer •
2 cloves, ground •
2 cinnamon sticks or
1 teaspoon
ground cinnamon •
1 teaspoon lemon zest,
minced, or
1/2 teaspoon dried
lemon rind •
1/2 cup honey •
2 egg whites •
1 whole egg •
1/2 cup rum •
1/2 teaspoon salt •

Place the beer, cloves, cinnamon, lemon zest and the honey in a saucepan; simmer for about 5 minutes. Beat the egg and egg whites together for several minutes until thickened and gradually add to the beer mixture, stirring constantly until blended. Simmer for a few minutes longer, but do not boil the mixture. Strain the mixture; add the rum and salt to taste. Serve hot.

BONUS IDEAS: An enameled, stainless steel, or ovenproof glass pot is recommended for preparing this toddy. This is a Bonus recipe using 1 egg yolk. For those who prefer not to use the yolk, replace the whole egg with 2 additional egg whites, or with 1/2 teaspoon of arrowroot dissolved in lukewarm water.

SAI GWAR JOONG Melon Delight

CHINESE

1 oval honeydew
or watermelon ·
1 peach, peeled
and cut in wedges ·
1 pear, peeled
and cut in wedges ·
1 tablespoon lemon juice ·
1 16-ounce can
lychee nuts ·
1 16-ounce can
mandarin oranges,
red or green cocktail
cherries,
or kumquats, singly
or in combination,
drained ·
1 jigger of
Grand Marnier or kirsch ·

The Chinese do not generally relish desserts, but this dish, which requires no cooking, is visually delightful and tastes as good as it looks.
YIELD: Eight servings

1. Cut the melon in half horizontally with a series of V cuts on each cut edge to form two shark-toothed melon boats of equal size (see page 48). Remove the pulp with a melon scoop, retaining the juices and discarding the seeds as necessary. Mix the peach and pear wedges in lemon juice to prevent discoloration.

2. Stuff the cavities of the lychee nuts with the cocktail cherries. Mix the melon balls, peaches, and pears with the syrup from the canned lychees; fill the melon boats with this mixture. Accent with the Grand Marnier and chill in the refrigerator for about 1 hour before serving.

BONUS IDEAS: If you are so inclined, you can make an interesting pattern by scoring the skin of the melon boats.

The combination of fruits is fully satisfying, but you may also wish to serve almond or Chinese fortune cookies with each serving.

PLANTER'S PUNCH

AMERICAN

1 tablespoon
date sugar or honey ·
2 jiggers
rum or brandy ·
1 dash
angostura bitters ·
1 dash grenadine ·
Juice of 1/2 lemon ·
Soda water ·
Cracked ice ·
Fruit for garnish ·

A traditional Southern specialty, refreshing on hot summer days, and colorfully presented garnished with fruits and served in frosted glasses. For a non-alcoholic version you can substitute HERB TEAS, or TISANES (page 180), and serve in the same manner.
YIELD: One serving

Dissolve the date sugar in the rum, combine the balance of the ingredients, and shake well. Fill a tall 14-ounce glass with cracked ice, pour in the rum mixture and soda water, to within 1/2 inch of the top of the glass. Churn the ice until the glass begins to frost. Decorate with an orange slice, a fresh strawberry or cherry, and a sprig of fresh mint. Insert a straw and serve.

BONUS IDEAS: The orange slice is generally cut 1 to 2 inches from the zest and anchored to the rim of the glass. You can substitute any of your favorite fresh fruits for garnishing, including sticks of pineapple, maraschinos, fresh cherries, or grapes.

MINT JULEP

AMERICAN

1 5-inch sprig
fresh mint ·
3 teaspoons
ground date sugar ·
1 tablespoon water ·
8 small top leaves
of fresh mint ·
1 large jigger
bourbon whiskey ·
1 dash
angostura bitters
(optional) ·
Cracked ice ·

The authentic mint julep comes from Louisville, Kentucky, and is served during the famous Kentucky Downs races. My first visit to Louisville occurred several weeks before the races were to start, and I was told it was too soon for a mint julep. My second visit occurred a month later—I was then told it was too LATE. The experts explained that a mint julep should be made only when the fresh spring mint, which grows along the banks of the Kentucky river, is at its peak flavor. Naturally I was frustrated until I met the chef of a restaurant who gave me his secret for making perfect mint juleps during any season. When the mint is at its peak in the spring, he harvests the delicate top sprigs and preserves them in a bottle of bourbon, which is an essential ingredient of the drink (see Bonus Ideas below). He is then prepared to serve mint juleps any time of the year, while still subscribing to the mandate that only fresh mint at peak flavor be used.
YIELD: One serving

Wash and drain the sprig of fresh mint and sugar it with 1 teaspoon of the date sugar. Bruise the 8 small leaves gently with a mortar and pestle. Combine in a bar glass or silver julep cup the remaining 2 teaspoons of date sugar and the water; when the date sugar is dissolved, add the bruised mint leaves and cracked ice, filling to the brim of the glass. Pour in the jigger of bourbon and the optional angostura bitters. Churn the ice and bourbon with a barspoon and add more ice as necessary, filling to within 3/4 inch of the top. The glass will begin to frost. Decorate the julep with the sugared sprig of mint, stem down; insert a long straw and serve.

BONUS IDEAS: Some experts insist on prechilling the glasses in the refrigerator for half an hour, but I find that the unchilled glasses frost satisfactorily once the cracked ice has been added. If not serving immediately, the glasses of mint julep can be kept on a tray in the refrigerator until ready to serve. Some hostesses like to serve mint juleps on a deep tray filled with a thick layer of cracked ice.

To prepare ALL SEASON MINT JULEPS, place 15 tablespoons of date sugar—or to taste—in a large measuring cup and add enough bourbon to dissolve the sugar. With a mortar and pestle, gently bruise the top leaves of fresh spring mint at the peak of its flavor. Press the leaves into the bottle of bourbon and pour the dissolved date sugar mixture into the bottle. Cap the bottle, shake the contents gently, and store for future use.

When preparing to serve an ALL SEASON MINT JULEP, shake the bourbon julep mixture well; fill glasses or mint julep cups with cracked ice and pour into each 1 large jigger of the mixture. Churn the ice with a barspoon and add more ice as necessary, filling to within 3/4 inch of the top. Sugar a sprig of fresh mint, whether it is at its peak flavor or not, and decorate the glass with the sprig stem down. Insert a straw and serve.

9.
Additional Hints and Approaches to Creating Your Own Minceur Recipes

As you have progressed through this book preparing a number of the dishes, you have probably compared them with some of your favorite recipes and possibly made some adjustments—as most cooks will do—to suit your own taste and preferences. Indeed, I would be disappointed if you had not, for my intent is to demonstrate how easily and how much fun it is to break our old habits and develop new, delicious, and attractively presented dishes that are both low-calorie and low-cholesterol.

Our objective, remember, is to eliminate or minimize, by using the smallest quantities possible, those ingredients that are neither healthful nor necessary to the inherent flavors and harmony of the basic foods we are preparing. Oil, butter, cream, flour, and sugar in large quantities have been habitually accepted as necessary to the preparation of international dishes—and particularly those of LA GRANDE CUISINE of France.

The excessive use of onions in sautéing is a prime example—a basic step in a large percentage of international recipes, whether the onions are used alone or mixed with other vegetables. The French begin the preparation of COQ AU VIN (chicken braised with wine) by sautéing onions with garlic; Italians begin their famous tomato sauce for pasta by sautéing onions, garlic, and occasionally diced pepper; and the Spanish begin their traditional PAELLA by sautéing onion and garlic. So it goes for many ethnic cuisines. In addition, the traditional process for sautéing has always called for considerable quantities of oil, butter, or animal fat.

186

In the MINCEUR approach, however, sautéing is accomplished AU SEC—in a Teflon skillet, or one sprayed with cookware spray, using a little water, broth, or white wine. Onions and other vegetables sautéed in this manner turn translucent rather than become brown, and otherwise prove more than satisfactory. By eliminating just one tablespoon of oil—whether polyunsaturated or not—you are removing over one hundred calories. Even when small quantities of oil are used, the preferred polyunsaturated oils such as corn or safflower should be selected. This applies to the use of polyunsaturated margarines as well.

Using lean meats with as much excess fat as possible removed also reduces calories and the cholesterol level without affecting the overall taste of the finally prepared dish. Chicken, especially, has pockets of excess fat in the cavity area; this should be discarded. A great deal of fat is also concentrated under the skin, and this fat as well as the skin can be removed in many recipes, depending on one's taste. Remember, every ounce of oil, cream, fat, flour, and sugar (other than natural sugar) you can eliminate from a recipe reduces both the calorie and cholesterol count and increases the healthfulness of your cooking.

The use of certain ingredients is largely a matter of habit. As I have pointed out earlier, I tend to use smaller amounts of salt than is customary in many recipes, and I generally use coarse sea salt, or coarse kosher salt, which is considerably less expensive. I recall that when Craig Claiborne visited my home to prepare his article on my concept of MINCEUR cooking for THE NEW YORK TIMES, he commented to the photographer, Bill Aller, while tasting my Roast Chicken in a Bag, "It's absolutely delicious! And did you notice he only used a half-teaspoon of salt?" Because I had come to take these smaller quantities of salt for granted, his remark took me somewhat by surprise. It does prove the point, however, that the judicious addition of spices and herbs to cooking can minimize the need for larger quantities of salt.

In planning this book, I purposely avoided establishing calorie and cholesterol counts for each recipe, since my aim was not to suggest a diet regimen but rather a cuisine that is both satisfying and healthful. I would prefer that you approach the recipes in this way, realizing that the more you eliminate every unnecessary ounce of oil, butter, cream, wheat flour, and refined sugar, the more healthful your finished dish will be. It is a concept of cooking in which you don't have to do away with anything you absolutely feel you must have, providing you reduce or eliminate those ingredients that are not essential to achieving a satisfying result. Think of it in terms of reserving unnecessary calories from one dish so that you may consume them later, if you so desire, especially when eating out. Needless to say, the overall calorie and cholesterol count will be considerably lower than in the standard cooking and LA GRANDE CUISINE recipes you have been used to.

Indeed, after I began following this eating regimen, my doctor reported that, in a matter of weeks, I had lost nine unneeded pounds, that my cholesterol was reduced by 56 mgs, and my triglyceride level was reduced by 59 mgs—all due to the reduction of starch and sugar basic to my new concept. During this period, I ate in restaurants regularly for business and social reasons, continued to have cocktails before lunch or dinner, and actually drank considerably more wine on a weekly basis than I had previously. More importantly, the MINCEUR dishes my family and I consumed were both delicious and often lavish. So it can be done. I want to emphasize, however, that I never considered myself on a diet, nor consciously gave up eating any particular food, including bread and butter, whenever I felt like it.

Here, perhaps, is the time for me to indicate a few instances of the calories you will NOT be consuming when you utilize the MINCEUR concept and eliminate or minimize the specific high-fat, high-calorie ingredients we have found are no longer necessary.

Food:	Calories:
Butter, 1 ounce	200
Cream, whipped, 1 tablespoon	60
Flour, wheat, 8 ounces	400
Ham, fatty, 4 ounces	440
Oil, salad, 1 tablespoon	125
Pork, salted, 4 ounces	300
Lard, 1/2 cup	990
Milk, whole, 8 ounces	165
Milk, condensed, sweetened, 4 ounces	360
Sugar, granulated, 4 ounces	440

Since this book is intended neither as a fad diet nor a medical treatise, perhaps it is sufficient to point out the following, additional benefits of the MINCEUR concept. None of the above foods are recommended by physicians for patients with elevated blood triglycerides and high cholesterol counts.

Triglycerides can be defined as blood lipids, which are fat-like materials. Elevated blood triglycerides can be generally controlled by reducing one's intake of carbohydrates, which are the starches and sugars in food. It is generally agreed, therefore, that the intake of sugar can and should be drastically reduced. (Since alcohol can also be a major factor in raising triglycerides, physicians are inclined to discourage patients who have elevated triglycerides from drinking too liberally.)

The level of one's cholesterol intake is equally important; an excess over the amount that the human body itself produces is considered dangerous in that it may contribute to coronary artery disorders in some people. Polyunsaturated fats, however, are believed by most authorities to help in lowering cholesterol in the body, so that using polyunsaturated fats and oils may contribute to preventing coronary arteriosclerosis.

It is easier to see the potential benefits if we calculate the specific calories we can eliminate by doing away with those ingredients that are not essential to our MINCEUR concept of cooking.

As an example, a standard recipe for a cake, exclusive of flavoring or icing, would call for one cup of butter (1,520 calories), one cup of sugar (800 calories), four whole eggs (300 calories), and one cup of all-purpose flour (400 calories). As you can see, the total for these basic ingredients alone is over 3,000 calories, not to mention the high cholesterol count involved. One could do far better to enjoy several four-course MINCEUR gourmet meals with wine on a weekend, consuming fewer calories, while simultaneously reducing one's cholesterol intake.

With these facts in mind, let's begin to create our own MINCEUR dishes, using as a basis some traditional favorite recipes or international classics that we had employed before our new awareness of the advantages of MINCEUR CUISINE and LA NOUVELLE CUISINE. First, out of deference to France, the country that originated these new concepts, let's begin with a traditional recipe for COQ AU VIN.

CONVERTING TRADITIONAL RECIPES: COQ AU VIN

Here is an old French recipe quoted in LAROUSSE GAS-TRONOMIQUE, an invaluable guide to any cook interested in French cuisine:

> Cut up a young chicken into six pieces. Heat in 3 tablespoons (45 grams) of butter in an earthenware pot, 3 ounces (90 grams) of lean breast of pork, cut into dice, and some little onions. When these are browned, put in the pieces of chicken, a garlic clove chopped fine, a BOUQUET GARNI, MORELS or other mushrooms. Sauté till golden on a lively heat, with the lid on; take off the lid and skim off the fat. Pour over a little good brandy, set light to it, and then pour on a pint (demi-litre) of old Auvergne wine. After cooking on a good fire for 15 to 20 minutes take out the chicken, and pour over it the sauce, thickened with the blood of the chicken mixed with the pounded liver and some brandy. Do not cook the sauce after this liaison, because the sauce will curdle. Lacking the blood, the sauce may be thickened with kneaded butter.

Studying this recipe, let's note whether any of its ingredients can be eliminated or reduced, and whether its methods of preparation can be adapted to our new concept of cuisine. First, I am certain that most readers will react negatively to the idea of thickening the sauce with the blood of the chicken. This happens to be an accepted practice in France, but one which we will not utilize. We will, however, need a thickening agent and can initially consider arrowroot, cornstarch, tomato paste, or another vegetable purée, until we do further research. Secondly, we see that the recipe calls for butter and a lean breast of pork, which, of course, will be high in fat. Let's make a note to eliminate the butter and pork and possibly to remove the skin from the chicken, where much of its fat is concentrated. In any case, as in all chicken dishes, we will remove and discard the excess fat found in the tail of the cavity and other parts of chicken.

Furthering our research, let's check another excellent traditional source: THE ESCOFFIER COOK BOOK. Here we find that the recipe for POULET DE GRAINS À LA BERGÈRE, Bergère Spring Chicken, calls for thickening a wine sauce with "a piece of MANIÉ butter, the size of a hazelnut, or a little arrowroot, flour, etc." Now we know we can use arrowroot for our new MINCEUR recipe.

Checking a well-known American stand-by, THE JOY OF COOKING, we find in a recipe for COQ AU VIN that our sauce of red wine will turn a rich, medium-brown if we add caramel coloring. In America, this is how the effect of cooked animal blood is often imitated by those who prefer to do so, especially restaurant chefs. For our purposes, however, we will use neither the blood nor the caramel coloring. (If we don't believe, incidentally, that a medium-brown sauce will be satisfying enough, we can do without the brown sauce altogether: white wine instead of red is equally permissible in preparing this dish. In fact, the dish takes its name from the type of wine used, as in COQ AU CHAMBERTIN, COQ AU AUVERGNE, or COQ AU RIESLING, and so on.) But the JOY OF COOKING recipe calls for certain ingredients we will want to consider:

> 3/4 cup mild onions, or 1/2 cup pearl onions
> 1 carrot, sliced
> 3 shallots, minced
> 2 tablespoons flour (which we will eliminate)
> 2 tablespoons minced parsley
> 1/2 bay leaf
> 1/2 teaspoon thyme
> 1 teaspoon salt
> 1/8 teaspoon freshly ground pepper
> 1 tablespoon brandy (optional)

The recipe calls for stirring in 1-1/2 cups of red wine or sherry. The chicken, vegetables, herbs, and spices are to be simmered in the wine for one hour; and 1/2 pound of sliced mushrooms are to be added during the last five minutes of cooking.

Clearly the preceding information helps determine for our new recipe the BOUQUET GARNI (the herbs and aromatic vegetables) we will use, as well as the amount and kind of wine, and the cooking time. Depending on taste or preferences, we can decide to use, say, the red wine, and to include onion, carrot, parsley, bay leaf and thyme in our BOUQUET GARNI (which I prefer to tie in cheesecloth). But let's delve on.

Researching further, we find that THE ART OF FRENCH COOKING by Fernande Garvin has a recipe calling for 1/2 cup each of red wine and chicken broth, and that THE NEW YORK TIMES COOKBOOK by Craig Claiborne has a recipe calling for one cup red wine and 1/4 cup of cognac, and includes one slice raw ham, chopped. We see that our cooking liquid can include red wine, cognac, and chicken broth. The ham seems an interesting touch, and we can make a note to consider adding one slice of Canadian bacon or a smoked pork chop, diced, to our new recipe.

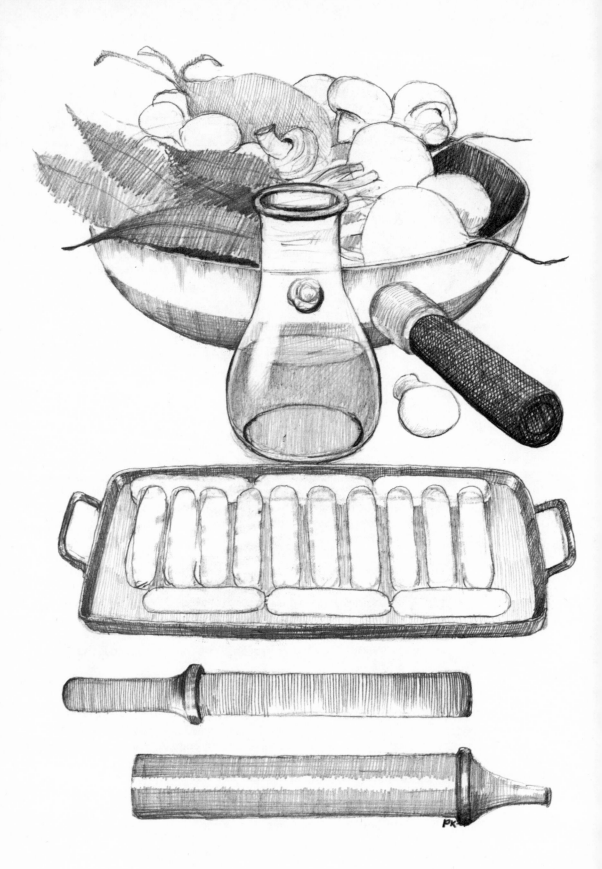

Referring now to FRENCH COOKING FOR PLEASURE by Mary Reynolds, we see that in her COQ AU VIN, she suggests the interesting idea of removing the backbone and leg shanks from the chicken and simmering them with the giblets, onions, and seasoning in just enough water to cover, to make a broth. Let's make a note to consider this for the preparation of our new recipe.

Our new MINCEUR recipe is taking shape, but let's research one more source: MASTERING THE ART OF FRENCH COOKING by Simone Beck, Louisette Bertholle, and Julia Child. The recipe includes the following suggestions: 1/4 cup cognac plus 3 cups red wine; 1/2 tablespoon tomato paste; 12 to 24 brown-braised onions; and 1/2 pound sautéed mushrooms. In addition, the recipe suggests cooking in a heavy, fireproof casserole or electric skillet, and adds that the sauce, when done, should be thick enough to coat a spoon lightly.

Now we have sufficient input to complete our new recipe for COQ AU VIN À LA MINCEUR. Before you turn the page to find my final version of this recipe, may I suggest that for the fun of it, you take the time to write out your own, using your own judgment of the various ingredients, their quantities, and the cooking time and process you would employ. Remember, there is no right or wrong in creating a new recipe like this; it is determined simply by personal taste, experience, and judgment. Now, compare your version with the one on the following page and make whatever adjustments you believe would improve it to meet your own needs. That's all there is to it; it couldn't be simpler.

∗ COQ AU VIN Chicken Braised with Wine

FRENCH

1 3-pound chicken, quartered or cut into serving pieces; chicken liver (optional) ·
3 small onions, peeled and diced ·
1 clove garlic, minced ·
1/4 pound Canadian bacon, or smoked pork chop, diced thickly ·
1 tablespoon each, water and dry vermouth ·
1/4 teaspoon coarse salt ·
5 twists of pepper mill ·
2 tablespoons cognac ·
2 cups wine, preferably red ·

Bouquet Garni, tied in cheesecloth:
1 celery stalk with leaves ·
1 carrot, cut into long strips ·
4 sprigs parsley ·
1 leek, or 3 scallions, white part only, cut into long strips ·
1/2 bay leaf ·
1/4 teaspoon each, thyme and basil ·
1 tablespoon fresh chervil or marjoram, or 1/2 teaspoon dried ·
8 green peppercorns, crushed ·

24 pearl onions ·
1/2 pound mushrooms ·
1/2 tablespoon tomato paste, canned ·
1 to 2 teaspoons arrowroot or cornstarch ·
Cookware spray ·

This traditional French dish can be prepared with any good red wine—a young, hearty Burgundy, a Beaujolais or Chianti—or with a fine white wine. In our home, we prepare the chicken with red wine for family meals, but when serving guests my wife prefers to use white wine, since she finds that the rich, almost mahogany color of chicken braised in the red wine is not always of general appeal. However, since I like the rich brown color and taste of the red wine sauce, I am suggesting the use of red wine in this recipe.

YIELD: Four to six servings

1. Quarter the chicken or disjoint into serving pieces; remove excess fat and discard. Place the chicken back, neck, wingtips, and optional chicken liver in a saucepan with just enough water to cover. Add 1 of the small onions, season to taste, and simmer 15 minutes over medium heat. If used, remove the chicken liver and reserve, continuing to simmer the broth for 15 minutes longer.

2. Apply cookware spray to a 10-inch fireproof earthenware or metal casserole with cover, or to an electric skillet. Cover and sauté the two small onions, garlic, and the Canadian bacon, adding up to 1 tablespoon each of water and dry vermouth as needed, until the onions are translucent.

3. Dip the chicken parts in cold water quickly, drain but do not pat dry. Place the chicken parts in the casserole, increase the heat, and brown both sides of the chicken, adding some of the chicken broth from the saucepan if necessary. Once browned, sprinkle with the salt and pepper. Cover the casserole, lower the heat to medium, and cook for approximately 5 minutes; then turn the chicken over and continue cooking, covered, 5 minutes longer. Uncover, add the cognac and ignite; or heat the cognac in a separate pan, ignite and pour over the chicken parts, shuffling the pot until the flames are spent.

4. Add the wine, the BOUQUET GARNI, and enough of the strained broth from the saucepan to completely cover the chicken. Cover and simmer for 30 minutes, or until the chicken is fork-tender. Remove the chicken parts to a platter and place in a warm oven, or wrap them in aluminum foil and set aside.

5. While the chicken has been cooking, in a separate skillet sprayed with cookware spray, sauté the pearl onions and the mushrooms, using as much of the chicken sauce as necessary; set aside.

194

6. Skim off fat from the sauce in the casserole, and bring it to a boil. Continue cooking until it has reduced to approximately one-third. Correct the seasonings to taste.

7. Blend the tomato paste and, if used, the mashed chicken liver with the arrowroot in as little of the cooking liquid as is necessary to form a paste. Beat the paste into the hot cooking liquid with a balloon wire whisk until the sauce is thickened.

8. Arrange the chicken parts in the casserole surrounded by the glazed onions and mushrooms, and cover with the sauce. Simmer several minutes until the contents are heated through, and serve in the casserole, or transfer to a warm platter. Garnish with some of the mushrooms, onions, and several sprigs of parsley.

BONUS IDEAS: You may wish to add 1 dozen stuffed olives, cut in half. Sliced carrots can also be added during the cooking process.

Boiled potatoes are a traditional accompaniment to this dish, but I personally prefer ROAST POTATOES A LA CABAÑA (page 111) or CAULIFLOWER PURÉE (page 137).

Here, an ideal dessert would be ORANGES GRAND MARNIER (page 22).

CONVERTING TRADITIONAL RECIPES: OSSO BUCO

Traditional Italian recipes can easily be re-created to yield personalized, yet still authentically Italian, MINCEUR dishes. Many classics of Italian cuisine have, of course, become international favorites; and the more popular a dish becomes, the more variation you will find in the way it is prepared, as each country or region lends its distinct touch to the original recipe. OSSO BUCO is one such dish—an Italian stand-by, now popular in many countries, and consequently subject to considerable variation in its creation.

I would like at this point to clarify the many confusing spellings of OSSO BUCO, which literally means "bone with a hole." The correct usage for both singular and plural forms is OSSO BUCO; OSSO is the bone, and BUCO is the hole. Since the cut of meat has a bone with only one hole, BUCO should never be pluralized into BUCHI, which would refer to a bone with more than one hole.

Before creating our MINCEUR OSSO BUCO, let's investigate and compare some of the different methods that have been used, and let's see what we can cull—and discard—for our MINCEUR recipe.

In his famous LA SCIENZA IN CUCINA E L'ARTE DI MANGIAR BENE (SCIENCE IN THE KITCHEN AND THE ART OF EATING WELL), written at the turn of the century, Pellegrino Artusi, one of the accepted authorities on Italian cuisine, comments on OSSO BUCO in his inimitable, chatty manner: "This is a dish that should be left to the Milanese to prepare for it is a specialty of the region of Lombardy. Therefore, in order to avoid possible ridicule, I shall only describe it briefly."

Artusi was famous for many contributions to Italian cuisine, but exactness in specifying measurements and the precise steps of preparation were never considered his forte. Here is his description, followed by his cooking instructions:

> The OSSO BUCO, or shank, is a piece of muscular bone, which is hollow, found at the end of the leg or the shoulder of milk-fed veal. When stewed, it is delicate and delicious. . . . Place as many veal shanks as there are people to eat them, into a pan over some raw, chopped bacon, chopped onion, celery, carrot and a piece of butter; season with salt and pepper. When the meat has absorbed the flavor of the other condiments, add another piece of butter blended with flour in order to color and thicken the

sauce. Cook until the meat is done with water, tomato pulp and juice or tomato paste. Sieve the sauce, skim off the fat and place the pan back on the fire. Flavor it with the zest of lemon cut into small pieces. Add a pinch of chopped parsley before removing the meat from the fire.

We have no exact measurements or instructions. But what have we learned thus far for our purpose of creating a MINCEUR recipe? First of all, we have learned that OSSO BUCO is a hollow bone surrounded by meat. We know, too, that aromatic vegetables are required in the initial braising (or stewing) of the meat. But we also see that the raw bacon and butter will have to be eliminated or minimized in our MINCEUR recipe. The sauce, in addition, will require a thickener, so a replacement for the additional butter blended with flour will have to be determined. And, of course, we need to know specific measurements of ingredients, cooking time, and whether or not the pan will be covered during the cooking process.

As we have done previously, let's proceed to evaluate additional ideas on this dish. First, we'll explore the thinking of the great Italian chef, Luigi Carnacina, a disciple of Escoffier. In his cookbook, GREAT ITALIAN COOKING, he has a recipe entitled OSSOBUCO CON GREMOLATA ALLA MILANESE (Veal Shanks with Gremolata Milanese Style). GREMOLATA is similar to the French MIREPOIX, a blend of diced aromatic vegetables used as a base for cooking meats, poultry, and shellfish. The Italian GREMOLATA, however, includes a mixture of seasonings, particularly the zest of the lemon (the rind without any of the bitter white part). For the GREMOLATA, Carnacina suggests: "a chopped mixture of 1 onion, 1 carrot, 1 stalk celery, 1 clove garlic, 3 sprigs marjoram (or 1 teaspoon dried), 1 small piece lemon rind (no white part)."

This famous chef begins with 6 veal shin bones, 4 inches long and well covered with meat. His preparation calls for dusting the meat with flour and browning it in butter, adding the GREMOLATA and 1/2 cup of dry white wine, then stirring and cooking until the wine evaporates. (Interestingly, he suggests that the pieces of meat be cooked standing upright so that the marrow will not fall out during the cooking process.) He then adds 4 peeled and seeded tomatoes and 1-1/2 cups of brown veal stock, brings the mixture to a boil, reduces the heat, covers the pot, and simmers the contents for about 1 hour. Ten minutes before the meat is fork-tender, the cover is removed, and the heat is increased in order to reduce the sauce slightly. Finally, 3 minutes before removing the pot from the heat, an additional crushed clove of garlic and 1 teaspoon each of grated lemon and orange zests are added. The dish is traditionally served with RISOTTO.

197

As I'm sure you've already noted, neither the wheat flour nor the butter is necessary to brown the meat. We know that we dip the meat quickly in cold water and achieve the same browning effect without using fats or oil. We can also make a note to serve the veal on a bed of puréed cauliflower instead of RISOTTO, if we wish.

Vernon Jarratt in his book, EAT ITALIAN ONCE A WEEK, gives us some further insights. He suggests that the butcher saw across the shank (or shin) of veal where it is 3 to 4 inches in diameter and that each piece be at least 1-1/2 inches long. This gives us important information concerning the ordering of OSSO BUCO. Depending on the number of pieces we will want for this dish, to obtain sufficiently large pieces, the butcher may have to cut from more than 1 shank. Because of this, it is wise to give your butcher advance notice so that he can reserve the number of shanks you will require. Also, I would like to caution you that the butcher may try to sell you the very end piece of the shank, which is mostly bone and has very little meat. If he insists, count this part as an extra piece when calculating how many servings you need.

Jarratt further recommends cleaning the surfaces of the OSSO BUCO with a cloth to remove any bone splinters. Actually, a good butcher should do this for you with his "scraper," or with a cloth.

Let's investigate just two more variations of this dish before we get to our MINCEUR recipe. The Arnoldo Mondadori Editore edition of FEAST OF ITALY has a recipe for OSSO BUCO CON FUNGHI (Veal Shanks with Mushrooms), which calls for a GREMOLATA using 1 celeriac, finely chopped, instead of celery. A good idea, but celeriac—when available—comes in various sizes, and I suspect the recipe intended merely 1 slice of celeriac, finely chopped. If celeriac is not available, the celery stalk or a slice of the base of a head of celery will do. This recipe also introduces 1 tablespoon of rosemary and uses clear stock in addition to white wine. In ITALIAN FAMILY COOKING, Edward Giobbi suggests a tablespoon of basil for seasoning.

I am now satisfied that we have sufficient information with which to create our personalized MINCEUR recipe for OSSO BUCO ALLA MILANESE. Take a few minutes to review your notes from our recipe survey for this dish; decide on the ingredients and their measurements, the cooking time and procedures, and any other considerations, including garnishing and serving suggestions, for your own interpretation of this dish. Then, compare your MINCEUR recipe with the one I suggest opposite.

Remember, there are no absolutes; creating a recipe is a matter of judgment, experience, and personal preference.

* OSSO BUCO ALLA MILANESE Braised
Shanks of Veal with Marrow

ITALIAN

**6 pieces of milk-fed veal
shank or shin,
each 3 to 4 inches in
diameter and
1-1/2 to 2 inches long,
with marrow in bone ·
1 clove garlic, minced ·
1 teaspoon coarse salt
and 6 twists
of pepper mill ·**

**Gremolata, consisting of
a diced mixture of:
1 onion ·
1 carrot ·
1 slice of celeriac,
base of head of celery,
or 1 celery stalk ·
3 sprigs of
fresh marjoram,
basil, or thyme,
or 1/2 teaspoon dried ·
1/2 teaspoon rosemary ·**

**1/2 cup white wine,
or dry vermouth ·
4 ripe tomatoes, peeled,
seeded, drained,
and chopped;
or 2 cups canned
Italian style tomatoes,
strained ·
1 cup beef or
chicken stock,
or canned consommé ·
1 teaspoon
arrowroot or cornstarch ·
1 tablespoon tomato paste ·
1 clove pressed garlic ·
1 teaspoon
lemon zest, grated ·
1 teaspoon
orange zest, grated ·
Cookware spray ·**

Although this dish is one of the crowning achievements of Milanese cookery, I certainly disagree with the famous Italian chef, Pellegrino Artusi, who claims that its preparation should be left to the Lombardians! It is a delicate and relatively simple dish to make, and also has the additional taste sensation of the distinctive bone marrow, which is the culmination of the harmonious blends of the basic ingredients.
YIELD: Six servings

1. Trim the meat of any excess fat and rub the pieces with a damp cloth to remove any splinters of bone. Apply cookware spray to a heavy pan. Dip the meat briefly in cold water, drain, but do not pat dry. Rub in salt and pepper, and brown the meat over high heat, with the minced garlic, being careful that the marrow does not fall out of the bone.

2. Add the GREMOLATA mixture, which may be wrapped in cheesecloth, and stir for 3 minutes. Add the wine, and continue cooking until it has almost evaporated. Adjust the meat so that the pieces are upright to prevent the marrow from falling out; add the strained tomatoes and the stock, and bring to a boil.

3. Cover the pot, reduce the heat, and simmer for about 45 minutes, or until the meat is not quite fork-tender. (At this point, begin preparing RISOTTO or whatever accompaniment you elect to serve as a bed for the cooked OSSO BUCO.) Uncover, and increase the heat to slightly reduce the sauce. Dissolve the arrowroot in 2 tablespoons of sauce, blend in the tomato paste, and stir the mixture into the sauce to thicken it. Cook over high heat 7 minutes longer. Add the juice of the additional garlic, the zests of lemon and orange, and a pinch of parsley before serving.

BONUS IDEAS: RISOTTO ALLA MILANESE is the traditional accompaniment to this dish. Our MINCEUR recipe for the RISOTTO follows, on page 200.

Unless you are adding mushrooms to the RISOTTO, which I recommend, you can add 1/2 pound of button mushrooms with sprigs of parsley to the OSSO BUCO as a garnish.

Other accompaniments are mashed potatoes or CAULIFLOWER PURÉE (page 137). When I use the cauliflower, I purée half of a large head, and reserve the florets from the other half, also cooked AU SEC, for garnishing the platter of OSSO BUCO. Glaze the cauliflower florets, pearl onions, and additional button mushrooms by sautéing them in several tablespoons of the OSSO BUCO sauce.

* RISOTTO ALLA MILANESE Risotto
Milanese Style

ITALIAN

2 cups unwashed
short grain rice •
5 cups of chicken bouillon
or canned consommé •
1/2 cup dry white wine,
dry vermouth, or Marsala •
1 tablespoon
water or
dry vermouth •
1 small onion, chopped •
2 ounces diced
raw beef marrow, or
2 tablespoons margarine •
1/2 teaspoon saffron
or tumeric •
1 teaspoon coarse salt •
5 twists of pepper mill •
1 tablespoon margarine
(optional) •
2/3 cup Parmesan cheese
(optional) •
Cookware spray •

As I have mentioned elsewhere, the Milanese love their RISOTTO, in many cases, more than they do pasta; it is not unusual for them to have rice as a first course practically every day. This version of the dish is traditionally served as an accompaniment to OSSO BUCO. Once you have mastered the basic RISOTTO, you can enhance it by adding chicken livers, seafood, cognac, or other ingredients for exciting new taste experiences.

YIELD: Six to eight servings

1. Place the bouillon in a saucepan, bring it to a boil, and let it simmer until ready for use. Apply cookware spray to large, heavy saucepan and sauté AU SEC the onions with up to 1 tablespoon of water, or dry vermouth, until they are translucent. Add the raw beef marrow, or the margarine, stirring until it melts.

2. Add the wine and cook over high heat until it is almost evaporated; add the rice, the salt, and pepper, and stir constantly for about 3 minutes, until the grains of rice are coated and have become transparent. Mix the saffron with 2 tablespoons of bouillon, or water, and stir into the rice, with 3 cups of the boiling bouillon.

3. Bring this mixture to a boil; stir well while the rice absorbs the liquid. Cover; lower heat to medium, and continue cooking for about 20 minutes, adding bouillon and stirring constantly, as the liquid is absorbed. It is important to add the additional bouillon gradually and in small quantities. If you want to add mushrooms or other ingredients, it is best to do this after 15 minutes of cooking. When the RISOTTO is cooked AL DENTE, add the optional margarine and Parmesan cheese; remove from the heat to set before serving. (Parmesan cheese is optional only when the RISOTTO is used as an accompaniment to OSSO BUCO; it is at other times an essential ingredient to RISOTTO, both in cooking and as a garnish to each serving.)

BONUS IDEAS: The Italians generally don't use saffron in their RISOTTO dishes, except in the case of RISOTTO ALLA MILANESE. The basic recipe can be varied with other ingredients such as mussels, clams, shrimp, and seafood. If any of these are used, saffron is not; instead incorporate the juices from the seafood, including the broth made with the shrimp skins, combining the juices or broth with the chicken stock or consommé.

Generally a grated carrot along with a stalk of diced celery are sautéed with the onions for added flavor and sweetness.

Try RISOTTO VALDOSTANO, which incorporates a cup of sliced pepperoni; RISOTTO AL SALAME, which incorporates 1/4 cup of dried mushrooms and 1 cup of fresh mushrooms, sliced, and is garnished along the border of the dish with 1 dozen thin slices of Italian salami; RISOTTO CON I CARCIOFI, which incorporates 1/2 cup of white wine and 7 ounces of frozen artichoke hearts; and finally RISOTTO CON LE CASTAGNE, which incorporates 1 cup of dried chestnuts soaked overnight in water, a little salt, and 1 bay leaf. (Reserve some of the larger chestnuts, grind the others, and cook in the RISOTTO, adding 1 cup of skim yoghurt or buttermilk before the rice. For garnish, prepare a mixture of chopped sausage and glaze the chestnuts in a skillet with the sausage and 1 tablespoon of white wine or Marsala. Cover and steam the chestnuts until they are golden and fork-tender. Use them to garnish the RISOTTO dish.)

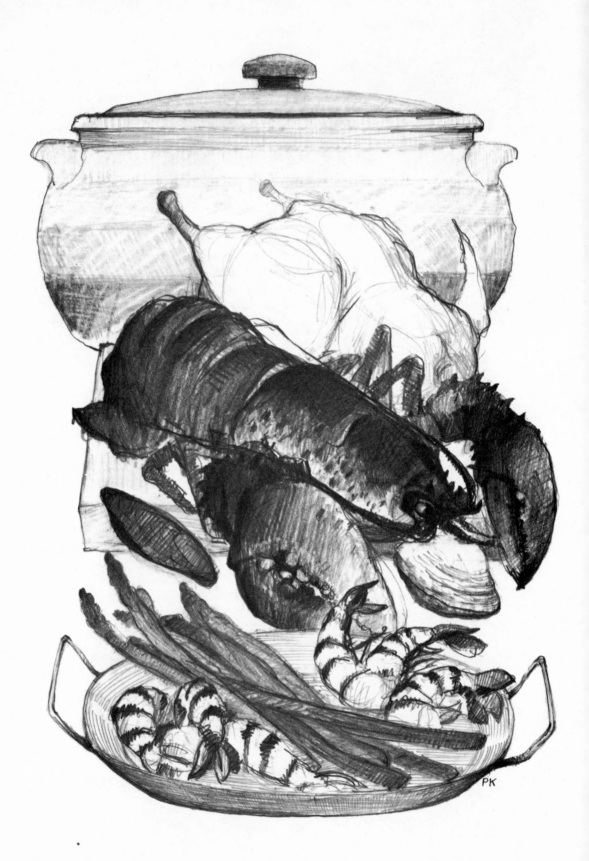

CONVERTING TRADITIONAL RECIPES: PAELLA

Now that we have proven to ourselves that we can convert traditional French and Italian dishes to our MINCEUR concept, let's consider Spanish cuisine and let's focus on PAELLA, Spain's most famous dish, and one that has been adopted internationally—a distinctive blend of chicken, seafood, vegetables, and saffron rice. The dish derives its name from the specially shaped pan in which it is usually cooked.

Most of us are already familiar with some version of PAELLA; but here again, I recommend making notes as we proceed. First, we must know that the PAELLA pan is important to the cooking process. Because it is broad and shallow, the liquid can evaporate easily, leaving the rice uniformly dry. If an authentic pan is not available, we will have to consider a relatively shallow, heatproof pan that is approximately 14 to 18 inches in diameter, depending on the volume of ingredients we will be including. Here is an opportunity to use your ingenuity in finding a substitute, if necessary, among the cooking pans you have on hand. Fortunately, I have a PAELLA pan, but I have also used large casseroles, a large ovenproof mixing bowl, and even the casserole-like lid to a large copper pot. Ideally, you will want to serve the completed PAELLA at the table in the same pan in which it is cooked. However, depending on your inventory of cookware, you may have to transfer the final dish to a large platter, or use two smaller casseroles. But let's continue with our evaluation of the dish itself.

There is an authentic Spanish interpretation of PAELLA A LA BARCELONA (Rice Barcelona Style) in THE SPANISH COOKBOOK by Barbara Norman. Here a recipe by María de Guadalupe Varela, serving 8, calls for: 1/2 chicken (with chicken liver and giblets optional), 1/2 pound squid, 1/2 pound any white fish, 1/2 pound shrimp, 1/2 pound pork spare ribs, 12 pork sausages (cocktail size), mussels, peas, canned artichokes, and 3/4 cup olive oil. Optional garnish includes slices of hard-boiled eggs, a lobster tail cut in pieces and canned pimientos. For our MINCEUR version we note that the spare ribs, pork sausages, and olive oil are dubious items, and require further consideration, as do the chicken liver and giblets. And this recipe appears to be a festive version of PAELLA; it involves a number of varied and expensive ingredients that would not necessarily be suitable for an everyday version.

The same book has a recipe for PAELLA VALENCIANA, serving 4 to 6, which is less elaborate. This calls for: 1 small chicken, 3-1/2 ounces lean pork, green beans, shelled peas, 8 crayfish, 1/2 pound clams, and 1/3 cup olive oil, among other ingredients and seasonings. Apparently, when the diversified possibilities of seafood are reduced, the quantity of chicken is increased, as this is one of the less expensive ingredients.

SPECIALTY OF THE HOUSE by Sandy Lesberg has two PAELLA recipes in the Valencian style. One, from The Matador restaurant in West Los Angeles, California, calls for 1 cut up broiler, 2 rock lobster tails, 1/2 pound shrimp, 1 large CHORIZO (Spanish sausage), 1 thick slice of ham, 1 dozen frozen or canned clams, 2 cups of rice (long grain), both peas and string beans (the standard ingredients) and red pimientos, as well as black and green olives. This serves 6 to 8 persons.

The second recipe, from the Alba Patio de Makati restaurant in the Philippines, calls for 2 ounces each of pork, chicken, CHORIZO, smoked ham, squid, jumbo shrimp, clams, string beans, and green peppers, plus 4 cups of rice and 1/4 package of frozen peas (which, if we checked, would probably equal 2-1/2 ounces). The dish is garnished with hard-boiled eggs, asparagus tips, or sliced lemon and chopped fresh parsley and it serves from 4 to 6 persons.

What have we learned from these interpretations of PAELLA? The combination of rice, meat, seafood, and vegetables is obviously a constant, with individual variations, of course. The quantities may vary considerably, especially in regard to the amount of rice included. Some new ingredients have appeared, such as squid, black and green olives, green peppers, and asparagus tips and fresh parsley for garnishing. We have also learned that, depending upon geographic location and the availability of fresh ingredients, frozen and canned ingredients may be substituted.

The ENCYCLOPEDIA OF WORLD COOKERY by Elisabeth Campbell also has two recipes for PAELLA. The first introduces some new ingredients: peeled tomatoes, cloves of garlic, a BOUQUET GARNI, and cayenne pepper. The second recipe uses diced bacon in place of pork.

We've made considerable progress, and I trust we've also made useful notes, either mentally or otherwise. Let's now do a quick survey of other interpretations before settling on our own personalized MINCEUR version of this exciting Spanish dish.

HOUSE & GARDEN'S NEW COOK BOOK has a recipe serving 6, that calls for: one 3-pound frying chicken, cut into 8 serving pieces; 1-1/2 cups (12 ounces) of rice; 1/2 cup peeled and chopped tomatoes; 12 each of unshelled clams and shelled shrimp; and 1 or 2 Spanish or Italian sausages.

Marguerite Patten's recipe, in CLASSIC DISHES MADE SIMPLE, calls for 1 small chicken, 4 ounces of rice, 1 small, cooked lobster, 8 to 10 prawns, 6 to 9 mussels, and other standard ingredients, to serve 4. AMERICA COOKS, edited by Ann Seranne, has a recipe for PAELLA CON VINO, which calls for 1/2 cup of dry white wine, 2 tablespoons of lemon juice, and a bay leaf. Wine, by the way, appears in a number of other interpretations of this recipe. Whether we use wine or not, we know we will need some cooking liquid and we can make a note to use chicken or beef broth.

We will end our survey with a Panamanian interpretation, which appeared in Craig Claiborne's NEW YORK TIMES article of April, 1974. The recipe was created by Mrs. Marco Robles, the wife of the former President of Panama. For 12 to 18 servings, Mrs. Robles' PAELLA calls for: 2-1/2 cups long grained rice (Vigo brand, available in Spanish markets), squid, scallops, oysters, clams, shrimp, shredded chicken, CHORIZOS, bay leaves, capers, oregano, and hot pepper sauce, among the standard ingredients. The dish is cooked entirely on top of the stove in a PAELLA pan with a 16-inch diameter, and the cooking instructions specify that "after the rice is added, the paella must be stirred constantly until the dish is finished." The paella is stirred gently back and forth in one small area at a time instead of with one large, circular motion.

Of particular note is the information on how to garnish the dish:

> The traditional garnishes for a paella include pimentos, generally cut into lozenges or strips; cooked green peas; Spanish olives stuffed with pimentos; and hard-cooked eggs, cut into wedges. The egg yolks may be put through a sieve and sprinkled over all (which we can do without). A piece of seafood such as a clam in the shell is centered in the pan. It is surrounded with wedges of egg white like the spokes of a wheel, with lozenges of pimento between. A cup of cooked peas generally serves as a border around the paella and the olives, approximately one cup, are scattered at random.

Now, as I'm sure you will agree, we have more than sufficient information to complete our MINCEUR recipe for PAELLA. In order to be consistent, let's plan to serve this dish to eight persons, and, in determining the amount of rice we will use, take into consideration that rice when cooked generally swells to three times its original volume. Before turning the page to the MINCEUR PAELLA recipe I have prepared, put the finishing touches on your own efforts so that you can compare your approach with the one I have chosen.
Ready?

205

PAELLA

SPANISH

5 small lobster tails,
fresh or frozen and/or
1 one pound whole lobster •
5 cups chicken
or beef broth, or
canned consommé •
2 cloves garlic,
skewered with toothpicks •
1 medium onion minced •
2 tablespoons
fresh parsley minced •
1 pimiento,
drained and chopped •
2-1/2 pounds chicken,
cut into serving pieces,
reserving the unused
chicken parts •
1 2-ounce slice
Canadian bacon or
smoked pork chop, diced •
1/2 cup squid,
fresh or canned,
cut into 1/2-inch rings
or strips •
1 cup medium shrimp,
shelled and deveined •
1 cup bay
scallops and/or
drained oysters
(optional) •
12 well-scrubbed mussels,
clams and/or oysters •
2 tablespoons capers •
1/4 teaspoon
crushed coriander •
1 bay leaf •
1/2 teaspoon
saffron or tumeric •
1 teaspoon coarse salt •
1-1/2 cups
long grain rice •
1/4 teaspoon Tabasco sauce,
or 1 chile serrano,
chopped •

PAELLA, unquestionably one of the most festive Spanish dishes, is now widely popular internationally. It contains a wonderful combination of poultry, seafood, and vegetables, and is served on a bed of saffron-colored rice. The dish is intended for parties and special occasions, since it is most unlikely one would take the time to prepare it for a meal that was not to be shared. And by varying its ingredients, adding to the standard recipe or leaving certain items out, PAELLA can be varied to suit each cook's particular taste. More than any other dish I know, except for Oriental ones, the preparation of this imaginative dish gives me a sense of creativity as well as anticipation—of the beauty, festivity and appreciation I know will be realized when the meal is finally served.
YIELD: Eight servings

1. Remove the undershell of the lobster tails. If frozen, place in hot water for a few moments; drain; partially separate the flesh from the upper shell. Cut each tail in half, lengthwise, right through the flesh and shell; set aside. Cut the underside of the lobster lengthwise, partially separating the flesh from the upper shell, and set aside.

2. In a saucepan, bring the broth to a boil and let it simmer gently until ready for use. Apply cookware spray to a PAELLA pan, or to a wide but shallow heatproof casserole with approximately a 16-inch diameter. Prepare chicken broth using the back, gizzards, and other parts of the chicken not being served with the PAELLA. Dip the serving pieces of chicken in cold water; drain, but do not pat dry. Sauté the skewered garlic and half the onions until translucent, then add the chicken parts and brown all surfaces over high heat, adding some of the hot broth, as necessary. Remove the skewered garlic and reserve. Add the remaining onion, the parsley, pimiento, and additional hot broth as necessary, and cook, stirring, for 3 minutes.

3. Add 1 cup of the hot broth, and reduce the heat to medium. Add the Canadian bacon and the squid to this mixture and cook 1 minute, stirring. Add the shrimp and optional bay scallops and/or drained oysters and cook several minutes, or until the shrimp turn pink. Add the capers and the crushed coriander and stir.

4. Add the bay leaf and, gradually, 2 cups of the hot broth until the mixture comes to a boil. Meanwhile, crush the saffron with the reserved garlic and the salt, blend with 1 tablespoon of the hot broth or warm water, and add to the mixture in the pan.

3/4 cup fresh or frozen peas ·
5 ounces asparagus tips, fresh, frozen, or canned (optional) ·
1 tablespoon Spanish sherry ·
2 lemons, cut in wedges ·
2 sprigs of parsley, washed and chopped ·
Cookware spray ·

5. Sprinkle the rice gradually into the pan so that it is evenly distributed, stirring constantly with a wooden spoon; use a gentle back and forth movement, concentrating on one small area at a time and making sure all areas of the pan are covered. Add the Tabasco sauce and additional hot stock, as necessary; cook 5 minutes, constantly stirring and adding small quantities of the hot stock as the rice absorbs the liquid. If you are preparing the dish ahead of time, remove the pan from the heat at this point and set aside in a warm place.

6. About one half hour before serving, arrange the chicken pieces over the rice and place the lobster tails or the whole lobster, the scrubbed mussels, clams, and/or oysters and the peas and optional asparagus tips, on top of the rice. Simmer uncovered for 10 minutes, until most of the liquid is absorbed and the shells are open. Sprinkle with sherry, cover with aluminum foil, and steam over a very low heat for about 5 minutes. Remove from the heat; let the PAELLA set for 5 minutes, then serve, garnished with the lemon wedges and parsley.

BONUS IDEAS: One of the traditional methods of garnishing PAELLA is centering a clam in the shell and surrounding it with strips of hard-boiled egg white, pimiento, cooked peas, and olives.

I prefer to use the asparagus strips and surround the center piece with alternating combinations of the egg, pimiento, and asparagus, and perhaps a sprinkling of peas. The lobster tails are placed on the outer circumference of the pan with their tail ends projecting over the edge. If a small lobster has been cooked with the dish, I make it the center-piece, with its cut side facing down. I then surround it with the colorful strips of the other garnishes in radiating lines, like the spokes of a wheel.

An excellent accompaniment is a robust SANGRÍA (page 177). Now you're prepared for a real FIESTA!

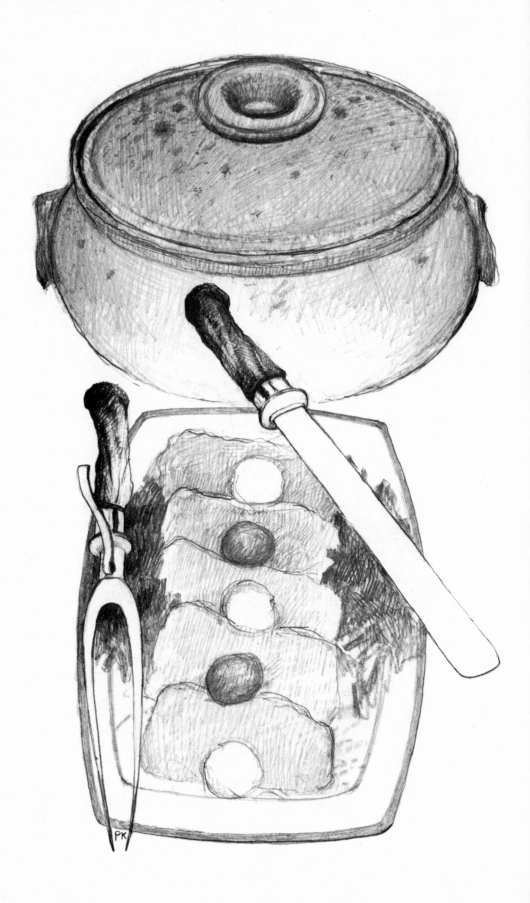

CONVERTING TRADITIONAL RECIPES: SAUERBRATEN

Moving along the European Continent, let's now investigate an internationally famous dish that originated in Germany: SAUERBRATEN—a spiced, braised pot roast. Contrary to the impression given by its name, this dish is not sour tasting, but has a delightful and often haunting blend of flavors derived from the combination of ingredients used in the pickling marinade, the preparation of which is a mandatory first step in this recipe. Estimates for marinating the meat vary from a quick version of 4 hours to at least 4 days—and, in an Austrian version of this German specialty, up to a week!

How to create a MINCEUR version of this German dish, and where will we start?

I'm sure you've found, as I have, that many of your favorite recipes have come not from cookbooks but from people—from a family member, a friend, or an acquaintance whose cooking you have both enjoyed and admired. In fact, whenever possible, I have sought out experienced and imaginative amateur cooks who, after trial and error over the years, have discovered for themselves the secret ingredients or best cooking processes for a particular dish. Here, for instance, is a recipe from Signora Dorothea Aldi, the mother of a business acquaintance, who obtained it from a neighbor, an elderly German woman, an excellent cook, who had migrated to the United States.

> Use 3 pounds of bottom or top round, or the top sirloin of beef. The meat is then soaked for 2-1/2 days to 4 days in a marinade consisting of the following: 1 cup red wine, 2 teaspoons of sugar, 1 cup wine vinegar, 2 onions, sliced, 10 peppercorns, 10 cloves, 1 bay leaf, 1 clove garlic, 1/2 cup of water to cover the meat, and the secret ingredient for tenderizing the roast: 1/2 pint of sour cream.

Signora Aldi doesn't mention whether the marinade should be refrigerated, but I would assume it should be. The recipe continues:

> Dust the meat with flour and brown the meat in oil. Add the entire marinade, cover the pot, and simmer until tender. Add 10 gingersnaps and simmer a while longer, before serving.

In the Aldi family, this dish is served with ROTKRAUT or red cabbage, and KARTOFFELKLÖSSE, German potato dumplings. The latter are made by mixing riced potatoes with bread crumbs to form dumplings, which are then boiled in salted water until they rise to the surface.

We now have an idea, of course, of the kind and quantity of meat necessary, presumably to serve 6. Most of the ingredients for the marinade are acceptable to our MINCEUR concept, except the sugar and possibly the sour cream, for which we'll have to find acceptable substitutes. Personally, I suspect the combination of the wine and vinegar in the marinade and plan to clarify this point, as we proceed with our survey of other interpretations of this dish. As for the flour and the oil, we know these are not consistent with our MINCEUR principles; the browning can be accomplished by quickly dipping the meat into cold water (which in this case isn't necessary, since the meat will have been marinated) before cooking it over high heat.

SPECIALTY OF THE HOUSE, by Sandy Lesberg contains a recipe for Old-Fashioned Basler Sauerbraten by chef Hans Moosberger of the Swiss Chalet in San Juan, Puerto Rico. This calls for 4-1/2 pounds bottom round of beef to serve 4, which seems to be a great deal of meat per person. (Depending upon the eating habits of your family and friends, 1/2 pound of meat per person seems adequate.) The meat is placed in a deep mixing bowl with a marinade of 2 large carrots and 2 onions (diced), 1 clove of garlic, 1 stalk of celery, 1/2 cup red vinegar, salt, bay leaves and rosemary. The meat is left in the marinade in a cool place for at least 4 days. (This is the first indication we have had so far that the marinating mixture should be kept cool or refrigerated.) The meat is then drained, browned in oil and sprinkled with flour, tomato paste, and brown sugar. The marinade plus 2 cups of red wine and 8 cups of beef stock are then poured over the meat, the pot is covered and the contents are cooked for between 2 and 3 hours until the meat is tender.

We have, then, gained some insight into at least one recommended cooking process and the time required for cooking. Interestingly, this chef adds the wine while cooking, but not to the marinade, as Signora Aldi had suggested. Hans Moosberger's recipe then calls for draining the meat, slicing it thickly, and serving it with the sauce, to which some dry raisins have been added. (Raisins, incidentally, would be a good substitute for the sugar.) He recommends buttered egg dumplings and braised red cabbage as accoutrements.

The famous SETTLEMENT COOK BOOK, which originated as an aid to turn-of-the-century immigrants in the Milwaukee, Wisconsin, area, also has an interpretation of this German specialty. Serving 4 to 6, it calls for 4 pounds beef, chuck, rump or round, rubbed thoroughly with salt and pepper, and marinated 3 to 4 days (turning occasionally), in a combination of onions, bay leaves, peppercorns, heated vinegar and water, with salt and sugar to taste. The container is specified as a deep earthen dish, well covered; the contents should be refrigerated.

A small portion of the marinade is used in braising the meat in a hot oven (400°F.) to brown. (This is also an acceptable MINCEUR method for browning meat.) The meat is then covered, and cooked in an oven reduced to moderately low for 3 hours, or until tender. It's then removed, sliced for serving, and kept hot while the sauce is strained, and the fat skimmed off. Then, 1/4 cup of brown sugar is melted in an iron skillet, and the strained liquid is added very gradually, followed by raisins and 4 to 6 gingersnaps. The sauce is cooked until thickened and smooth, and poured hot over the sliced meat. An alternate suggestion recommends straining the liquid, thickening it with flour to make a brown gravy, and if desired adding sour cream. This has been the first recipe that suggests baking the meat in an oven; and note the gingersnaps and the possibility of adding sour cream to the final sauce.

THE JOY OF COOKING also recommends heating the marinade before pouring it over the meat. The container is then covered and the mixture is refrigerated for 24 hours to a week. Some of the more interesting information we learn from this recipe is: "The longer you leave it, the sourer the meat will get; and some cooks add raisins, catsup and gingersnaps to the gravy." Finally, the recipe points out that this dish doesn't freeze successfully.

We have surveyed sufficient interpretations of this famous dish to begin preparing our own MINCEUR recipe. I will ask you to bear with me a bit further, however, since there are two recipes I would like to bring to your attention; they provide information on the length of time for marinating the meat and an alternate cooking process. First, James Beard and Sam Aaron in HOW TO EAT BETTER FOR LESS MONEY have a recipe for Quick Sauerbraten to serve 6. This calls for marinating the meat, refrigerated, for only 4 hours. What makes the process "quick" is that instant meat tenderizer (about 1/2 teaspoon per pound of meat) is sprinkled instead of salt over all surfaces of the meat before the meat is marinated. The authors admit, though, that "the roast is even better if soaked overnight." The rest of the recipe fairly closely follows the procedures outlined in the others we have looked at, except that the marinade includes 2 cups of buttermilk and lemon (optional) and these rather than sour cream are added to the final sauce.

The last recipe we will discuss is interesting because of the cooking process utilized, which is implicit in the title of the book it comes from: CROCKERY COOKERY by Mabel

Hoffman. Entitled Old World Sauerbraten, this recipe calls for marinating the meat for 24 to 36 hours, then placing it in a slow-cooking pot with 1 cup of the marinade. The pot is covered and cooked on low for 6 to 8 hours. Of course, this dish lends itself admirably to being cooked in a microwave oven, as well.

We certainly have enough information at this juncture to complete our MINCEUR recipe. To be consistent, let's establish that we will use a 4-pound roast of beef, to serve 8 to 10. Before looking at my recipe for SAUERBRATEN MINCEUR, choose your own ingredients, marinating time, cooking process, and your preference for the final sauce. Now, let's look and compare our respective personalized MINCEUR versions of this famous German dish.

SAUERBRATEN MINCEUR Minceur
Spiced German Pot Roast

GERMAN

**4 pounds rump or
silver tip roast of beef** •

**Marinade
consisting of:**
2 cups red wine vinegar •
1 cup water •
1 clove garlic •
2 bay leaves •
6 cloves •
**6 each, whole black and
green peppercorns** •
1 cup sliced onions •
1 unpeeled lemon, sliced •
1 carrot, chopped •
1 stalk celery, chopped •
1/4 cup raisins •
**8 ounces skim buttermilk,
or plain yoghurt** •

**1 tablespoon
tomato paste, canned** •
1 cup red wine •
8 gingersnaps, crushed •
**4 ounces skim buttermilk,
ricotta, or plain yoghurt
(optional for sauce)** •
**1 tablespoon cornstarch
(optional for sauce)** •
**1 tablespoon lemon juice
(optional for sauce)** •
**1-1/2 teaspoons
coarse salt** •
6 twists of pepper mill •
1/4 cup rasins •
Cookware spray •

Although this famous German specialty requires days for the meat to properly marinate, it is not a difficult dish to prepare, and I'm sure it will become popular with your friends and among members of your family. It also lends itself to various cooking processes and to variations in the sauce served over the meat. I strongly suggest you try the sauce made with gingersnaps for thickening, as well as the variation calling for buttermilk, or "MINCEUR cream"; or you may want to serve both versions, as I have done on several occasions, permitting your guests to taste both and decide for themselves which they prefer.
YIELD: Eight to ten servings

1. If the meat is a solid piece, it need not be tied and rolled. Trim off all excess fat, and rub it thoroughly with salt and pepper. Place it in an earthenware crock or ceramic bowl of sufficient size, with a lid.

2. Bring the vinegar, water, garlic, cloves, and bay leaves to a boil, then let the mixture cool for 5 minutes. Pour the vinegar mixture over the meat, then add the balance of the marinade ingredients. Add sufficient hot water to barely cover the meat. Stir this pickling mixture and turn the meat over once before covering. Let it stand in a cool place, or in the refrigerator, for at least 3, and preferably 4, days, turning the meat over twice a day with a wooden spoon.

3. Apply cookware spray to a large heavy pan. Remove the meat and strain the marinade, forcing the vegetables through a sieve; this produces between 2-1/2 and 3 cups of strained marinade; do not pat the moist meat dry. Over high heat, brown all meat surfaces with enough marinade to maintain this thin layer until the browning is completed. Add the balance of the marinade, cover the pot, and simmer gently on top of the stove; or place in an oven at 350°F. for about 3 hours, basting occasionally with marinade, until tender.

4. Remove the meat and reserve it in a warm place; or, if you are preparing the dish ahead, wrap the meat in aluminum foil. Continue cooking the sauce over low heat and stir in the tomato paste and the red wine, then add the crushed gingersnaps; if making the optional sauce, instead of gingersnaps, stir into the sauce gradually a blend of skimmed buttermilk, ricotta, or yoghurt, and the cornstarch and lemon juice. Stir constantly, and continue cooking either version of the sauce until it is thickened and smooth. Strain the sauce, add the raisins, heat as necessary and serve hot over the meat, and in separate sauce boats.

BONUS IDEAS: SAUERBRATEN can be served over noodles or, preferably, with potato dumplings (page 215) and red cabbage, which can be prepared while the meat is simmering.

Garnish with red cabbage as a border around the sliced meat, and top the meat with a pattern of alternating dumplings and cherry tomatoes or stewed prunes. Add apple rings with their centers filled with raisins from the sauce or with additional dry raisins. Chopped parsley and/or chopped blanched almonds can be sprinkled on top of the dish.

SAUERBRATEN can be cooked in a microwave oven or in a slow-cooking crockery pot, after the meat has been browned. When using a microwave oven, cover a non-metal casserole, containing the meat and marinade, with wax paper and cook for 25 minutes. Baste the meat with the marinade, turn it over, and cook 25 minutes longer, or until the meat thermometer registers 150°F., being sure not to place the thermometer in the oven while cooking. Baste the meat, and let it stand for 20 minutes, when the thermometer should register 160°F. Continue basting until you remove the meat to a warm place. Skim fat from the sauce, add the sauce ingredients and cook in the oven for about 3 minutes, or until it bubbles.

If using a slow-cooking crockery pot, place the meat and 1 cup of the marinade in it; cover and cook on low for 6 to 8 hours. Remove the meat and keep warm. Strain the juices, return to the pot and add the ingredients for the sauce of your choice, and cook on high for 15 minutes.

* KARTOFFELKLÖSSE German Potato Dumplings

GERMAN

2-1/2 to 3 pounds
mature Idaho potatoes ·
1/4 teaspoon salt ·
1 clove garlic,
minced ·
1/8 teaspoon
ground nutmeg ·
3 egg whites ·
1 whole egg, optional ·
1/3 cup potato starch ·
3 slices gluten bread,
toasted and cut into
1/4-inch-square croutons ·
1 teaspoon coarse salt ·

An excellent accompaniment to any roasted meat dish, but traditionally served with SAUERBRATEN and red cabbage.
YIELD: Eight to ten servings

1. Boil the potatoes in their skins for about 30 minutes, or until firm but tender. Cool, peel and rice or coarsely grate the potatoes in a mixing bowl. Add all the ingredients except the gluten-bread croutons and the teaspoon of salt. Mix the batter well, and form it into balls about 1 inch in diameter. The cleaner and drier your palms are, the easier the balls will form without sticking. Now press 1 crouton into the center of each ball. (At first the tendency may be to make the balls larger than required; if so, trim them as necessary so that your final count is approximately 70 dumplings.)

2. Bring a pot of water and 1 teaspoon of salt to a boil. Drop the balls into the boiling water; remove the pot from the heat and let stand for about 20 minutes, after which the dumplings will rise to the surface. Remove, drain, and serve.

BONUS IDEAS: A simple method for draining dumplings is to place a saucer upside down in a soup bowl. Place the dumplings on top of the inverted saucer and let them drain into the bowl.

You may use 3/4 cup of corn flour instead of potato starch.

Another traditional way to make dumplings is to grate 5 pounds of raw potatoes (reserving 1 potato), and squeeze them dry in a cloth towel, reserving the liquid; let stand until the starch settles. Cut the reserved potato, unpeeled, into sixths, and cook it in 1/4 cup of water until tender. Drain, mash with a fork, and combine with 3 cups of boiling skim milk. Add salt and a dash of nutmeg to taste. Drain the water from the reserved potato liquid and combine it with the grated potatoes and mashed mixture. Form into balls and cook as called for in the recipe.

The dumplings can also be made by rolling the potato mixture into a long cylinder 2 inches in diameter, placing the roll on a cutting board dusted with potato starch or corn flour, and slicing it into 2-inch thicknesses. The slices are cooked in the same manner as the balls.

ROTKRAUT German Red Cabbage

GERMAN

1 large head
red cabbage •
1 large onion, chopped •
3 cups water •
1/4 cup wine vinegar •
6 cloves •
1/3 cup raisins •
2 unpeeled apples,
sliced •
1 tablespoon cornstarch •
1/8 teaspoon
ground nutmeg •
1/2 teaspoon salt •
1 tablespoon honey •
Cookware spray •

Of course, you could use green cabbage just as well, but the red cabbage is typically German, and adds a pleasant color that complements the roasts this dish is often served with. An intriguing sweet-and-sour taste combination, ROTKRAUT is ideal when served with cooked pork and sauerkraut, and especially as an accoutrement to SAUERBRATEN.

YIELD: Eight to ten servings

1. Remove and discard the outer leaves, the core, and the coarse ribs of the cabbage; cut the balance into sections, and reserve. Apply cookware spray to a large, heavy saucepan and sauté the onions with 1 tablespoon of the water, until translucent. Add the cabbage and 1/4 cup of the water and sauté for 5 minutes.

2. Add the vinegar, cloves, raisins, apples, and the balance of the ingredients except for 1/4 cup of the water, the cornstarch, the nutmeg and the honey. Cover, and cook over medium heat for about 15 minutes, stirring occasionally, until tender but still crisp. Stir in the cornstarch mixed with the nutmeg and water, then add the honey and continue cooking, stirring constantly, until the mixture thickens. Cover, let set for 5 minutes, and serve.

BONUS IDEAS: Instead of sautéing the onions, the pickled onion from the SAUERBRATEN marinade may be used. Simply add all the ingredients except 1/4 cup of water, the cornstarch, the nutmeg, and honey, and bring to a boil. Lower the heat and simmer for about 15 minutes until the cabbage is crisply cooked. Then proceed with the thickening and sweetening of this PICKLED ONION ROTKRAUT, before serving.

CONVERTING TRADITIONAL RECIPES: ORIENTAL

We have learned a great deal thus far about creating MINCEUR recipes by converting traditional dishes from several major European cuisines; let's now turn to Oriental cuisine, focusing on the Chinese and the Japanese recipes. But isn't the very idea of improving on these cuisines somewhat presumptuous? The MINCEUR concept itself is borrowed, in part, from the Chinese and Japanese cuisines, and most experts agree that the Chinese cuisine in particular is the most healthful, as well as the lowest in calories and saturated fats, of any of the other cuisines we have explored thus far.

Let's see, therefore, how the principles and techniques of MINCEUR CUISINE can be used to create MINCEUR recipes for both Chinese and Japanese dishes. Since both cuisines are steeped in traditional approaches, I believe you will find that the relatively minor variations in their recipes do not warrant the survey of interpretations that we have employed previously in this chapter for other ethnic cuisines. I will therefore begin by presenting an authentic Chinese recipe that is a mainstay in our household, and two Japanese recipes we have enjoyed. And I will show you how I have adapted them to MINCEUR recipes.

In Chapter 4, we saw that Chinese Chicken and Peppers is a prime example of the art of garnishing. The dish is made with diced bits of red and green fresh peppers—even though for taste and texture, two fresh peppers of either color could be used. The combination of colors remarkably enhances its visual appeal. The dish is, moreover, extremely popular in my family, and before the advent of MINCEUR CUISINE, we had enjoyed it hundreds of times.

Here, then, was a real test of my concept. It would have been easy enough, perhaps, to create a MINCEUR recipe for some authentic—but unfamiliar—Chinese dish. But could I successfully create one for a dish so beloved by my wife and daughters—and one (to make matters worse) that one of my daughters had assisted me in cooking, in the old style, on numerous occasions? When I announced that I was going to prepare Chinese Chicken and Peppers, my daughter immediately set out the ingredients as she usually does. These included: 1/2 cup each of green and red fresh peppers (seeded and diced); 1-1/2 pounds of boned chicken, cut into 1/2-inch cubes; 2 egg whites blended with 1-1/2 tablespoons of cornstarch and beaten until fluffy; 1 tablespoon sherry; 2 tablespoons soy sauce; 1 teaspoon sugar; and 1/2 teaspoon Tabasco sauce.

Having studied the ingredients for the original, non-MINCEUR recipe for Chinese Chicken and Peppers, I realized, of course, that sugar was not consistent with the MINCEUR concept; and, although only 2 tablespoons of oil are called for, the real test would be if I could make the dish equally well without using sugar and any oil at all. Thanks to our new MINCEUR techniques, we can sauté onions and other vegetables AU SEC, or with small quantities of added water, chicken or beef stock, or a wine such as dry vermouth. Why not adapt these precepts to Chinese cooking in order to reduce the calorie and cholesterol content to even more favorable levels than they already are?

For this recipe, I generally start by boning a broiling chicken and reserve the neck, back, wings, and other bones for later use in preparing chicken broth. Therefore, my daughter, who expected to assist me in the preparation of this favorite meal of hers, was somewhat surprised when I actually completed the chicken broth, sieved it, and set it aside before getting ready to cook the intended recipe. I turned on the heat beneath the WOK, and had all the other ingredients ready, when I conveniently remembered an errand my daughter could do for me upstairs—away from the kitchen. Fortunately, she obliged and rushed off. As soon as she left the kitchen, I poured 3 tablespoons of the strained chicken broth, instead of the customary 2 tablespoons of corn oil, into the WOK. By the time my daughter returned, I was stirring the cubes of chicken over high heat (as one should, for 5 minutes, until the pinkness of the surface meat turns white).

While she hovered over me, I added a tablespoon more sherry than we generally use in the traditional recipe, but I managed to sneak it in without her noticing. The next problem was to add the soy sauce and Tabasco sauce without adding the teaspoon of sugar. To solve this, I remembered another emergency errand, and as she left, I made the additions without the sugar, and continued the preparation of the dish. When my daughter returned, it was time to add the diced red and green peppers, and to cook, while stirring constantly, until the dish was completed and ready to serve. Meanwhile my daughter had been preparing the rice to accompany this dish. I was pleased that I had gotten away with my little ruse, but the real test would be when we all sat down to our prized Chinese dish.

Suffice it to say that the meal was consumed, as usual, with tremendous gusto and appreciation. My daughter and a visiting friend had second helpings. When I later asked how everyone had enjoyed the dinner, a simple "as always" was my welcome answer. I must say my wife, who was aware of my ruse, and I agreed that the MINCEUR version was equally as delicious as the traditional version we had been accustomed to. Actually, we have saved only slightly under 300 calories, in the entire preparation, by adapting this dish to our MINCEUR concept; it does prove, however, that in other Oriental dishes similar reductions of calories and cholesterol can be achieved without minimizing taste and attractiveness.

On the following pages you will find my recipe for MINCEUR CHINESE CHICKEN AND PEPPERS and MINCEUR adaptations of two traditional Japanese recipes.

✳ LA SZE CHOW GAI DING Minceur
Chinese Chicken and Peppers

CHINESE

1-1/2-pound chicken, or 1 pound chicken breasts and thighs, boned and cut into 1/2-inch cubes • 2 egg whites • 1-1/2 tablespoons cornstarch • 1-1/2 tablespoons cornstarch • ` 3 tablespoons chicken stock, or canned consommé • 1-1/2 tablespoons sherry • 2 tablespoons soy sauce • 1/2 cup each, green and red fresh peppers, seeded and diced • 1/2 teaspoon Tabasco sauce • Cookware spray •

Relatively easy to make, this dish requires the preparation of the ingredients in advance, but no more than fifteen minutes of actual cooking time. The Chinese specify a combination of diced green and red fresh peppers. Of course the two different colors of peppers don't contribute to the taste or texture, since either pepper alone would work as well. But the combination of the two colors enhances the attractiveness of the dish, and we therefore consider it an essential part of its preparation and presentation.

YIELD: Four to six servings

1. After boning and cubing the chicken, set aside the bones, the neck, back, and other parts to prepare chicken stock for later use (see page 253–54).

2. In a mixing bowl, blend the cornstarch and egg whites; whisk until fluffy. Stir in the chicken cubes and mix well so all parts of the meat are coated. Apply cookware spray to a WOK or skillet; add the chicken stock or consommé. Increase the heat to extremely high. Add the chicken, and stir continuously for 5 minutes, or until the surfaces of the cubes have turned from pink to white.

3. Add the sherry; stir until the pan has become very hot again; add the soy sauce and Tabasco sauce and stir continuously for another 5 minutes, until the sauce is bubbling. Add the combination of diced peppers and cook for about 5 minutes more. Remove from the heat; cover until ready to serve—which should be as soon as possible, over a bed of rice.

BONUS IDEAS: This dish calls for no additional garnishing, since the combination of the red and green peppers are sufficiently colorful.

Prepare the rice in advance, but time its cooking carefully to coincide with the time required for this dish. Extra Tabasco sauce may be added, according to taste, before serving.

If cooking well in advance, prepare the chicken stock early, so that you can use strained tablespoons of the broth for this recipe, reserving the balance for other uses.

Freeze leftover portions, or double the recipe for further use. If doubling the recipe, however, do not try to cook all the ingredients at the same time; only cook the equivalent of one recipe first, then cook the ingredients of the second later, since a single WOK often cannot properly cook too large a volume of ingredients at the same time.

ABURAGE WITH MEAT Fried Bean Curd
Stuffed with Meat

JAPANESE

1 egg white ·
1/2-pound ground
lean veal ·
2 scallions,
white part only, minced ·
1 tablespoon sherry ·
2 tablespoons
light soy sauce ·
4 fried bean curds,
available in
Oriental markets ·

Taught to me by a Japanese friend many years ago, the original recipe calls for the fried bean curds to be stuffed with ground pork. Although the pork is a traditional ingredient, by substituting veal we can save 68 calories. I served this HORS D'OEUVRE to the Japanese friend who originally introduced me to it. Half was made with ground veal À LA MINCEUR, and the other half with the traditional ground pork; and neither he nor any of the other guests were able to tell the difference.

Easy to make, unusual and attractive to present to guests. You will find this dish versatile as an appetizer, an HORS D'OEUVRE, or a savory snack when you're in the mood for something delicious and off-beat.

YIELD: Four servings

1. Whisk the egg white until fluffy and combine with the ground meat and balance of the ingredients, except the bean curds. Mix well.

2. Cut the bean curds into 2-inch squares and open one of the cut sides to form a pouch. If smaller bean curds of the desired approximate size are available, make crisscross cuts on one end to form a pouch. Fill each pouch with rolled balls of the meat mixture, each about 1-1/2 inches in diameter, adjusting the size of the meat balls so that all pieces of bean curd are evenly filled.

3. Arrange the stuffed bean curds on a heatproof platter and place in a steamer, or on a rack over sufficient water in a standard tightly covered pot. Be sure the water level is sufficient to avoid total evaporation during cooking but not high enough to reach the level of the platter. Steam over high heat for 12 minutes.

4. Spoon the cooking liquor over the stuffed bean curd, and serve hot.

BONUS IDEAS: Try preparing the stuffing with any ground meat, or combinations of meats you may have on hand.

Here are other variations you might try: Increase the quantity of sherry, adding 1/4 teaspoon of minced garlic, 1/6 teaspoon of ground ginger, and 1 tablespoon of diced water chestnuts for texture; serve additional minced scallions for individual garnishing to taste.

The Chinese, especially in Hong Kong, use stuffed bean curd in preparing the famous HONG KONG HOT POT (page 54–58). In this case, the sherry is eliminated since the bean curds are cooked, as are the other ingredients, in boiling chicken broth, which eventually is enriched by the cooking juices of the ingredients; sherry, then, would not be harmonious with the overall flavor of the dish.

Another famous Japanese dish is Sukiyaki, which can be made with either thinly sliced beef or a combination of seafood. On the following page is my preferred recipe for MINCEUR SUKIYAKI, in which I have used beef.

SUKIYAKI is equally authentic when made with shrimp, or a combination of white-fleshed fish, instead of the lean slices of beef. All other ingredients remain the same. It is not necessary, however, to marinate the shrimp beforehand, even though some experts insist that marinating the fish and seafood for as little as 5 minutes improves the overall flavor of the dish.

Watercress may be used in place of the spinach; the quantity of celery may be reduced to 1 stalk if Chinese cabbage is used instead of spinach; and 2 cups of bean sprouts may be used in place of the SHIRATAKI, or cellophane noodles.

MINCEUR SUKIYAKI

JAPANESE

2 pounds lean beef:
sirloin tip, filet, or
tenderloin, thinly sliced ·

Marinade, consisting of:
1-1/2 cups beef stock,
or consommé ·
1/4 cup sherry,
sake, or mirin
(sweet Japanese liquor) ·
1/3 cup soy sauce ·
1 tablespoon honey ·
1/8 teaspoon
powdered ginger ·

3 medium onions, sliced ·
10 spinach leaves,
or 6 ribs Chinese cabbage,
chopped coarsely ·
3 stalks celery,
sliced diagonally ·
1 cup mushrooms,
or 4 large Japanese
mushrooms, thinly sliced ·
5 ounces water chestnuts,
drained and sliced;
or julienne strips
of 1 turnip ·
1 cup bamboo shoots,
drained and sliced ·
2 cups boiled and
drained shirataki
or cellophane noodles
(4 ounces uncooked) ·
1/2 cup bean curd
(tofu), cut into
1-inch squares ·
6 scallions,
cut into 2-inch lengths,
white part only ·
Cookware spray ·

The preparation of SUKIYAKI is a festivity in itself—almost a ritual: the ingredients are sliced and artfully arranged well in advance, and the actual cooking is performed in full view at the table in a chafing dish, an electric skillet, or any suitable pan over an HIBACHI or brazier. The actual cooking takes less than a half-hour. This is considered the king of NABEMONO dishes—saucepan foods—with SUKI meaning "to thinly slice," and YAKI meaning "to fry."

In converting this famous dish to a MINCEUR version, we need only eliminate the small amount of oil called for in the traditional recipe, and use honey instead of sugar as a sweetener. For an authentic Japanese touch, serve sukiyaki with individual bowls of beaten eggs, into which the morsels are to be dipped before eating.

YIELD: Four to six servings

1. Prepare the marinade by combining the beef stock, soy sauce, sherry, honey and ginger; marinate the sliced beef for at least 1 hour (preferably 2 hours), turning at least once. In order to slice the meat as thinly as possible, place it in the freezer for about 15 minutes before slicing.

2. Cut and prepare the vegetables and arrange them decoratively on separate platters or trays. Apply cookware spray to the cooking utensil to be used at the table. Remove the meat from the marinade and arrange the moist slices attractively on a platter, reserving the marinade in a pitcher. Arrange all the items to be cooked on the table near the cooking utensil.

3. Heat the cooking pan; when very hot, add the sliced meat and cook for 3 minutes, turning the meat occasionally. Push the meat to the edges of the pan; add the onions, celery, spinach, mushrooms, water chestnuts, and bamboo shoots, and half the marinade; cook for 7 minutes. Add the cellophane noodles, which have been cut with kitchen shears into 2-inch lengths, the bean curd, and scallions, and the balance of the marinade. Gently stir and mix the meat with the other ingredients, and cook for 5 minutes, being sure not to overcook the mixture. Serve over, or with, boiled rice, which should be prepared in advance. If your cooking utensil is not sufficiently large to permit cooking all of the ingredients at the same time, cook a portion sufficient to serve some of the guests, then repeat the process, until all ingredients have been utilized.

BONUS IDEAS: Traditionally, warm SAKE is served with SUKIYAKI.

224

CONVERTING TRADITIONAL RECIPES: CHILI CON CARNE

Our final challenge is to convert one of our great American dishes into MINCEUR recipes. Offhand, despite its Spanish name, I can't think of another dish that can be called our most typical one. And if recipes go through numerous variations as a result of regional interpretations and variations, chili con carne has so many variations that an entire book could be written on this one dish alone.

Suffice it to say that the household is rare indeed that has not prepared this dish. And so is the cook who is not convinced that he has found the secret combination of ingredients for "the best chili you ever tasted." The Lone Star State of Texas officially declared chili as the official state dish over twenty years ago, and this fabulously popular and controversial meal is equally well known in virtually every part of our country.

Let's see what we can do to convert the many variations and interpretations of chili into a MINCEUR recipe, and let's explore several possibilities. Chili is essentially a dish made with beef, onions, tomatoes, chili powder, and a variety of additional ingredients depending on taste and personal preference. At almost every stage of a recipe, there can be possible disagreements. First, the beef—is it ground, as many prefer; or is it cut into cubes? Should other meats be cubed or ground and combined with the beef? Onions always seem to find their way into the dish, but should diced peppers or other vegetables be added? Then tomatoes—are they fresh, cooked whole, in sauce, or are they necessary at all? Chili powder invariably does get into every recipe. And that's about as far as consistency goes with this tremendously variable dish. Even the dish itself is spelled CHILI, CHILE, CHILLI, and even CHILLEY!

In view of the impossibility of finding a typical, authentic, and overwhelmingly accepted recipe for chili con carne, I can only resort to my own favorites, experiments, and personal appraisals of the most outstanding chilis I have encountered, and savoured. Let me begin with Marion Dystel's chili, which is very well known to many, especially in literary circles, where this dish has been served both in intimate groups and in large gatherings; and generally with such success and approbation that the recipe is clamored for.

This recipe, which serves 6, calls for: 6 tablespoons of cooking oil; 2 large onions, chopped; 2 green peppers, diced, 2 pounds ground beef; 2 bay leaves; 2 (16-ounce) cans tomatoes; 1 teaspoon paprika; 2 teaspoons Worcestershire sauce; 1/4 teaspoon cayenne pepper; 2 tablespoons chili powder; 2 cloves garlic, crushed; 2 teaspoons salt; and finally 2 cans (16-ounce) of kidney beans. This latter ingredient is another subject of considerable controversy: should beans be included at all? Or, if so, should they be red kidney beans or the more delicately colored Mexican pinto beans, or whatever. But, at least, we have an auspicious start with a widely accepted recipe for outstanding chili.

From the basic starting point of a good recipe, one learns of myriad possible ingredients that might be included in a personalized version, hopefully in finding the "secret" ingredient that makes a dramatic difference. I have investigated more possible ingredients for chili than I care to specify in detail. One of my major efforts came when I prepared the "World's Greatest Chili," as ordained by a competition in Texas. The recipe was published in one of the leading magazines, and not only called for several kinds of meat, but also boasted the fact that it utilized between thirty and forty secret ingredients. It was probably one of the most expensive and difficult-to-make chilis in history! But when I presented it with pride to my family, who are chili-lovers, they found it merely "interesting." By chance, I had some frozen chili made from a simple and relatively inexpensive version of another recipe. I quickly defrosted the second chili, and offered it to my family as an alternative; I was surprised as well as pleased to find the simpler version was overwhelmingly the favorite.

I think this proves the point that whatever the extra ingredients or seasonings, they must be used judiciously. You may wish to compare the following list with one of your own, but I now present some of the recommended ingredients for the perfect chili:

Herbs and Spices: basil, bay leaf, black pepper, cayenne, caraway seeds, celery salt, CHILI PASILLAS (dry, red chili peppers), CILANTRO (fresh coriander leaves), crushed red pepper, dehydrated onion flakes, dried green chili peppers, green peppercorns, jalapeño peppers, MSG, oregano, parsley, sesame seeds (toasted), sugar, Tabasco, white ground pepper, whole or ground cumin seed.

Oils and Fats: bacon and/or drippings, butter, lard, olive oil, peanut oil, salad oil, shortening, suet, vegetable oil.

Vegetables: canned Italian style tomatoes, diced potatoes, grated carrots, green fresh pepper, lima beans, peeled and seeded tomatoes, pink or pinto beans, red kidney beans, Spanish onion.

Meats: chopped pork, ground lamb, ground beef.

Miscellaneous: buttered crumbs, cornmeal, flour, oatmeal, pasta, saltine crackers, crushed; beef broth, bouillon cubes, consommé, tomato juice, tomato paste, tomato purée, tomato sauce, wine vinegar, Worcestershire sauce; grated cheese; un-sweetened chocolate.

And believe me, this is not intended to be a complete list of possible ingredients that reputable cooks use, recommend, or insist upon as being essential to the "perfect chili." So whatever your orientation, please feel free to add or delete any of the ingredients I will recommend for the MINCEUR versions of MY favorite chili con carne.

Obviously, I have my own secret ingredient, as does virtually every cook who has prepared this dish. Many years ago, I studied dozens upon dozens of recipes, and I soon determined that one, if not THE, secret ingredient was cumin seed. The chili I made for my family proved an instantaneous success and became a favorite; but as time went by, I learned the "secret" of "the secret"; that if the cumin seed is toasted first, then ground, it adds a superb taste and aroma to the dish. I tried, and it does.

As there is no standard recipe for this dish, I am going to offer two alternatives—a MINCEUR version of Marion Dystel's chili, and the recipe for my own favorite chili, also À LA MINCEUR, both of which permit consideration of some of the many ingredients we have discussed. In addition, since my "secret ingredient," toasted, ground cumin seed, is not compatible with some seasonings like paprika, cayenne, and Worcestershire sauce, used in Ms. Dystel's very tempting recipe, and since one of the principles of MINCEUR CUISINE is to use all ingredients judiciously, especially herbs and spices, I would prefer presenting two alternate and satisfying MINCEUR recipes, rather than overburdening either one with too many favorite ingredients. No doubt you will make further alterations in either or both of these MINCEUR versions to satisfy your own personal preferences. That is fine, for there's no better recipe in the whole world of cookery with which a cook can assert his or her own sense of individuality.

* MARION DYSTEL'S MINCEUR CHILI

AMERICAN

2 pounds lean ground beef, preferably top round; (it is optional to cut the lean beef into 1/2-inch cubes) •
2 large onions, peeled and chopped •
2 green peppers, diced •
1 32-ounce can Italian style plum tomatoes •
1 32-ounce can red kidney beans, drained •
2 bay leaves •
1 teaspoon paprika •
2 teaspoons Worcestershire sauce •
1 tablespoon dry vermouth •
1/4 teaspoon cayenne pepper •
2 tablespoons chili powder •
2 cloves garlic, skewered with toothpicks •
2 teaspoons salt •
Cookware spray •

A dish that has been known never to fail for entertaining a large group on a festive occasion, for an intimate family meal, or a satisfying snack. CHILI CON CARNE is always the dish that hits the spot. Vary it to your preference, and make sufficient quantities to freeze for future use; serve it immediately; or preferably, make it well in advance, for its blended flavors seem to improve with reheating.

YIELD: Six large servings

1. Apply cookware spray to a large, heavy pan. If using cubed beef, dip pieces briefly in cold water, drain but do not pat dry and brown in the pan over high heat. If using ground beef, brown the meat until the surface portions lose their pinkness. Add the onions and green peppers, and stir occasionally until the onions become translucent.

2. Add the tomatoes, and the balance of the ingredients, stirring until the entire mixture is blended. Bring to a boil.

3. Cover pot tightly, reduce the heat, and simmer for about 1 hour, stirring occasionally. If there is time before serving, continue to simmer over very low heat for an additional 1/2 hour, since this dish improves with additional cooking. Remove bay leaves and garlic, and serve.

BONUS IDEAS: You can decide on your own garnishes, but I prefer to serve CHILI CON CARNE with boiled rice. I vary the accoutrements that I serve, depending on my mood, the guests, and what's available, but usually provide Tabasco sauce, or hot pepper; saltine crackers or TACOS (crackers); chopped onion and/or chopped lettuce; grated Iceland cheese; or extra red kidney or pinto beans.

* PUNGENT MINCEUR CHILI CON CARNE

AMERICAN

2 pounds
lean chuck roast,
cut into 1/2-inch cubes;
or ground, if you prefer ·
2 medium onions,
peeled and diced ·
2 green peppers,
seeded and diced ·
2 teaspoons cumin seeds,
whole ·
1 32-ounce can
Italian style
plum tomatoes ·
2 16-ounce cans
pinto beans, drained ·
2 whole bay leaves ·
1 garlic clove
skewered with toothpick ·
1 teaspoon coarse salt ·
2 tablespoons
chili powder ·
1 tablespoon
dry vermouth ·
1/8 teaspoon
Tabasco sauce ·
Cookware spray ·

From the moment you begin toasting the cumin seeds, and the aroma permeates the entire house, there will be a great sense of anticipation for this delightful dish. You can easily prepare it in advance, but be sure to make enough of it—I find that members of my family keep dipping into the simmering pot, diminishing the chili before I can get a chance to serve it. This dish freezes very well, so make portions sufficiently large to permit you to reserve some for future use, an impromptu meal or a well-deserved snack.

YIELD: Six large servings

1. Apply cookware spray to a large, heavy pan. Dip the pieces of cubed beef briefly into cold water, drain but do not pat dry and brown over high heat. If using ground beef, brown the meat until the surface portions lose their pinkness, stirring occasionally. Add the onions, green peppers, and dry vermouth stirring until the onions become translucent. Place the cumin seeds in a small skillet and toast over medium heat for 5 minutes, being careful not to burn them; then grind into a powder.

2. Add the tomatoes, and the balance of the ingredients, stirring until the entire mixture is blended. Bring to a boil.

3. Cover the pot tightly, reduce the heat, and simmer for a minimum of 1 hour, stirring occasionally. After a maximum of 1-1/2 hours remove from the heat, and let set covered. Reheat before serving, removing the bay leaves and skewered garlic beforehand.

BONUS IDEAS: Whether you use pinto or kidney beans, you may begin with one pound of dried beans, washed and drained, and then simmer with one chopped onion and salt to taste for 2 hours, after which they can be added to the chili. Or, you can bring the dried beans to a boil in 6 cups of water and simmer for 15 minutes; then remove from the heat and let stand, covered, for 1 hour.

After browning the meat and sautéing the onions and peppers, you may transfer the total ingredients to a slow-cooking crockery pot and cook, covered, on high for 2-1/2 hours; or transfer all ingredients except the beans to a glass casserole with cover, and cook in a microwave oven (uncovered for 15 minutes; then add the beans, stir well, and cook 5 minutes covered, or until hot, stirring occasionally.)

I prefer to serve this chili with pinto beans, which complement the dark brown sauce, and over boiled rice.

Serve with any of the garnishes of your choice but preferably the refreshing light ones that go best with the special pungency of the dish, such as: plain yoghurt with 1 teaspoon of lemon juice; minced onions; bits of fresh tomatoes, chilled, and mixed with 1 teaspoon vinegar and sprinkled with oregano; chopped lettuce; or grated Iceland cheese.

CONCLUSION

Our survey of various ethnic cuisines has shown that most old-style recipes employed cooking techniques and ingredients that we no longer deem necessary. Peoples living in cold and damp climates naturally tended to use fats and oils, for example, the Eskimos; the Scandinavians, who had difficulty growing a variety of fresh vegetables because of their climate, tended to include potatoes in virtually every meal; and so forth. However, with improvements in transportation and technology, especially the availability of frozen foods, our options have changed, even if the old habits have not always kept pace. Also, there have been major changes in living and working habits around the world, with fewer agricultural workers, and more urban and office workers, more sedentary living, and more frequenting of restaurants. Proper nutrition is therefore more important than ever, and especially a diet that is lower in carbohydrates and fats.

Now that we have seen how ingredients and habitual methods and processes of cooking can be modified or changed with our MINCEUR approach—and seen its advantage to our health—we can analyze and approach ALL recipes and ALL our cooking experiences in the light of the new French style of cookery.

My wife has been doing something of the kind all along. I have always admired her talents as a cook, especially her uncanny ability to enumerate the ingredients contained in a dish merely by tasting it. She is like a musician having perfect pitch who, hearing a sound, can identify the specific note. But my wife's habitual approach to a new recipe was, unlike mine, to analyze it, and, before even trying it, to make changes to suit her particular preferences. This used to appall me since I always wondered what the original recipe would taste like, and whether there was some secret I might have missed. My approach had always been to meticulously prepare a recipe as it was presented, then vary it on future occasions whenever I felt I could improve upon it or modify it more to my own personal taste. Now, with our MINCEUR concept, this conservatism is no longer necessary, so perhaps my wife's approach was correct in the first place!

In any case, I suggest that you analyze every recipe you may be considering, especially noting the ingredients and cooking processes that are not consistent with MINCEUR CUISINE. Then, utilizing the techniques we have learned, you can modify the old recipes or create your own MINCEUR versions, suiting your individual preferences and needs. This applies to the recipes contained in this book as well. I myself find it tremendous fun—and most rewarding—to analyze old recipes with our new MINCEUR insights. It has become second nature to me; I hope it will to you.

10.
Planning Ahead:
Time-Saving Approaches

None of us are as perfect as we would like to be. Too often we are comfortable just doing things as we always have—habitually, without asking whether or not there could be a better way. Putting it succinctly, we don't always plan ahead. For the busy homemaker, however, with business, civic, social, or other additional responsibilities, NOT to plan ahead can only be considered the height of folly. Yet we've all heard someone close to us say: "Plan ahead? I'd love to, but I'm just too busy!" But the truth is that intelligent planning is the simplest way of all. We accept this fact in our business lives, organizing our work so that it will proceed step by step, as smoothly and efficiently as possible. Why doesn't this also hold true at home, and especially in the kitchen—where, probably, more of our waking lives are spent than in any other room of the house?

Since no one likes being lectured to, I will simply offer you some of my ideas on planning and will share some of the experiences that have proven helpful within my own household, which is as busy as you would probably find anywhere. My wife not only teaches school but also is the editor for a publishing firm specializing in foreign language textbooks, and I have various interests as a business executive, playwright, and, of course, a cook. With three active daughters having varied careers of their own, I had for years been amazed how well we did at household management, but I kept wondering why we couldn't do better. The problem seemed to be the lack of planning. Yes, we too were just too busy to take the time to do it. If we had deadlines such as friends coming for dinner, or a special party for a member of the family, everyone pitched in and things got done in an efficient manner. A great help is our efficient kitchen with many time-saving aids—a good-sized freezer, a microwave oven, a dishwasher, and so on; but it does take time to use these aids properly. Merely drawing on the freezer's reserves, for instance, without replacing them, is not enough.

But the time came when I had to prove to myself the real advantages of planning ahead and developing time-saving approaches in the kitchen. This is easiest to do when you are absolutely alone, on your own—and when there is no one else you can complain to if things aren't done well.

This was the situation for me when, one summer, my wife accepted an assignment to conduct a large group of foreign language students on an educational tour of Europe for six weeks. My wife and I agreed that this would be a worthwhile activity for her and two of our daughters. Because of business responsibilities I couldn't get away, and having traveled so much the rest of the year, I preferred staying home with my eldest daughter, who had just returned from school in Paris.

Obviously, there was a lot of planning to do: three women had to decide on luggage, clothing, and accessories; arrangements had to be made concerning the care of our two dogs while I was at work, and possibly on business trips; occasionally, I would need someone to come in to help with the cleaning, and some assistance with the gardening. We didn't give too much thought to food, at this point, since my eldest daughter loves to cook, and she promised to introduce me to some of the many recipes she had mastered in France.

Thanks to the imminent deadline, planning for the trip went quite well. Two days before the scheduled date of departure, however, we received word that the principal in charge of the tour had become seriously ill. My wife was to be in charge! Her first assignment as the new principal, moreover, was to find someone qualified to supervise her original group of students—and to do so in two days. And where could this problem be solved? In my own household! The only qualified applicant available, with a knowledge of the languages and the countries involved in the tour was—my eldest daughter! Before I knew what was happening, the whole matter was settled and approved by the sponsors. Now my entire family was leaving for six weeks. All I could do was accept the inevitable.

Anyone with a family, especially one comprised of three daughters, can imagine the ensuing chaos: packing and unpacking, trying this outfit on, and leaving that one aside, making up one's mind and then changing it just as readily, carefully folding clothing before packing and then stuffing it mercilessly into bulging luggage. Finally, it was time to drive my wife and daughters to the airport—and then return to a house that had mercilessly been pulled apart. It was now eleven o'clock at night, and I found myself wandering through the rooms unbelievingly surveying the disarray. "My dear," I remembered hearing my wife say just before leaving

233

the house, "the maid will be in tomorrow to help put things in order!" I found myself laughing out loud at the absurdity of the situation, as I began picking up item after item, attempting to achieve some sense of order. I checked the refrigerator and found it to be replete with cheerful notes from my wife suggesting menus for my first meals alone. But I realized that one of the advantages of cooking for oneself is the comforting thought: "You probably will make more exciting meals for yourself!" And so it started: six weeks completely on my own in running a big house.

The next day, however, I only managed a makeshift dinner. But then I decided to do some food shopping. I bought sufficient supplies for a week, and added staples to our larder to be sure I would have everything I would need. When I got home, I checked recipes and found those I would use the next evening; I carefully lined up all the staples, cookware, and utensils I would need. The rest of that night I was able to relax, reading and enjoying some of my favorite recordings, with the comforting knowledge that I was fully prepared for the next evening's meal. Before I went to bed I even set the table!

The next evening, thanks to the maid's arrival during the day, I returned to a sparkling clean and orderly house. She left me a pleasant note telling me how surprised she was that she had so little to do and how well I seemed to be doing. Soon I was preparing my meal for that night, veal chops ALLA MILANESE, including several portions for additional meals, either alone or with company, which I reserved in the freezer. Although I was starting to plan ahead, I knew that if I didn't keep building up my reserves, I would have veal chops every night of the week; so, each night after dinner, I contributed a reserved meal from another recipe to the freezer. As a result, I repeated only one meal during that first week.

During my first weekend alone, I used one full day for shopping and cooking ahead. I made a large quantity of tomato sauce, several portions of CORDON BLEU of chicken breasts, a number of small TERRINES of pâté, as well as many other favorites. The rest of the weekend, I was free to work in the garden and socialize with friends. By the following Tuesday, I was ready to entertain friends at dinner, which I did—and with a sense of great aplomb. From then on, I entertained several times a week.

It became evident to me that all this was a matter of planning ahead. Before I left work each morning, I would take the items I needed from the freezer to begin thawing, if I knew I couldn't take the time to thaw them in the microwave oven, before my guests arrived. Also, I prepared a shopping list for the items I had to pick up on my way home—fresh

234

fruit, bread, milk, and so on. And I found it all so easy to do; once I began planning, everything worked beautifully.

Here are the things that proved most helpful to me in planning my meals and in entertaining. I offer them as suggestions for your own planning needs:

1. Make yourself aware of the foods that are available, in season and at the peak of their freshness, in any given week. Check your newspapers for ads that indicate the best buys for the items you need.

2. Determine how you will prepare the ingredients you plan to purchase, first checking your recipe to refresh your memory on important details.

3. Take the time to make a shopping list, as specific as necessary for particular dishes, but flexible enough so that you can revise it, if you discover items of special quality or appeal while shopping. Buy in economic quantities, but don't buy impulsively, and don't buy more than you are prepared to use or store properly within a given period of time.

4. Before preparing a recipe, line up all the necessary ingredients, very much as the Chinese must do since their cuisine calls for so little actual cooking time. This assures that you won't leave out any essential item. I find this procedure is less confusing, as well as more organized and less messy.

5. I find it easier to clean up as I proceed in preparing a recipe. This is a personal preference, and you might prefer to concentrate on the preparation of a recipe and leave the cleaning up for a later time. But the advantage of cleaning as you go along is that often you can re-use a pot or pan for several stages of a recipe instead of cluttering up a sink with several used ones.

6. Double, even triple, many recipes—especially those that are complicated or bothersome in their preparation—so that you can reserve one or two additional meals in the freezer.

7. While cooking any main dish, try simultaneously during the cooking time to prepare other dishes to supplement the meal, or, to add to your reserves for future meals. Often, for example, while preparing chicken, I simultaneously make chicken stock to be reserved for later use with the parts of the chicken unnecessary for that particular meal.

Most important, learn as many time-saving devices as you can from expert cooks. Just as you do in other areas of life, learn to simplify and improve the techniques you need in order to perform the repetitive but important tasks in the kitchen. I have found these "tricks" not only time-saving but fun to learn. In the next chapter, you will find the tricks of the trade (LES TOURS DE MAIN) that chefs, experienced cooks, and busy homemakers like myself have learned to use—devices that make preparing meals both simple and efficient. And all simply due to planning ahead.

11.
Les Tours de Main

Les Tours de Main means "tricks of the trade" and is a catchword among chefs in France. Every French chef has his professional secrets and favorite techniques, and in fact serious cooks of all nationalities have developed their own methods of expediting and simplifying many of the steps necessary in cooking, especially cooking in quantity. These trade secrets can be most useful to anybody interested in cooking; not only are they functional and time-saving, but they are also fun, and they can increase one's sense of creativity and participation in completing a recipe. Indeed, I am certain that every experienced cook has a number of such tricks of his own. Here are some that have become part of my repertoire.

Almonds **Peeling and Blanching:** Simply pour boiling water over the unpeeled almonds, and drain; with a knife, remove the brown hulls, which will be loosened. An alternate method is to steep the almonds up to five minutes in boiling water, drain, and with your fingers, squeeze one end of the almond until the hull slips off.

Artichokes **How to prepare:** First of all, in selecting globe artichokes, avoid any vegetables whose leaves are spreading or are discolored. This indicates that they are past their tenderness. Cut and discard the top one-quarter of the tip of the artichoke, then trim the upper part of each leaf. Some chefs trim the tips of the leaves with scissors, while others prefer to bend them back and simply snap off the upper green tough parts of each leaf, leaving the tender, whitish bottom parts attached to the artichoke. Rubbing the leaves with a cut lemon helps during the trimming operation to avoid discoloration.

The prepared artichoke should be placed in acidulated water, using vinegar or lemon juice. One famous chef insists that adding 1 tablespoon of oil is far more effective in preventing discoloration. To maintain its firm shape during cooking, another chef likes to tie twine around the middle of the pre-

237

pared artichoke, then up over its top, and knot it at its base. This chef removes the choke after the artichoke has been placed in water, brought to a boil, then simmered for 10 minutes. The artichoke is then stuffed. Other chefs prefer to remove the small yellowish and purple inner prickly leaves of the choke by scraping the inside with a knife with a rounded end, or with a grapefruit knife, before cooking. Not so incidentally, many Italians believe that there are male and female artichokes, and that the preferred female has little or no choke; the male is identified by the top of each leaf, which has a thorn-like point, while the leaf of the female is somewhat heart-shaped at the tip.

If the stems are to be left on for a recipe, its tough outer layer should be trimmed with a knife or vegetable peeler. In all cases, the green outer parts of the leaves at the base of the artichoke should be pared and discarded and the base rubbed with a cut lemon.

Asparagus **How to cook:** Cook asparagus standing up, with the tougher base at the bottom of a tall steamer pot, tightly covered, in 1-1/2 inches of water; this permits the delicate tops to be steamed, while the bottoms are boiled. Special asparagus cookers are available and work wonderfully. I have a copper one that doubles as a steamer for other items, for serving cheese or beef fondues, and even as a wine cooler at the table. Any narrow, deep pot can be adapted—some types of double-boilers (use the deep base pan), corn steamers, or bottle sterilizers.

Scrape the tough, outer skin off the asparagus stems, then line up the heads before cutting off parts of the base stems; all the spears should be about equal in length. You can also tie small bunches of the spears with kitchen twine, before steaming, which makes them easier to remove from the pot and arrange for individual servings.

Basting When basting with a basting bulb or spoon, it is preferable to remove the pan from the oven. When testing or turning, avoid piercing the flesh of poultry with a fork, as this will release the juices. Use large wooden spoons, or Chinese stir-frying implements, to turn poultry, and when using metal forks, avoid piercing.

Boning **How to do a whole bird:** Unfortunately, too many American-trained butchers don't know how to bone chickens and smaller birds such as Cornish game hens—or prefer not to do so. Using a sharp knife, however, this is simple to do if you follow these steps:

1. Cut off and discard the wing tips and the first wing joint of the bird; this is what I do first but is a matter of personal preference. I prefer to leave the wing bones, since when the

boned bird is stuffed, the wings contribute to a more attractive form.

2. Slit the skin along the backbone, and use the knife to scrape away the skin and flesh from both sides of the bird, until the shoulder and thigh joints are revealed. Sever these joints, and cut away the skin and flesh around and over the breast until you have scraped the thighbones clean, and then the legbones, first on one side of the chicken and then the other. Cut through the knee joints and remove first the thighbone; continue the scraping and then remove the legbone.

3. Carefully cut away the skin from the top of the breastbone, but do not split the skin or separate the two sides of the chicken since you will want it all in one piece for stuffing. The bird should now be boneless, except for the optional wing bones, with the meat and skin intact and ready for stuffing. Once stuffed, secure the skin with skewers or poultry pins and string, or sew together.

How to bone a breast: With a sharp knife, pierce the breast from the cavity side, and cut off the slender bones to either side of the neck end. Separate the halves and pull off the skin. Slice the meat away from the breastbone and press heavily on the breast; scrape and pull each side until they slide down and away from the bone, and you've done it!

Bouquet Garni

Making a garni without cheesecloth: When cheesecloth and twine are not available to isolate a BOUQUET GARNI during cooking, substitutes are available, even if they are not preferred by some expert cooks. Small quantities of ingredients for a BOUQUET can be enclosed in perforated metal tea balls, which, having served their purpose during cooking, can be lifted out easily, emptied of their contents, and washed. For larger quantities, a metal, perforated ball-shaped rice cooker—similar in shape and design to the tea ball, but larger in diameter—can be used. The one I have was given to me years ago, and since I never found it to be particularly advantageous for cooking rice, I began using it for larger BOUQUET GARNI, just to justify its existence among my BATTERIE DE CUISINE.

Carrots and Celery

How to dice: So many ethnic cuisines call for chopping, dicing, or mincing long narrow vegetables. To do this rapidly by hand, line up as many stalks as you plan to use for a specific recipe. After scraping the vegetables and trimming the ends as necessary, make slices lengthwise 1/4 inch apart, halfway through from the tip to a midway point in the length of each stalk if they are very long; for shorter stalks, make the slices right up to, but not through, the base. Rotate the vegetables 90° and make similar sized slices. Then line up the partly-cut items in parallel rows, and make 1/4-inch slices diagonally across the already sliced sections of all the vegetables together, until the diced pieces fall away. If large quantities of carrots or celery are being prepared, slice and dice in convenient batches, repeating the process with each batch, until all have been diced. To chop or mince, simply adjust the thicknesses of your slices, as desired.

Charcoal Table Cookers **Hints on using:** To avoid uncomfortable smoke within the house, be sure to use smokeless charcoal, available in most Oriental markets. A favorite trick for starting charcoal for Chinese hot pots, or for a hibachi to be used at the table, is to put the charcoal in a metal pan and place it under the broiler or in a 500°F. oven for about 20 minutes until the coals are white-hot and can be set aflame easily when transferred to your cooking utensil. When using a hot pot, be sure it has a protective base; or use a marble slab beneath it, or any other attractive but protective material, to avoid burning your table top.

Chestnuts **Reconstituting dried forms:** Soak the dried chestnuts in water overnight, drain and use as required by the recipe. Italian dried chestnuts are generally conceded to be sweeter than those from Spain or Portugal.

Chinese Cleavers **Master-knives for cutting, chopping, and slicing:** Used singly, these versatile cleaver-knives can handle most of your food-preparation chores. The blades are big—about 3 inches deep and 8 inches long, with a 4-inch handle; they are usually razor-sharp and easy to use singly or in tandem. I use a lighter cleaver for scraping the scales off fish, and for slicing softer meats and vegetables. The heavier version can perform the same tasks, but can also chop bones and seafood shells, and mince meat. Many experts recommend getting two medium-weight cleaver-knives, and using one in each hand as the Orientals do. This method can accomplish virtually every kitchen cutting task you can think of; it also permits you to scoop up the cut ingredients with the broad blade surfaces to transport them from cutting board to cooking utensil.

You may consider a third, heavy-weight, cleaver for cutting through bones to avoid dulling the sharp edges of your regular cleavers. The side of the extra cleaver can also be used to pound meat cutlets. With two cleavers, one in each hand, experts can cut food ingredients wafer-thin, without losing any valuable juices—and faster than is possible with a mechanical device. The blades are made of tempered steel, which holds a sharper edge; but they rust unless dried thoroughly after each use, and occasionally they should be rubbed with cooking oil. As a word of caution, however: the

Chinese cleavers are sharp and will take practice to use, especially before you start working with two simultaneously.

Chinese Stir-Frying **The minceur version:** The Chinese fry their sliced vegetables over high heat in a small amount of oil—a tablespoon or so—stirring constantly for about 5 minutes; then they lower the heat and simmer, stirring frequently, for an additional 5 or 10 minutes, depending on the amount to be stir-fried. You can substitute concentrated chicken or beef broth or bouillon for the customary polyunsaturated oil used in most recipes calling for the Chinese stir-frying techniques. And with excellent results, as we have indicated in the recipe for CHINESE CHICKEN WITH PEPPERS (page 218–21). Reduce the broth or bouillon by half over heat before using, or dissolve bouillon cubes in half the amount of boiling water you would normally use (1 cup per bouillon cube). Although the Chinese, admittedly, have one of the most healthful cuisines we know, this "trick of the trade" will permit you to eliminate unnecessary calories without minimizing flavor. You can also enrich any stock you have on hand by bringing it to a boil and dissolving in it 1 bouillon cube per cup of stock. Depending upon the particular recipe, consider pre-dipping briefly in cold water meats to be browned, or dip them into cold broth. Drain, but don't pat them dry, and then sear them in a hot pan, to which cookware spray has previously been applied.

Citrus Fruits **Cutting into sections:** Perseverance and a sharp knife will produce attractive skinless orange and other citrus fruit sections, without an untidy mess. If you plan to use the zest, remove it first with a vegetable peeler; then cut away the skin and pith, working over a bowl or soup dish to catch any juices that drip off. Run the sharp blade of a knife against the thin wall of skin separating each fruit section, then reverse the knife and free the section from its surrounding membrane. Repeat this process with each fruit section.

Clarifying Stock To eliminate undesired cloudiness from soup, use 1 egg white and the shell of the egg. Whisk the egg white for about 1 minute until foamy and grind the egg shell with a mortar and pestle, then mix both into the COLD soup. Bring the mixture to a boil, stirring constantly with a wooden spoon. Once it begins to boil, stop stirring, but continue to boil for 3 minutes longer. Lower the heat, and simmer for 10 to 15 minutes. Strain the mixture through cheesecloth, reheat, and serve in its new clarified state.

Defatting a Hen **Preparation for soup:** Wrap the hen in tinfoil and place in an oven at 500°F. for 15 minutes. Remove the foil. The skin of the chicken will fall away easily, and with it the fat concentration that lodges under the skin.

Eggs   **Beating the whites:** It's easier to separate eggs when they're cold. Before beating egg whites, however, for best results you should always bring them to room temperature. A wire balloon whisk is recommended here because it permits greater air infusion into the mixture; and for more volume an unlined copper bowl reacting with the steel of the whisk causes a chemical reaction that does the trick. An electric mixer can be used, but when it is, one must be careful not to overbeat. Egg whites when beaten for about 1 minute are foamy; when beaten for longer periods they are considered "stiff," at which point they form peaks and can be scooped onto the whisk. Be sure your equipment is clean and especially devoid of any type of grease which will work against your beating efforts.

Boiling: As easy as it is to boil an egg, there are a number of tricks that assure greater success. Begin with eggs at room temperature, to avoid their cracking while cooking. A glass or enamel pan is preferable for boiling, and the eggs should first be completely covered with cold water. Use medium heat, not high heat, until the water comes to a boil, then lower the heat and simmer the eggs for 15 minutes. If you plunge the cooked eggs into cold water instantly, you will prevent discoloration of the yolks, and you'll find that the shells will peel off more easily.

Separating the yolks: For those who have difficulty in separating egg whites from the yolks, try poking a hole in the narrower end of an egg and placing it, hole side down, onto the top of a narrow-necked empty jar, the neck only large enough to hold the egg in place with its top protruding. As you go about your other chores, you will find that the egg white will ooze through the hole into the base of the jar, leaving the yolk within the shell. When finished, simply crack the shell and remove the yolk, reserving it, if you desire, for future use.

Other devices I have found helpful are to use a large-necked funnel to hold the egg; a butter warmer, with a top section· that is lipped on either side, placed over its base (which is intended for hot water) has also proven helpful in separating eggs: crack the egg and place its entire contents in the top section; invert the base of a spoon to hold back the yolk, and tip the section so that the egg white will fall into the bottom section of the butter warmer. I have a ceramic, heat-proof steamer meant for baking pies which looks like an inverted funnel with several steam vents in its base; I often use this instead of a funnel in separating eggs. The eggs generally separate more quickly when refrigerator-cold, but remember that egg whites should be at room temperature (about 70–75°) when beating, for best results.

Emergency Meals   Because we are busy homemakers, my family and I have made it a policy, as I have stressed elsewhere, to plan ahead and reserve a number of meals in the freezer for emergency use. As indicated in many instances throughout this book, specific recipes, unlike others, lend themselves to freezing. When we have depleted our reserves, however, or when we just don't feel like whatever is in the freezer, we like to keep the ingredients on hand for what we call "blizzard meals," which also fill the bill in an emergency or when it is difficult to shop. Many an evening, we resort to one of these easy-to-make MINCEUR favorites for a leisurely but satisfying meal. Here are some you may wish to consider: they all take relatively little time to prepare and can be made from canned items in your pantry, or from ingredients you can arrange to have available in your freezer or refrigerator.

#1:   Emergency Bouillabaisse (page 87)
#2:   Whitecap Omelet with Fruit (page 28)
#3:   Anchovies and Pimiento (page 15–16)
#4:   Pasta with Clams (or.Shrimp or Tuna)
#5:   Tuna or Salmon with Mixed Bean Salad
#6:   Mia's Mediterranean Fish Salad (page 106)
#7:   Chinese Abalone Soup (page 163)
#8:   Steak with Tomatoes and Oregano (page 35)
#9:   Milanese Veal Chops with Handles (page 94–95)

Fish   **Carving whole bass, or large fish like salmon:** With a sharp knife, make a cut immediately behind the head and through the backbone of the fish and lift off the skin on both sides. Make several 2-inch cuts diagonally across to the backbone, but do not cut through it; then lift out the flesh, and reserve. When the bone is exposed, lift it from the tail end so that the bone structure separates from the flesh of the bottom-side of the fish. The head remains in place. Discard the bone, and cut the remaining bottom-half of the fish into serving pieces, free of the skin.

Carving trout, bluefish, and similar kinds: Remove the head and tail, but reserve them. Cut the center part of the fish lengthwise, up to but not through the backbone, beginning at the point where the head has been removed. Use the knife to separate the top level of flesh from the backbone; lift off into a plate, and reserve. Repeat this operation on the under side of the flesh, then lift out the backbone, and discard. Replace the reserved flesh of the fish in the original form of the body, then replace the head and the tail, and present the boned fish for serving.

Fileting sole: Pierce the flesh of the fish with a fork to anchor it, then using the angled back of a spoon scrape away the many small bones along the extreme edges of the fish. Sepa-

rate the filets from either side of the central backbone, using the fork and spoon, always using the fork to anchor the backbone, and the spoon to gently separate each filet from the bone. Then lift out the backbone and discard, and reshape the boned fish before serving.

Scaling fish: Scaling fish is easier if you steep the fish in boiling water briefly for 1 minute. If you are steaming the fish, however, it isn't necessary to scale it; you can easily do this after the fish is cooked. (See SEABASS STEAMED WITH SEAWEED, page 13.)

Testing fish for freshness: Avoid any fish with skin that is loose and not close to the body. The flesh of fresh fish will be hard under the pressure of your finger; stiffness is a positive sign that the fish is fresh, as are clear eyes and red gills. When preparing a recipe calling for fish, select the freshest fish available regardless of the size called for, and make adjustments, rather than compromise on freshness.

Flaming Brandy   **How to ignite:** Some recipes call for adding the liquor to the cooking mixture, then igniting it. Most chefs prefer to heat the liquor separately in a small long-handled pan (I often use long-handled copper measuring pans for this purpose.) When warm, the liquor is ignited, then poured into the cooking mixture or over a finished dish, as required. A non-MINCEUR trick is to add a teaspoon of sugar to the liquor, which encourages flaming, but I really don't find this to be necessary. Shuffle the pan or dish until the flames die out.

Fresh Herbs   **Freezing for future use:** Of course, you can always use freeze-dried, or simply dried herbs instead of the fresh ones, but why do so? If you are as fond as I am of using fresh herbs, it is simple to freeze them when they are at their peak and, thus, have them on hand throughout the year. Devotees of PESTO (page 126–27), of which I am one, freeze as many fresh basil leaves as possible, when the fresh are available, for future use. The same can be done with fresh parsley, coriander, tarragon, and other fresh herb leaves of your choice. Many experts insist these fresh herb leaves must be blanched for a number of seconds by parboiling or parsteaming, then plunged into cold water, and dried before freezing. I have found this generally unnecessary. I simply wash and dry the leaves I plan to freeze and place them in tight containers in the freezer. This process is a lot easier than the fuss of blanching, and I have found it consistently successful. I have one friend who uses this method except when it comes to his precious basil; before freezing this one, he separates each sprig of leaves with a sheet of wax paper. The flavor of dried herbs is stronger than that of fresh herbs. When substituting dried ones for fresh herbs called for in any recipe, therefore, you should reduce the quantity specified by half.

Ginger   **How to store:** Ginger is a must to have on hand, especially if you wish to explore the delicacies of Oriental cuisine. I have used a number of tricks for storing ginger so that it is readily at hand when needed. Of course it will remain fresh for a reasonable amount of time in the refrigerator. But if you have to reserve extra ginger, this is what you can do. The easiest method is to simply freeze the ginger whole, unpeeled, wrapped in a tightly closed plastic bag. When needed, remove the frozen whole ginger, and with a heavy sharp knife slice off the quantity you need. Trim off the skin, and in a few moments it is ready to use. Since ginger is often combined with sherry wine in Oriental recipes, another trick is to slice the fresh ginger and store it, covered with sherry wine, in a tightly closed jar. In both cases, the ginger will last for many months, ready whenever you are to use it.

Homemade Mustard   **Dijon style:** Use 1/4 cup ground or powdered black, brown, or white mustard seeds, singly or in combination, mixed preferably with 3 tablespoons of VERJUS, or verjuice—the acid juice from large, unripened grapes. Some say that VERJUS was the original SAUCE VERTE sold years ago on the streets of Paris. If verjuice is not available, you can use 3 tablespoons of tarragon vinegar, which is made by adding 1 quart of vinegar to 1 pint of fresh tarragon leaves (or 1/2 pint of dried); steep for about two weeks before straining and discarding the leaves. For greater flavor, add 1 ounce of cayenne, 1 minced garlic clove, and 1 tablespoon of any combination of fresh thyme, mace, or parsley (or 1/2 tablespoon dried). Combine the verjuice or tarragon vinegar with the ground mustard seeds to form a smooth paste. If the mustard is too hot, tone it down with a teaspoon of polyunsaturated oil. Once prepared, it needn't be refrigerated, but it does help to store it in a closed container, with a lemon slice on top, before closing the lid; the slice of lemon should be replaced about once a week.

Quick mustard: In an emergency, you can always prepare MOUTARDE VITE, or QUICK MUSTARD, by simply blending dry mustard powder with a proportion of liquid—water, beer, any dry white wine, or evaporated skimmed milk—to form a smooth paste. Let it settle for 15 minutes until the flavor blossoms. Then, if it is too hot, tone it down with as many drops of polyunsaturated oil as necessary.

Japanese Half-Cutting   For the preparation of small roots, such as turnips, for garnishes, the Japanese have a simple trick for half-cutting—preventing cutting too far down and through the base: First they pare the root, then line up two chopsticks, one to either side of the root, and then slice down to the level of the chopsticks. Barbecue skewers, or even pencils will serve the same purpose. This technique is used particularly in preparing a "chrysanthemum" for garnishing (see page 47 of The Art of Garnishing).

Knucklebones   **How to use for stock or soup:** One of the ways restaurant chefs eliminate most of the need for skimming soups is to preboil the soup bones: first place the bones in a large pot with water to cover, bring to a boil, then remove and drain the bones; discard the first water. I generally tie the bones in cheesecloth; and, when I want a more richly colored broth, I place the bones or knuckles, after the initial boiling, in an oven at 500°F. for 15 minutes until they are browned. Then I proceed with making the stock or soup.

Lettuce   **How to decore:** This works best with Iceberg lettuce. Rotate the head of lettuce so that its base faces down. With a quick motion, slam the base against your cutting board. Then turn

246

the lettuce up and simply lift out the broken core; proceed to separate the lettuce leaves. This eliminates the necessity of trimming off any of the unwanted hard core.

Mushrooms How to clean: Never wash or soak mushrooms. They should be rubbed or wiped clean with a soft cloth or paper towels, and dipped in acidulated water made by mixing about 1 tablespoon of lemon juice to each quart of water. It may be easier to quickly dip the individual mushrooms into the acidulated water, then to rub them dry.

Mussels How to clean: Mussels must be cleaned thoroughly. Washing them with several changes of water and scrubbing them with a stiff brush will generally do the trick. One famous chef recommends adding 2 teaspoons of dry mustard to the water, and leaving the mussels to soak for 2 or more hours. This is guaranteed to loosen any accumulations of barnacles clustered on some of the mussels. Another trick is to add 1 teaspoon of flour or oatmeal to the water, after the mussels have been cleaned, which permits them to ingest some of the flour and become fattened before they are ready to be cooked. Always discard any broken-shelled mussels before cooking. Clip off the beards with a pair of scissors.

Another school of experts recommends cooking the mussels first, with aromatics and a pinch of bicarbonate of soda; after they are cooked and have opened, remove and discard the beard (or see MUSSELS À LA MARINIÈRE, page 72). Discard any cooked shell that has not opened, and be sure to reserve and use all the juices. When serving, I like to use the Parisian trick of scooping out each mussel with its accompanying shell, rather than to use special forks or other utensils. Mussels can be refrigerated before using, but always in fresh water. Once cooked, they freeze well.

Onions How to peel, chop, and mince: Onions must, of course, be peeled before cooking by any method, and for easy peeling, one trick is to drop them into boiling water momentarily and remove; the skins will then peel off instantly. There are also a number of hints for quickly chopping or mincing onions. All of these have one point in common—always cut the onion from its top down to but not through its base. This helps hold the onion slices together until they are completely chopped or minced. For example, a TOUR DE MAIN I learned from a Portuguese friend: hold the onion, base down, in the palm of your hand. Then make slices, as close to one another as desired for chopping or mincing, down to 1/4 to 1/2 inch from the base. Rotate the onion 90°, and repeat the slicing. Then, holding the crisscrossed onion in your fingers, slice diagonally, permitting the bits of onion to fall into a mixing bowl, or directly into the mixture you are cooking. The first time I saw this done, I was alarmed, sure that my friend would lose a hand; but if you have the confidence to try it, it works beautifully.

Another method is to slice the onion in the same manner, resting the base on a chopping board. Rotate the onion, slicing always not quite down to the base, so that it will hold together. Then lay it on one side, cutting off a small section of its rounded edge so it will lie flat; then slice through to within a fraction of an inch from the base, permitting the bits of onion to fall into place before you. A third method is to cut the peeled onion into halves. Lay each half cut side down, and make slices of the desired width through the onion, again not through the base. Then make similar cuts along the diagonal of the onion, which creates the bit-sizes you want; repeat with the second half.

In all of these methods, you will end up with a small base section that is unchopped; simply chop this part to conform to the sizes of the rest. If your first series of cuts results in a larger dice than you desire, continue chopping until you have reduced to the desired size or have minced the onion.

Pasta **How to cook:** Always use at least 4 quarts of water per pound of pasta, or about three times the volume of the pasta used. Do not add salt until the water is boiling, and to prevent the pasta from sticking together, add a tablespoon of oil. Add the pasta gradually so as not to disturb the brisk boiling; and, if long pasta is used, using a wooden spoon push it gently into the boiling water. Different pastas require different cooking times, but should never be overcooked, but rather AL DENTE, to your taste. Once cooked, drain and instantly pour cold water over the pasta, which stops the cooking process. To avoid the cold water technique, many chefs don't bother with a collander but prefer forking the strands of pasta (and using a slotted spoon for the shell-types) directly from the hot water. In either case, the cooked pasta should be mixed with some of the hot sauce to be used, and kept warm before finally and completely saucing, adding cheese, and serving. A wooden fork or spoon is considered preferable for stirring and handling pasta. A pleasant variation is to mix both regular and green spaghetti, to be cooked and served together, for a welcome "straw and hay" effect. If the pasta has to be cooked in advance, moistening it with hot bouillon, tomato juice, or some of the sauce you plan to use, will prevent it from drying out.

Peppers **How to roast:** There are a number of techniques for this relatively simple operation. First, you can place the peppers under a broiler, and rotate them regularly until they blister all over. Then, if desired, peel off the outer skin and discard. If you happen to have deep fat or oil available, the peppers can be blanched in the hot liquid and then peeled. My mother's favorite trick was to skewer the stem-end of the pepper with a long cooking fork, then cook it on all sides on top of the range over high heat. When the outer skin blistered, it was easily peeled off. But for superb taste, you must try barbecuing fresh peppers until they are charcoal-broiled; you'll love them whether you remove the outer skin or not. No matter how you want to handle the skins, be sure that you remove the seeds and the inner membranes.

Potatoes   **Classifying types:** Potatoes are classified by many chefs as waxy or mealy. The older potatoes are the mealy ones, and are generally preferred for making such dishes as GNOCCHI (page 26). The waxy ones are preferred for stews. An old trick of the trade for testing the two different kinds is to place the potatoes in a pan with 2 quarts of water and 4 tablespoons of coarse salt; VOILÀ—the mealy potatoes sink to the bottom of the pan, while the waxy ones rise to the surface.

How to boil: When cooking potatoes, it is also recommended that you select them as close to the same size as possible, so that they will cook equally in approximately the same period of time. To boil them it is generally suggested that the potatoes be washed, scrubbed with a vegetable brush, and cooked unpeeled, in sufficient water to cover. Always cook over moderate heat, and avoid puncturing them too often to test for doneness since you can waterlog them in the process. New potatoes are best peeled with a scrubbing brush or coarse towel after they are cooked.

How to peel when hot: To avoid burning your hands, first flour them before handling hot items like potatoes, which (for making GNOCCHI or similar items) should be peeled while still hot.

Rice   **Varieties and methods of cooking:** Unlike Americans who favor rice only occasionally, most cultures utilize rice as an essential ingredient for the daily diet. And we should not be misled into thinking that these cultures use rice because they are impoverished or have no alternatives; rice is a prized food, used in thousands of variations—as main courses with other ingredients, as accoutrements, and even as desserts. Since the quality of rice, including both the size of the grain and its particular starchiness, varies, there are a number of processes of cooking and preparing it. It can be boiled, broiled, or steamed; it can be combined with oils, herbs and spices; with vegetables, coconut milk, saffron or achiote; with tumeric, lemon juice, tomato or other sauces, and so on, AD INFINITUM. Rice can be washed a number of times before cooking, or soaked and/or tenderized with other ingredients. When cooked, its crust can be eaten as we do bread, and its residue water can be prepared into a delightful tea. There is white and brown rice, there is freshly harvested and old rice, and then there is rice flour—all of which have their precise applications in the preparation of special dishes.

I do not recommend processed rices, but if you elect to use them, simply follow the cooking instructions on the package. Generally, however, I recommend the long-grained Carolina rice, which is the most readily available. Follow the instructions on the package of the brand you choose, but here are some additional helpful hints.

First, allow for the expansion of raw rice when cooked—1 cup of raw rice yields between 3 and 3-1/2 cups of cooked rice. Always use a pan that can hold double or more the capacity of the raw rice you are cooking, and be sure it has a tightly closing lid. The simplest and most effective recipe I know for Carolina rice is to combine 1 cup of rice with 2 cups of cool water, 1 teaspoon of coarse salt, and 1 tablespoon of polyunsaturated margarine. Place in a heavy pan and just before boiling, reduce to low heat, cover and simmer for 12 or 13 minutes, until the liquid is absorbed. Then let it set, off the range, for 5 minutes.

If reheating, I prefer to steam in a Chinese double-tiered steamer, or heat in a microwave oven. For those recipes calling for oven-cooked casseroles with rice as a principal ingredient, I like to boil the rice (using the same ingredients and proportions for boiling Carolina rice indicated above) for 15 minutes. The rice is then drained, and boiling water is poured over it to remove any remaining starch. After this, it is transferred to a casserole, covered with aluminum foil, placed in an oven at 225°F. for 20 minutes, then dried. Now the rice is ready to be incorporated with the other ingredients called for in the casserole dish. If you live in a hard-water area, add 1 tablespoon of vinegar to the water, before cooking, and the rice will remain attractively white.

Rose Water   **How to prepare:** Of course you can buy rose water in gourmet shops and in pharmacies, and vanilla can be substituted for it in emergencies. If you want to make your own, however, here are a few pointers: It's best to try this during the summer months when roses are plentiful and there are plenty of fragrant rose petals to draw on, preferably on a dry morning so that the leaves are not overly moist. Fill a metal basin—preferably a silver one—with the petals of full-grown roses, without the green leaves, and fill with fresh water—preferably rainwater—to 2 inches below the brim. Place the basin, covered, in a larger pan or BAIN-MARIE of boiling water and cook over moderate heat for 1 hour, then squeeze the petals, leaving their liquor in the basin. Discard the petals, and refill the basin with more petals, but don't add additional water. Repeat this process 4 more times and bottle the water immediately. Be sure to use moderate heat throughout, since the covered basin containing the mixture should simmer slowly for best results.

Sauces   **How to thicken:** It is generally assumed wheat flour is the best ingredient for thickening sauces. Not only is this unacceptable from a MINCEUR point of view, but even in LA GRANDE CUISINE, French chefs favor potato flour for thickening, especially for delicate sauces.

Seasoning Meats   When grilling meats, salt and certain other seasonings should be applied after each side of the meat is browned, not before; otherwise these seasonings will draw the juices out of the meat, leaving it dry.

PK

Selecting Oysters   If you are able to pry open an oyster, you'd better discard it right away. Select only those that are tightly shut and resist your attempts to pry them open. The so-called "R" months have nothing to do with the quality of oysters, which are edible at their place of origin at all times. The months not containing "R" happen to coincide with those stages of maturation when the oysters don't lend themselves to traveling well, which is the reason that if the oyster has traveled to reach your location during the non-"R" months, it will no longer be safely edible.

Selecting Poultry   **For broiling:** Select a chicken of approximately 2-1/2 pounds, which will be about 3 months old.
For pan-frying: Select one that is approximately 3-1/2 pounds, about 5 months old.
For roasting: Select one that is 4-1/2 pounds, about 9 months old.
Roosters over 4-1/2 pounds, and old fowl (hens) can best be used for stews, soups, mousses, and boiled meat salads.
Capons range in weight from 5 to 10 pounds and have a greater percentage of white breast meat than other poultry. Poach or roast.
Turkeys can weigh up to 24 pounds, and the larger ones yield more tender meat per pound in percentage to the bone structure. I often will halve a 24-pound turkey, cooking one-half only and using aluminum foil to contain the stuffing—rather than purchase a smaller turkey. The other half can be frozen and reserved for later use.

Soup   **Correcting overly salty soup:** It's remarkable how an experienced cook's suggestions, even those dating back many decades, can still be DE RIGUEUR with today's famous chefs. Although I learned this trick from my grandmother, it is still strongly recommended by the experts. If soup is too salty, add slices of raw potatoes and boil them in the soup for 5 minutes. They will absorb the excess salt. Remove the potatoes with a slotted spoon and discard. Should it be necessary, repeat this process until the undesired salt has been eliminated.

Stale Bread   **Reviving for use:** Plunge the loaf of stale bread into cold water briefly, then place on a pie plate and into an oven at 350°F. for 10 to 15 minutes. The same process can be used with stale rolls; however, in both cases, it is recommended that you serve the bread or rolls immediately.

Steamers   **Adapting other types of pots:** While a pot specifically designed for steaming is both efficient and convenient, almost any adequately sized pot with a tight-closing lid can be easily adapted. The insertion of a footed trivet, rack, vegetable steamer, or any inverted ovenproof dish that will support the platter of food to be steamed will do the trick. Just be sure that the water level at the base of the pot is high enough not to evaporate during the cooking process, but be sure it doesn't reach the level of food being steamed. If the lid seal needs to be improved, use wet paper toweling. If you want to improvise a double boiler, or a BAIN-MARIE, simply place a small pan on top of the trivet or rack arrangement and raise the level of water so that it reaches 2 or 3 inches from the rim of the inner pot.

Steaming **Improving the seal between pot and lid:** Improving the seal for efficient steaming can be accomplished easily by using paper toweling or aluminum foil. When steaming on top of the range, use wet paper toweling placed between the lip of the pot and the covering lid. Fold the edges of the toweling extending beyond the diameter of the pot, back over the top of the lid, to avoid its drying out during cooking and possibly igniting. Because of its greater resistance to high temperatures, aluminum foil is used in the same manner between the pot and lid for cooking in the oven. Many European-trained cooks make a paste of flour and water and brush it on the rim of the pot to form a seal after the lid is put on. After cooking, the paste seal can be sliced with a knife if necessary.

Stocks **Some valuable secrets:** First of all, don't throw away vegetable peelings, such as those from carrots, scallions, or celery, including the leaves at the top of the stalk—all of which can add extra natural flavor to your stock pot. For other stocks, the same applies to saving fish heads and bones, chicken and turkey carcasses, and veal and beef bones—perhaps you can convince your butcher to give them to you even if they are not part of your order. These and the cooking liquors you have reserved from cooking vegetables all can add richness to your stocks. Restaurateurs privately admit that once the stocks and sauces are made, the chef can go home—during off-peak hours—and the second chef can carry on, providing the master chef's sauces are prepared.

Most chefs will recommend that you prepare three basic stocks, which you can freeze in ice-cube trays in 1- or 2-tablespoon quantities for use as you require them. These instructions apply to BASIC CHICKEN STOCK (page 117), BASIC VEAL STOCK (page 117), and BASIC FISH STOCK (page 127). Of course, you will want to freeze and reserve quantities of DEMI-GLACE SAUCE (page 105) which is used as the base for many French sauces that can be made rather quickly if this essential basic sauce is available. Other experts in the kitchen have reduced the number of stocks to one basic chicken stock and one basic fish (or fumet) stock. There is a "mahogany" stock that Escoffier is said to have perfected for use in cooking when he traveled. This stock was "perpetual," which meant that it was kept on the stove and added to each day with the trimmings of whatever meats and vegetables had been cooked—but not, of course, with seafood and fish. Every 5 days or so, it was brought to a boil and if necessary, Madeira wine or sherry was added. I have known several persevering cooks who have maintained this "master" stock for dozens of years, and even passed on some as starters to their family's next generation. Indeed, I have tried it for a period of months, enjoyed it, but found it too limiting for my taste and certainly too much effort for the benefits derived.

Probably the most famous, as well as the most used, of the "master" stocks is the CHINESE MASTER SAUCE, which is prepared for red-simmered meat or poultry dishes. Once the meat is consumed, the sauce is reserved, strained through cheesecloth, and skimmed of any fat. The sauce is then used to prepare the next red-simmered dish, adding to the flavoring of the meat as well as being enhanced by the added juices from the cooked meat. From time to time, soy sauce, sherry, scallion, salt, and ginger are added, as well as a number of spices like star anise. Like all perpetual sauces, if it has not been used for a week or so, it has to be boiled, cooled, and then refrigerated again to avoid souring. This sauce is known to have been passed on from generation to generation, and gone from continent to continent; and there are reports that it has outlived some of its users!

Stuffing a Bird In many recipes it is standard to suggest rubbing salt before stuffing on the inside of the cavities of birds such as turkey or chicken, or into the cavities of game. Instead, many well-known chefs recommend that the cavity be first rubbed with a cut lemon for extra flavor, then stuffed. Do not stuff a bird too far in advance before roasting. When refrigerating, it is preferable to refrigerate the stuffing separately, rather than in the bird, since the coldness of the refrigerator may not penetrate the stuffing inside the bird. Shortly before roasting, place the stuffing loosely in the bird, and fill no more than three-fourths of the capacity of the cavity (if you like extra stuffing, bake it separately in aluminum foil, or in a covered casserole); cover the cavity opening with a piece of aluminum foil, then secure with skewers, or a trussing needle and heavy thread. The neck cavity can be stuffed with the same stuffing or with a second one of your choice—but always leave room for the stuffing to expand when cooking. Before roasting, turn the stuffed bird on its back, tie the legs close to the body, leaving enough string to tie the wings close to the back, and connect the two tied areas with additional string so that the bird is firmly trussed. Avoid running any string across the breast of the bird.

Tenderizing Eggplant Many chefs advocate treating eggplant to tenderize it and remove an inherent bitterness they find objectionable, while others find this process completely unnecessary. If you feel you agree with the former experts, slice the eggplant into 1/2-inch thicknesses, peeled or unpeeled—depending upon your recipe. Lay the slices in salted water—one on top of the other—with a plate on the top slice to keep all the slices under the briny liquid, and soak them for 1 or 2 hours. Wipe them dry and proceed with cooking. Another school of thought avoids the use of water in this operation, and simply places salt between each of the slices. The topmost slice is then covered with a plate that is heavily weighted with anything from an old iron to a heavy stone. The bitter juices are discarded after several hours of tenderizing, or after soaking overnight; then the slices are cooked as called for.

Tomatoes **How to peel and seed:** My mother peeled tomatoes in a manner similar to the method she used for peeling peppers—by skewering a long cooking fork into the stem end and rotating it over the top of the range until the skin becomes, not blistered as in the case of peppers, but shiny and tight. Then the seared tomato is dipped briefly into cold water and easily peeled. I find it easier to press the unsharpened end of a knife against the skin of the tomato, without bothering to sear it first, until it shrivels and lifts off easily, although my mother would insist her technique is better. Another trick is to plunge the tomato briefly into boiling water, remove and dip into cold water; then drain and peel off the skin. All of these techniques are fun to try; then you can determine which suits your particular style.

Truffles **How to store:** Truffles are expensive, and I am often surprised to discover friends using an entire can or jar of them for a single meal, merely because they assume truffles cannot be stored for any period of time. There is, however, a simple trick that works well here. First transfer the drained truffles into a jar with a tight lid (I use a glass apothecary jar for this purpose), and fill the jar with Madeira wine or sherry so that all the truffles are covered. They will keep for many weeks in the refrigerator. When ready to use, let them air-dry for several hours and you'll believe you have freshly harvested truffles. This works equally well with either the black or white truffle.

Vegetables **How to select and store:** MINCEUR CUISINE requires using harvest-fresh vegetables and fruits as close as possible to their peak of flavor. If this is not possible, I find it preferable to use frozen items rather than to accept wilted or overly ripe vegetables and fruits well beyond their peak. If you purchase large quantities in excess of your needs, and are unable to store the excess properly, you will end up with a portion that will no longer be in peak condition. You should get to know the produce manager of your local market in order to find out when their freshest shipments are scheduled. Generally, this is in the latter part of each week, in preparation for the usually sizable week-end business, but it can vary with each establishment. Managers usually respond to customers who show an interest in their department—if, of course, they are approached at the right time. Usually, they will tell you which are the youngest and most tender items of each variety you may be considering, and often help you vary your shopping list to include a special item you may not have thought of.

Once you have made your purchases, proper storage is essential. If cleanliness is important in your kitchen, it is even more so in the storage compartment of your refrigerator, which is usually enameled or glass. This area should be cleaned with any mild disinfectant weekly, to avoid encouraging spoilage. It was designed to be closed, reasonably air-tight, cold, and away from direct sunlight—all of which help maintain the vitamins in the food being stored. Unless it contains unusual soil deposits, don't wash the produce before storing it. But if you think it absolutely necessary to do so, wash but be sure the produce is shaken or patted dry as soon as possible after purchasing, and refrigerated immediately thereafter. And if you place a thin layer of water or a wet paper towel at the base of your vegetable container beneath a rack, before storing the vegetables, they will maintain their quality for longer periods of time. Keep them completely uncovered, and let them breathe. If you use them as soon as is convenient, you will benefit from your efforts to select the freshest possible produce in the first place. Of course you will wash all vegetables thoroughly when ready to use.

Zests of Citrus Fruits How to store: The zests of oranges, lemons, and other citrus fruits can be stored in plastic bags and frozen in your freezer. Remove when required, and thaw sufficiently to cut, grind, or whatever is called for in your recipe.

These, then, are LES TOURS DE MAIN. I trust that you will find them helpful in expediting many of the dishes you will be cooking. As I am sure you noted, some of these tricks vary in technique, simply because chefs and other fine cooks are often strong-minded people with often unbending points of view: C'EST LA VIE. There is one point, however, that virtually every expert does agree upon, especially the chefs: they insist on organization, order, and planning. For a professional, the kitchen is where he spends most of his time; a hot, chaotic kitchen can be confusing and inefficient as well as uncomfortable. I realize that each reader will have his own personal approach to operating in the kitchen. Nonetheless, let me share some advice on which virtually all professionals are unanimous:

First of all, be comfortable while working in the kitchen. Dress comfortably, and that includes especially your shoes. Don't preheat your oven—especially on hot summer days—until about 10 minutes before you're ready to use it. Of course, a microwave oven can be especially helpful during summer months.

Learn to plan your menu two or even three days in advance—as most professional chefs do. This will permit you to find foods that are at their seasonal peak, shop for good buys, and give yourself an opportunity to check that you have all the necessary staples, cookware, utensils, and any other items you will require. If you can't plan days in advance, prepare a shopping list specific enough to include items you must get, but flexible enough to permit you to improvise with desirable items you may find available while shopping. If at all possible, shop personally rather than by telephone, so you can check the quality of foods you are purchasing.

For the Chinese, as we have learned, preparing well in advance is mandatory because of the relatively little amount of time required for the actual cooking. This same principle, however, is recommended generally by all experienced chefs. Read your recipe and follow it carefully, as professionals do. Even when experienced chefs prepare dishes from recipes they know by heart, they still find it advantageous and more efficient to plan and work ahead. Invariably, they have all the ingredients lined up for instant use; they have the necessary chopping, beating of egg whites, dicing, or slicing done in advance, and measured in advance essential ingredients. The same effort and amount of work has to be done in any case, of course. Chefs, however, agree that doing such chores in advance, without the pressure of the cooking processes upon one, makes them far lighter tasks. It's much easier to reach for cheese already grated than to start grating it when the recipe calls for it; trimming and preparing meat or poultry in advance is certainly easier and less confusing than doing so at the last minute.

Clean up as you go along—this is a virtually unanimous recommendation of the experts. Start with a sink full of water and suds, and either soak or wash and dry your cookware and utensils as you use them. As I have said elsewhere, I make it a practice to return to storage every staple and utensil after I have used it; this not only makes for greater neatness, but serves as an excellent reminder of which items are still to be used. You can have just as much fun, and will have more confidence and satisfaction, if your kitchen remains neat and clean no matter how exuberantly you may be cooking.

You'll find that following these tips will yield rewards; no recipe will be overwhelming since preparing some steps beforehand will make it that much easier and, having studied the recipe with care, cooking will always be a matter of approaching it one step at a time. The chefs I have discussed these matters with are not interested in moralizing. If you could spend a few hours in a busy, professional kitchen preparing hundreds of meals under pressure, you would realize these tenets are advocated not only in the interest of preserving the quality of the finished product served to the customers; they are advocated in the interest of preserving the chef's sanity! Should we ask for any less in our own home?

12.
What the Doctors, the Heart Association, and Other Experts Say

As we have previously emphasized, the objective of this book is not to create a new dietary fad, nor is it a medical treatise; it simply represents a new approach to eating well that is both satisfying and stimulating, and at the same time results in the consumption of fewer calories and less cholesterol than many of us have previously believed was possible. While you are enjoying these MINCEUR, or "slimming" recipes, therefore, as well as those you can now create on your own, you will benefit from the medical advantages that most doctors and experts agree result from their recommendations for improved eating habits.

We now know that by eliminating or minimizing the saturated fats and oils, butter, cream, wheat flour, and sugar (other than the natural sugars found in foods), we are consuming fewer calories and are lowering our individual cholesterol levels. This, most experts believe, has many advantages, including minimizing the danger of coronary artery disease.

The extreme importance of the kinds of foods we consume and of our eating habits in general, however, is not a new discovery. We have already seen that, as far back as twenty centuries before the birth of Christ, the Chinese Emperor Fu Hsi had advocated the proper cultivation of land, and, for the general population, the proper cooking of food. Indeed, probably the first refined effort along these lines was made by the Chinese. As Dr. Lee Su Jan says in his excellent book, THE FINE ART OF CHINESE COOKING, "The search for longevity has always been a subject of continuous interest for the Chinese. They have always placed great value on living to a vigorous old age. From the earliest stages of their history, they have been keenly interested in the relationship between food and health. An old Chinese proverb says that all man's diseases enter his mouth and all of his mistakes fly out of it." He then makes an interesting and pertinent observation: "In our calorie-conscious times, it is interesting to note the emphasis which Taoism and Buddhism placed on the avoidance of rich, heavy meals. The Chinese eat a low-calorie, low-fat diet, and do not really enjoy oily or overly sweet foods. They delight in light, crisp, and delicate food, and prefer savories to sweets. Because of its low percentage of animal fats, the Chinese diet is attracting the attention of doctors investigating the relationship between cholesterol and impairment of the circulatory system."

The importance of diet has been a major consideration of many cultures for hundreds of years. There are, of course, many instances in history of rulers and religious leaders establishing dietary laws and giving attention to other nutritional considerations. A prime example, as everyone knows, is the Jewish dietary laws, which categorize foods into non-kosher and kosher, or those permissible for consumption. Of course, many of the ceremonial rituals and laws established over the years were consistent only with the exigencies and the knowledge available in a specific period; not all kosher foods, although acceptable to Jewish dietary laws, are necessarily consistent with our contemporary notions of a healthy diet.

Many strong voices today are striving to update the old Chinese precept that all man's diseases enter his mouth. So great has been the concern that the American Heart Association has put out an authorized cookbook. In its foreword, Campbell Moses, M.D., Medical Director of the AHA, says: "Medical research has shown that too many fatty foods can be damaging to the heart and blood vessel system. This is true for persons of normal weight as well as the thin and fat persons, although overweight may bring a higher risk of cardiovascular disease." Dr. Richard Hurley, Deputy Vice President of AHA, tells us of a "new 'light food' consciousness that is happening everywhere." Writing in HOUSE & GARDEN magazine, he says: "Diet has changed for many reasons. People are getting more information about nutrition, based upon the diet recommendations of various groups. People are more health conscious because they believe in the role of diet in reducing risk of heart disease."

Max Ellenberg, M.D., Clinical Professor of Medicine, Mount Sinai School of Medicine, in his preface to DIET FOR A HAPPY HEART, adds: "Heart attacks due to coronary artery disease constitute one of our greatest health problems. They are associated with a high mortality rate and prolonged disability. Therefore, it is mandatory that we avail ourselves of all measures that offer protection against their occurrence. At the present time, one of the most readily available, most reliable and most rewarding approaches is diet. The constitution of this diet is based on three fundamental features that play a definite role in this disease: sugar, fats and total calories."

Because of the extremely high consumption of sugar by many Americans, let's take a moment to try to understand some of the kinds of sugars we ingest. Cane and beet sugars are predominantly sucrose, which when consumed, triggers the pancreas to secrete insulin into the blood stream. In some cases, when excessive amounts of these sugars are taken, hypoglycemia—low blood sugar—or diabetes can result. On the other hand, fruit sugars are composed of a mixture, in various proportions, of fructose (levulose) and sucrose (dextrose). The proportion of fructose is reportedly close to 75 percent more effective as a sweetener than that of sucrose; and fructose has the added advantage of not stimulating the production of insulin.

Of course, there are artificial sweeteners, including sorbitol, saccharin, and sucryl—all of which are, however, excreted by the body and therefore cannot enter the blood stream; for the same reason, they do not add to the caloric intake. However, these artificial sweeteners, though apparently effective for many individuals, have not been sufficiently researched to warrant wholehearted endorsement. Therefore, for the time being, as you will note in the introduction to Chapter 8, I have recommended the use of honey and the more readily available fruit sugars, such as date sugar.

A viable substitute, however, for pure cane and beet sugars—if honey and fruit sugars are not used—would be a commercially available blend of dextrose refined from corn and sucrose sugars.

THE ILLUSTRATED CORONARY FACT BOOK: AN AUTHORITATIVE LOOK AT HEART DISEASE—ITS CAUSES, TREATMENT AND PREVENTION—BY TWO NATIONALLY KNOWN CARDIAC PHYSICIANS has a valuable and interesting section on dietary recommendations. The two physicians are Jesse E. Edwards, M.D., and Bernard Goott, M.D , and they report the following dietary recommendations, made by national leaders in the field of arteriosclerosis. These recommendations appeared in a 1970 report of the Inter-Society Commission for Heart Disease Resources, published in CIRCULATION, December, 1970:

Americans should be encouraged to modify habits with regard to all five major sources of fat in the U.S. diet—meats, dairy products, baked goods, eggs, table and cooking fats. Specifically, a superior pattern of nutrient intake can be achieved by altering habits along the following lines:

Use lean cuts of beef, lamb, pork, and veal, cooked to remove saturated fat and eat moderate portion sizes;

Use lean meat of poultry and fish;

Use fat-modified (reduced saturated fat and cholesterol content) processed meat products (frankfurters, sausage, salami, etc.);

Use organ meats (e.g. liver) and shellfish in moderation since they are higher in cholesterol than muscle of red meat, chicken and fish;

Avoid fat cuts of meat, addition of saturated fat in cooking meat, large meat portions, and processed meats high in saturated fat;

Preventive Approaches

Use low-fat and fat-modified dairy products;

Avoid high-saturated-fat dairy products;

Use fat-modified baked goods (pies, cookies, cakes, sweet rolls, doughnuts, crullers);

Avoid baked goods high in saturated fat and cholesterol;

Use salad and cooking oils, new soft margarines, and shortenings low in saturated fat;

Avoid butter, margarine, and shortening high in saturated fat;

Avoid egg yolk, bacon, lard, suet;

Avoid candies high in saturated fat;

Use grains, fruits, vegetables, legumes.

I notice that Edwards and Goott warn against shellfish (although it is acceptable in moderation); but more recent medical and health authorities have changed their views concerning this matter. The U.S. Department of Health, Education, and Welfare has issued a booklet containing dietary instructions to assist patients who have specific kinds of hyperlipidemia (amounts of certain fats in the blood that are considered higher than normal). For many years this manual excluded shellfish from acceptable diet management. The most recent issue, however, contains this footnote: "Please note that shellfish are now included in the diet in accordance with 1972 figures for cholesterol content of food published by the U.S. Department of Agriculture."

All this, certainly, is good advice, but I wonder how many of us really tend to be put off by philosophies of "Don't Do" and "Avoid"—even when these may be of great benefit. Perhaps the reason is that the good advice we're given is so didactic and inflexible. If you tell me what I can't do, or should avoid, please tell me also what I can do, and can enjoy. The purpose of this book is to suggest what you CAN do and CAN enjoy, while at the same time satisfying our physicians' concern for a safer diet.

In fact the physicians I know personally, and who were aware of my interest in MINCEUR CUISINE, were the first to encourage me to write this book. Almost all of them echoed the chorus: "I keep telling my patients they have to change their diet, and I give them these dull manuals and recipes. They invariably try to stick to a new regimen but always complain they just don't enjoy eating any more."

Now that we are satisfied that we have a diet that meets the approbation of the medical profession, let's get back to our foremost concern of cooking creatively and enjoying our Confucian "first happiness"—good food, well prepared, artfully presented, and thoroughly enjoyed!

13.
Appendix I
Sources for
Hard-to-Get Items

Herbs, unusual spices (such as green peppercorns), and special ethnic ingredients called for in some of the recipes in this book are generally available in gourmet food shops and the delicacy shops of leading department stores. If not currently in stock, shop managers probably can help you obtain the items you require.

If you prefer to order these ingredients yourself, the following firms will honor mail orders, as indicated; sources followed by (C) have catalogues available. When there is a charge for these catalogues, we have so indicated. Some of these firms have retail shops, also indicated.

EAST COAST

Cardullo's Gourmet Shop (C)
6 Brattle Street
Cambridge, Mass. 12138
**$5.00 minimum for mail orders,
plus postage**
(Retail Shop available)

Italian, Oriental, Indian, Middle Eastern

Casa Moneo Spanish Imports
210 West 14th Street
New York, N.Y. 10011
**$15.00 minimum for mail orders,
plus postage**
(Retail Shop available)

Mexican, Spanish, South American, Puerto Rican

H. Roth & Don (C)
1577 First Avenue
New York, N.Y. 10028
$5.00 minimum for mail orders
(Retail Shop available)

Middle Eastern, Russian, Indian, Indonesian, Hungarian French

House of Spices (C) 76-17 Broadway Jackson Heights, N.Y. 11373 **No minimum for mail orders** (Retail Shop available)	Indian, Middle Eastern
Italian Food Center 180 Grand Street New York, N.Y. 10013 **No minimum for mail orders** (Retail Shop available)	Italian
Katagiri & Company, Inc. 224 East 59th Street New York, N.Y. 10022 **No minimum for mail orders** (Retail Shop available)	Japanese, Chinese, Indian
Kiehl Pharmacy 109 Third Avenue New York, N.Y. 10003 **$15.00 minimum for mail orders** (Retail Shop available)	Herbs for tisanes, imported herbs
Manganaro Foods (C) 488 Ninth Avenue New York, N.Y. 10018 **No minimum for mail orders** (Retail Shop available)	Italian, French
Mario Bosco Company 263 Bleeker Street New York, N.Y. 10014 **$25.00 minimum for mail orders** (Retail Shop available)	Italian
Maryland Midtown Gourmet (C) 1072 First Avenue New York, N.Y. 10022 **No minimum for mail orders** (Retail Shop available)	Indian, Middle East- ern, Oriental and International herbs and spices
Near East Market 602 Reservoir Avenue Cranston, Rhode Island 02910 **No minimum for mail orders** (Retail Shop available)	Middle Eastern, Oriental

Paprikàs Weiss Importer (C)
1546 Second Avenue
New York, N.Y. 10028
Send $1.00 annual subscription
for catalogue
No minimum for mail orders
(Retail Shop available)

International herbs, spices and teas; Indian, Russian, Middle Eastern, Turkish, Spanish, and South American

Trinacria (C)
415 Third Avenue
New York, N.Y. 10016
No minimum for mail orders
(Retail Shop available)

Italian, Indian, Indonesian

Wing Fat Company
35 Mott Street
New York, N.Y. 10013
$30.00 minimum for mail orders
(Retail Shop available)

Chinese, Japanese, Philippine and Thai

Wing Wing Imported Groceries   Chinese
79 Harrison Avenue
Boston, Mass. 02111
No minimum for mail orders
(Retail Shop available)

MIDWEST

American Tea,   Greek, Middle Eastern
Coffee & Spice Company (C)   Russian, Turkish,
1511 Champa Street   Indian
Denver, Colorado 80202
$5.00 minimum for mail orders
(Retail Shop available)

Il Conte Di Savoia (C)   Italian, Indian
555 West Roosevelt #7
Chicago, Ill. 60607
No minimum for mail orders
(Retail Shop available)

Kam Shing Company (C)   Chinese, Oriental
2246 South Wentworth Street
Chicago, Ill. 60616
No minimum for mail orders
(Retail Shop available)

SOUTH

Antone's (C)   Indian, Caribbean,
P.O. Box 3352   Greek, Hispanic
Houston, Texas 77001
$3.50 minimum for mail orders
(Retail Shops available)

Antone's Import Company (C)   Indian Caribbean,
4234 Harry Hines Boulevard   Greek, Hispanic
Dallas, Texas 75219
$3.50 minimum for mail orders
(Retail Shops available)

Central Grocery   Herbs, teas
923 Decatur Street
New Orleans, Louisiana 70116
$20.00 minimum for mail orders
(Retail Shop available)

WEST COAST

Haig's Delicacies (C)   Indian
441 Clement Street
San Francisco, California 94118
$10.00 minimum for mail orders
(Retail Shop available)

Kwong On Lung Company   Chinese
686 North Spring Street
Los Angeles, California 90012
No minimum for mail orders
(Retail Shop available)

Shing Chong & Company   Chinese
800 Grant Avenue
San Francisco, California 94108
No minimum for mail orders
(Retail Shop available)

CANADA

S. Enkin, Inc.   Indian, Chinese,
1201 St. Lawrence Boulevard   European and
Montreal, Quebec H2x 2S6   Philippine
Canada
No minimum for mail orders
(Retail Shop available)

Leong Jung   Chinese, Oriental
999 Clark Street
Montreal 128, P.Q., Canada
No minimum for mail orders
(Retail Shop available)

14.
Appendix II
Comparative
Measurements and
Conversion Tables

OVEN TEMPERATURES

FAHRENHEIT		CENTIGRADE
500°F.	Extremely Hot	260°C.
450°F.	Very Hot	235°C.
400°F.	Hot	215°C.
350°F.	Moderate	175°C.
325°F.	Slow	160°C.
275°F.	Very Slow	135°C.
225°F.	Cool	105°C.

A thermometer is an essential item of equipment in the kitchens of most countries, but especially in France, since the ovens there rarely are uniform; nor are they consistent with American standards. French ovens, like those in England, have a range of No. 0 to No. 10, which can be related approximately to American temperature ranges as follows:

REGULO NO. 1/2 Cool, or TRÈS DOUX: 225°F.

REGULO NO. 1 Very slow, or FOUR DOUX: 275°F.

REGULO NO. 2 Slow, or MOYEN: 325°F.

REGULO NO. 3 Moderate, or ASSEZ CHAUD: 350°F.

REGULO NO. 5 Hot, or CHAUD: 400°F.

REGULO NO. 7 Very hot, or TRÈS CHAUD: 450°F.

REGULO NO. 10 Extremely hot, or TRÈS, TRÈS CHAUD: 500°F.

COMMON MEASUREMENTS

3 teaspoons = 1 tablespoon = 1/2 fluid ounce
2 tablespoons = 1/8 cup = 1 fluid ounce
8 tablespoons = 1/2 cup = 1/4 pint = 4 fluid ounces
1 cup = 1/2 pint
2 cups = 1 pint
4 cups = 1 quart
2 quarts = 1/2 gallon

VOLUME

1 teaspoon = 5 grams (.5 deciliter)
1 tablespoon = 15 grams (1.5 deciliters)
1 fluid ounce = 30 grams (3 deciliters)
1 quart = 900 grams (.95 liter)
1 gallon = 3.60 kilograms (3.8 liters)
1.06 quarts = 954 grams (1 liter)
1 cup = 200 grams (237 milliliters)

CONVERSION TABLE

Centigrade into **Fahrenheit:**   multiply centigrade temperature by 9, divide by 5, and add 32

Fahrenheit into **centigrade:**   subtract 32 from the Fahrenheit temperature, multiply by 5, then divide by 9

Ounces to **grams:**   multiply ounces by 28.35

Grams to **ounces:**   multiply grams by .035

Centimeters to **inches:**   multiply centimeters by .39

Inches to **centimeters:**   multiply inches by 2.54

PACKAGED FROZEN FOODS

STANDARD PACKAGE	CONTENTS
Vegetables	9 to 16 ounces
Juice concentrates	6 and 12 ounces
Fruits	10 to 16 ounces
Soups	10 ounces

AMERICAN WEIGHTS AND EQUIVALENT MEASURES FOR COMMONLY USED FOODS

FOOD	WEIGHT OR UNIT	VOLUME
Beans, dried	1 pound	2-1/2 cups, uncooked
Beef	1 pound, raw	2 cups, ground
Cheese, grated	1/2 pound	2 cups, grated
Cornmeal	1 pound	3 cups
Cottage Cheese	1 pound	2 cups
Egg whites	4 to 5	1/2 cup
Potato starch	4 ounces	1 cup
Mushrooms	1 pound, raw	4 cups, sliced
Oil	1/2 pound	1 cup
Potatoes	1 pound	2 cups, cooked and mashed
Raisins	1 pound	2-3/4 cups
Rice	1/2 pound	1-1/4 cups, raw 4 cups, cooked
Spaghetti	1/2 pound	2-1/2 cups, raw 8 cups, cooked

DRY OR SOLID INGREDIENTS

INGREDIENT	AMERICAN/ENGLISH		METRIC
Rice	1 teaspoon	1/6 ounce	5 grams
Salt	1 tablespoon	1/2 ounce	15 grams
Margarine	1 cup	8 ounces (1/2 pound)	240 grams
Dried fruit	2 cups	16 ounces (1 pound)	500 grams
Spices	1 teaspoon	1/12 ounce	2-1/2 grams
Grated cheese	1 cup	4 ounces	100 grams
Rice flour	1 tablespoon	1/2 ounce	15 grams
	1 cup	4 ounces	120 grams
	2 cups	8 ounces (1/2 pound)	240 grams
	4 cups	16 ounces (1 pound)	500 grams
	8-1/2 cups	2 pounds, 3 ounces	1 kilogram

STANDARD CAN SIZES

CAN SIZE	WEIGHT	CONTENTS
6-ounce	6 ounces	3/4 cup
8-ounce, or buffet	8 ounces	1 cup
No. 1, flat	9 ounces	1 cup
No. 1, picnic	10-1/2 to 12 ounces	1-1/4 cup
No. 300	14 to 16 ounces	1-3/4 cups
No. 303	16 to 17 ounces	2 cups
No. 2	20 ounces	2-1/2 cups
No. 2-1/2	1 pound, 13 ounces	3-1/2 cups
No. 3 cylinder (46 ounces)	3 pounds, 4 ounces	5-3/4 cups
No. 10	About 7 pounds	12 to 13 cups

COMPARATIVE MEASURES

AMERICAN/ENGLISH		METRIC
1 ounce	---	32 grams, or .035 kilograms
1 pound	16 ounces	454 grams
2.2 pounds	---	1000 grams, or 1 kilogram
---	3-1/2 ounces	100 grams
1 teaspoon	1/6 ounce	5 grams (5 milliliters)
1 tablespoon	1 dessertspoon, or 1/2 ounce	15 grams (15 milliliters)
4 ounces	1/5 pint	1/10 liter
8 ounces	2/5 pint	1/4 liter
16 ounces	---	1/2 liter
20 ounces	1 pint	---
32 ounces	---	1 liter
34 ounces	1-3/4 pints	---
64 ounces	---	---
68 ounces	---	2 liters

Glossary

À la Mode: In the style of; generally refers to braised beef or the deluxe manner in which it is served. Apple pie À LA MODE is a deluxe serving of pie with ice cream.

À la Russe: In the Russian style or manner. (See RUSSIAN DRESSING, page 121.)

Al Dente: Normally refers to the tender, but firm, texture to which Italian pasta is cooked. In MINCEUR CUISINE, the concept is extended to vegetables which should be cooked until tender but still crisp.

Amandine: Using almonds in the cooking or garnishing of a dish.

Aromatics: Vegetables, fine herbs, or other ingredients such as seaweed and fennel that are placed under meats and fish during steaming to impart their particular aroma to the food being cooked. (See BLANQUETTE DE VEAU, page 20.)

Armagnac: A region in the French province of Gascony that is famous for the brandies bearing its name.

Aspic: A jelly made generally from meat or fish stock and used for coating or molding meat, fish, vegetables, or fruits. The aspic both contributes to the appearance of a dish and enhances its flavor. (See TONGUE IN ASPIC, page 59.)

Au Naturel: Cooking ingredients in their own natural juices.

Au sec or Étuver à sec: A basic process in MINCEUR CUISINE involving the cooking of many items of food, without added water, in tightly covered cookware, utilizing the natural moisture contained in the ingredients.

Auvergne: An ancient province of France noted for its excellent produce. Wine from this province is often used in braising chicken, which becomes COQ AU VIN AUVERGNE.

Bain-Marie: A large pan or pot, containing boiling water, into which a second pot is placed. Delicate ingredients, such as a hollandaise sauce, may be cooked in this manner, or in a double boiler (which contains boiling water in the lower compartment).

Bisque: A thick soup composed of a purée of shellfish.

Blanch: The process of pouring boiling water over food or placing it in boiling water for several minutes, then plunging it into cold water to arrest the cooking process; often referred to as parboiling. The purpose is to remove undesirable flavors, and to preserve color or nutrients.

Bouillabaisse: A fish stew made with a variety of fish and shellfish.

Bouillon: From the French BOULLIR, to boil; refers to the clear broth made by simmering meat or poultry with seasonings in water. Also a synonym for white stock. COURT BOUILLON is made by simmering fish with seasonings in water.

Bouquet Garni: A selection of herbs and spices usually tied together in cheesecloth, used for flavoring stews, soups, and many other dishes. Generally consists of small quantities each of parsley, thyme, bay leaf, celery, and often leek, cloves, and marjoram.

Braise: The process of browning meats over high heat to preserve their inner juices, and then simmering covered, for long cooking periods, in small quantities of liquid.

Brazier or Hibachi: From the French, BRASER; a brazier refers to any metal pan that contains coal or charcoal and is used for cooking purposes. The Japanese hibachi is one of the more efficient and economical braziers available, especially for cooking at the table. (SUKIYAKI, page 223–24; and SWISS FONDUE, page 88–89.)

Brochette: A spit or skewer used in cooking or broiling meats or other foods.

Bruise: The process of gently crushing the leaves of herbs such as mint or basil to release their inner essence.

Calvados: A French brandy made from apples, originally produced in Calvados in Normandy. Similar to applejack, which is also made with apples.

Canapé: A thin slice of bread or a cracker on which cheeses or other foods are spread; served as an appetizer or hors d'oeuvre.

Caramel and Caramelize: Caramel is burnt sugar, used to color stews, sauces, and gravies. Caramelizing means converting into caramel—or cooking foods with sugar to the point at which it caramelizes. (See VIOLET ONION MARMALADE, page 29.)

Cardoon: A vegetable related to the artichoke; only the root and stalks are edible, not the flower.

Casserole: An ovenproof dish, usually made of metal, glass, or earthenware ceramic, used for baking as well as serving. Foods prepared in such a dish are referred to as casseroles.

Cassoulet:	A thick stew that originated in the south of France; includes white beans, fresh pork, bacon or mutton, and often goose fat.
Caviar:	A delicacy prepared from the roe of sturgeon or other large fish; the roe is salted or marinated, seasoned and consumed in the form of a relish, a garnish, or as part of an hors d'oeuvre. (See CAVIAR PIE, page 148-49.)
Celeriac, Knob Celery or Celery Root:	A turnip-shaped vegetable generally used in slices as an aromatic; or served with a white sauce as an accoutrement.
Charcuterie:	A pork butcher; in France they are famous for specialties such as pâtés, sausages, and hams made from pork.
Charlotte:	A dessert pudding generally made with layers of stewed fruit and cake or bread. CHARLOTTE RUSSE adds whipped cream in the center; a charlotte mold, made out of metal specifically for the preparation of this dish, can be used for molding many other dishes as well (see MOUSSAKA IN A MOLD, page 30-31).
Choke:	The inner purple, sharp and pale, prickly leaves in the cavity of an artichoke, which should be removed before serving. (See ARTICHOKES MONTREAL, page 147; ARTICHOKES WITH PARMESAN CHEESE, page 153; and PREPARING ARTICHOKES, page 237.)
Cholesterol:	Naturally produced and necessary to the functioning of the human body. However, saturated fats and oils can increase the cholesterol levels to proportions many physicians consider harmful.
Chorizo:	Spanish hot sausage, used in Hispanic dishes; generally available in Spanish-American markets.
Clarify:	The process by which liquids are made clear by removing any impurities.
Cocotte:	French cookware of the casserole type that is either oval or round in shape, used tightly covered for cooking meats, poultry, or fish. (See POULET À LA CHINOISE, page 63-64.)
Condiments:	Aromatic ingredients added to foods to enhance their flavor.
Consommé:	Meat bouillon or stock that has been reduced to intensify its flavor and then clarified.
Cooking Liquor:	The enriched broth that results from cooking foods in some form of liquid and intensifying the flavor by reduction.
Coquille:	A shell; foods served in scallop shells or in shells made of other materials—glass, ceramic, or metal. COQUILLE also refers to pastry shells when filled with savories.
Coral or the "Lady":	The delicious roe of the female lobster that reddens when cooked. The green substance found in both male and female

lobsters is known as the tomalley, or liver, and should be incorporated into any recipe using lobster as a prime ingredient. (See LOBSTER BISQUE, page 145.)

Cornichon: French for gherkin—a small, pickled cucumber served with many cold dishes, particularly pâtés.

Crayfish: A fresh-water crustacean similar in appearance to, but much smaller than, a lobster and more readily available in European waters than elsewhere. Large prawns or lobsters are often substituted for crayfish when the latter are not available.

Crème: Cream; also whipped cream, or custard. French heavy cream is known as CRÈME FRAÎCHE or CRÈME DOUBLE because of its thickness and slightly nutty flavor. (See CRÈME FRAÎCHE MINCEUR, page 168.)

Crêpes: Thin pancakes rolled with mixtures of food and sauces, served as a main dish or, more often, with fruits, sweeteners and liqueur as a dessert. CRÊPES SUZETTE are the famous dessert crêpes and are cooked with a mixture of orange, butter or margarine, sugar, cognac, and Grand Marnier. Crêpes are similar to Italian MANICOTTI or Russian BLINTZES.

Croquette: A mixture of foods, bound with a thick sauce and rolled into the shape of a ball or sausage, and breaded and fried.

Croûtons: Bread cut into small pieces and baked, fried, or toasted, used as a garnish for various hot entrées or as the base upon which other ingredients are mounted, such as ROUILLE (page 130).

Crudités: Crisp fresh raw vegetables served as an appetizer.

Déglacer: Deglaze; the process of using the food particles or glazes that stick to a pan after cooking, to make sauces; the particles are stirred with broth or wine; also used as a base for special sauces.

Duxelles: Mixture of mushrooms, onions, and shallots, used to intensify the flavor of certain dishes or stuffings, or in the preparation of sauces and gravies.

English Dessertspoon: A British unit of measure equivalent to the American teaspoon. (See Comparative Measurements, page 269.)

Escabeche: The Portuguese word for cooking marinated foods. (See PORTUGUESE MARINATED CHICKEN, page 68-69.)

Escalope: From the French ESCALOPER—to cut meats, chicken, or fish into thin slices. Often refers particularly to thin slices of veal cut from the leg; known as SCALLOPINI in Italy and SCHNITZEL in Germany.

Farcir or Farci: Stuffed or filled, as in MOULES FARCIES, page 150.

Fines Herbes: A mixture of fresh herbs, usually equal parts of parsley, tarragon, chives, and chervil; generally used in omelettes or added shortly before serving sauces and soups.

Floret: A small flower; usually one of a larger cluster of composite flowers as in broccoli or cauliflower.

Foie Gras: Goose liver, considered a great delicacy in France, especially for pâté; geese are specially bred and fed for the purpose of producing FOIE GRAS.

Fondue: From the French word FONDRE, to melt. Generally a dish of melted cheese and wine, but can be made with other foods as well. (See SWISS FONDUE, page 88–89; FONDUE BEEF BOURGUIGNONNE, page 88–89; and ITALIAN VEGETABLE FONDUE, page 89.)

Fritters, or Beignets: Generally any food dipped in a batter and fried. (See BANANA FRITTERS, page 128–29.)

Fromage Blanc: White cheeses used in MINCEUR CUISINE; Iceland cheese, imported ricotta, Monterey Jack or other low-fat cheeses that can be grated. (See SWISS FONDUE, page 88–89).

Fumet: Stock that has been reduced and intensified in flavor, extracted from fish, meat or vegetables. Fumets are used to give additional flavor to other stocks or sauces (see ENRICHED SAUCE ESPAGNOLE, page 103.)

Galantine: An aspic dish prepared with boned meat or poultry, pressed into a symmetrical or formal shape.

Gazpacho: A "soup-salad" of Spanish origin made with fresh vegetables.

Giblets: The heart, liver, and gizzard of poultry; usually cooked separately.

Glaze: Adding an ingredient to produce a glossy surface on meats or pastries such as PIROZHKI (page 152–53). Glaze or GLACE also refers to the food particles that stick to a pan after cooking (see DÉGLACER).

Gluten: A combination of plant proteins found in cereal grains such as corn and wheat; used instead of flour. Gluten bread is made with gluten and hence has a low starch content.

Gnocchi: Italian dumplings generally made with potatoes or semolina flour; green dumplings are made with spinach and/or parsley.

Gratin: The hard crust formed on the surface of a baked or broiled dish; also the name applied to dishes—often made with cheese, potatoes, or puréed vegetables—with this hard crust.

Gremolata: An Italian version of BOUQUET GARNI, used in preparing sauces and gravies and distinguished by the addition of lemon zest and sometimes garlic.

Haricot of Mutton: HARICOT is the French word for BEAN and has probably been confused in translation with the word HALICOT, which means to chop fine. In English, however, "haricot of mutton" refers to thin strips or finely chopped lamb or mutton.

Harness for Chinese Cooking: An improvised basket or harness made of heavy twine, used to facilitate the lifting of heavy and hot foods after cooking, as in CHINESE WINTER MELON, page 92–93.

Hors d'oeuvre: Canapé or appetizer served before a meal, or with cocktails.

Jarret: The knuckle or the shank of an animal, similar to the Italian OSSO BUCO, page 196–98. (See also JARRETS DE VEAU, page 61.)

Kebab, Kebob, or Shish Kebab: Marinated or seasoned pieces of meat, skewered and roasted or grilled; a Middle Eastern specialty.

Klösse: A German version of potato dumplings; instead of being round or oval, the dumplings are rolled into 2-inch lengths and then sliced into pieces about 2 inches thick.

Kneading: Blending a mixture that is not liquefied sufficiently to stir. Dough is generally kneaded with one's hands dusted with flour.

La Grande Cuisine: The great cuisine, also known as HAUTE CUISINE (fine cookery or cookery in its highest form); a major influence in world cookery. The beginning of LA GRANDE CUISINE is often attributed to the arrival in France in 1533 of Catherine de Medici with her Venetian chefs. Auguste Escoffier, the great French chef, is credited with being the dominant influence in the refinement of LA GRANDE CUISINE.

La Nouvelle Cuisine: The new cuisine, or the new wave of French cooking; begun by Paul Bocuse in his restaurant at Collonges, near Lyon; emphasizes the natural ingredients of each dish. Bocuse's influence has proven so strong that he has been joined by a number of famous Michelin-starred chefs who are referred to as LA BANDE À BOCUSE, or the New Wave chefs.

Larousse Gastronomique: A comprehensive encyclopedia of food, wine, and cookery by Prosper Montagné, first published in 1938 in Paris with a preface by Auguste Escoffier. It is considered by most chefs and gourmets to be the authority on LA GRANDE CUISINE.

Liaison or Binding: Thickening or binding sauces, soups, and other liquids using flour, starch, eggs, creams, and cereals. Often a ROUX is prepared to form the necessary liaison.

Macédoine: A mixture of either fruits or vegetables cut into pieces of varying shapes and sizes (page 46).

Manié Butter: From the French MANIER, to work; refers to the kneading of butter or margarine with a quantity of flour to prepare a ROUX.

Marinate: Steeping food for a period of time in a seasoned liquid that imparts its flavor and tenderizes the food; facilitates cooking or increases the length of time food may be kept without refrigeration. Some marinades are used for "cooking" raw foods without heat, such as CEVICHE (page 160).

Marinière: Cooking fisherman style. (See MOULES À LA MARINIÈRE, page 72.)

Matignon: See MIREPOIX. (page 46.)

Médaillon: A round or oval cut of meat such as beef or veal which is especially tender.

Minceur Cuisine: "Slimming cookery" that eliminates, or uses in minimal quantities, such high-calorie and high-cholesterol ingredients as oil, fat, butter, cream, egg yolks, refined wheat flour, and sugar—other than the natural sugars found in fruits and vegetables. Whenever oil or margarine is used, it should be of the polyunsaturated variety. Michel Guérard, a member of LA BANDE À BOCUSE, is credited with founding CUISINE MINCEUR.

Mirepoix: A diced mixture of carrots, onions, and celery to which herbs and occasionally ham or bacon is added. When the ingredients are minced, rather than diced, the mixture is called MATIGNON.

Mirin: A sweetened liqueur of rice wine, used in Japanese cooking.

Mousse: A smooth light dessert like custard, made with egg whites or whipped cream and served either hot or cold. (See FRUIT MOUSSE, page 15.)

Nabemono Dish: Like the casserole, this Japanese dish is a one-pot meal and is identified with the cooking pan itself.

Nassi Goreng: Indonesian fried rice, popular in the Netherlands.

Papillote: Cooking EN PAPILLOTE refers to steaming delicate foods such as seafood, snails, and sweetbreads in parchment paper or aluminum foil. These foods may be sautéed first, then cooked for short periods in the packet, which preserves the aroma of the ingredients until served at the table; also refers to the paper frills placed on the bones of chops and crown roasts.

Pâté: Generally a savory pie, made with a purée of goose or other liver, but also includes minced meats, poultry, or fish.

Patna: A type of long-grained rice used in Indian dishes. Carolina rice is a suitable substitute.

Petite Marmite: A strong, clear soup garnished with meat, vegetables, and CROÛTES, served in individual pots. Also a covered earthenware pot, generally taller than it is wide, that imparts a particular flavor to the soup of the same name. (See PETITE MARMITE, POULE-AU-POT or POT-AU-FEU, page 84.)

Pinch:	A small quantity of an ingredient such as seasonings, herbs, or spices, often considered to be 1/8 teaspoon or the approximate equivalent. In French, the expression is POINTE, since the small quantity is often applied with the point of a kitchen knife.
Poaching:	Cooking foods over very hot, but not generally boiling, water and periodically basting with the hot water.
Prawns:	Edible crustaceans closely resembling and related to shrimp but generally much larger in size.
Pressure Cooking:	A method of cooking with water in a partial vacuum, permitting faster cooking at higher temperatures than is permissible in standard pots. Generally pressure cooking is done at gauge reading of 15 pounds of pressure, which can reduce the total time of cooking by as much as two-thirds. An effective method of cooking when canning foods.
Provençal:	In the style of Provence, France; food prepared in this manner is generally rich in the use of tomatoes and garlic, or garlic alone. Provençal garlic is less strong than the garlic found in other areas.
Puffing of Dried Foods:	Dehydrated foods, such as raisins and mushrooms, are reconstituted in warm water for about a half-hour—causing them to puff up before they are used in cooking.
Purée:	Blending food to a smooth consistency, sometimes with added liquid, by using a mortar and pestle, a sieve, a food mill, or electric blender. The thickness of the purée is determined by the amount of liquid used.
Quenelle:	Forcemeat of meat or fish, pounded or finely ground, and bound with eggs, shaped and cooked in boiling broth and served with an appropriate sauce as an entrée or appetizer.
Quiche:	A seasoned custard tart, believed to have originated in the French province of Lorraine. There are many versions of this popular dish. (See QUICHE NIÇOISE, page 151.)
Ramekin:	Individual, small-sized molds used for terrines, pâtés, mousses, and other dishes.
Red-Simmering or Chinese Braising:	The slow simmering of meats, poultry, or game in soy sauce and other aromatics that produce a reddish color. The resulting sauce is often reused for other red-simmering dishes or can become the starter for CHINESE MASTER SAUCE (see page 134–35).
Reduce:	To boil a liquid mixture such as a sauce, gravy, or soup in an uncovered pan so that a portion of the liquid will evaporate, reducing the original volume of the mixture, thickening it, intensifying its flavor.
Ricing Potatoes:	The process by which cooked potatoes are forced through a

"ricer," a hand-operated cookware utensil; results in thin strings of puréed potatoes, which come through the many holes at the base and sides of the machine.

Risotto: Italian dishes in which rice is the basic ingredient.

Roux: A blend, usually in equal proportions, of flour and either butter or margarine, which is then cooked to the desired color. Hence, one may use either a brown, golden, or white ROUX.

Sake: Japanese rice wine, often served with Japanese meals.

Sateh: Skewered and broiled meats of Indonesia, increasingly popular in the Netherlands.

Sauté: Derived from the French word SAUTER, to jump, which suggests the action of food cooked over high heat in fat and oil. In MINCEUR CUISINE, however, sautéing is achieved by using, instead of oil, minimal amounts of water, stock, broth, white wine, or vermouth.

Sea Salt or Coarse Salt: Also referred to as Bay Salt; made by evaporating sea water. Kosher salt is a coarsely grained version of sea salt, which is considered more flavorful than other types of salts because of its natural supply of iodine and other minerals.

Shirataki: Cellophane noodles used in Oriental cooking, composed of vermicelli-thin yam threads. (See SUKIYAKI, page 223–24.)

Shuddering: The rippling effect of a sauce, especially tomato sauce, that is simmering over very low heat.

Shuffle: The brisk sliding back and forth—without stirring or necessarily uncovering—of a pot of cooking food to avoid the food's sticking.

Simmer: To cook a sauce or stew over low heat. The liquid should shudder but not break into bubbles. Generally, the liquid is first brought to a boil, then the heat is lowered for relatively long cooking periods.

Sprinkle: Adding droplets of liqueurs or other liquids to accent desserts and other dishes, such as ORANGES GRAND MARNIER, (page 22.)

Soufflé: A light fluffy mixture of varying foods that are incorporated with egg whites, and can be served either hot or cold. Mousse is often included in the category of soufflés.

Terrine: Related to pâtés, but generally doesn't have any pastry-crust covering, nor are the terrine ingredients blended as finely as in a pâté. The name is derived from an earthenware cooking dish in which the potted meats or fish are cooked.

Timbale: A molded custard dish similar to the soufflé, except that the timbale is steamed.

Tomalley or Liver:	The greenish substance found in both male and female lobsters, considered a delicacy. (See LOBSTER BISQUE, page 145.)
Vermicelli:	Extremely thin pasta.
Wok:	A Chinese cooking pot with a curved bottom; many food experts consider the WOK one of the most efficient pots ever conceived. It permits rapid cooking with the use of very little liquid or oil.
Zest:	The rind of citrus fruits, without any of the bitter, white, pithy membrane that connects it to the fruit.

Index

W

Walnut sauce, 140
Watermelon, 159, 183
Wa yium, 82–83
White sauce, basic, 125
  velvet-smooth, 125
Wine:
  hot, spiced, 181
  pudding, chilled Italian, 171
Winter melon soup, whole, 92–93, 159
Witlof, 115
Wright, Russel, 37–38, 41–42

Y

Yam, 105
Yoghurt:
  cucumber salad, 107
  and rose water highball, 177

Z

Zabaglione freddo, 171
Zucchini, breasts of chicken with, 99–100
Zupa szczawiowa, 162–63
Zuppa di pesce, 87